Major Trends and Issues in Early Childhood
Education: Challenges, Controversies, and
Insights, 2nd Edition
JOAN PACKER ISENBERG &
MARY RENCK JALONGO, Eds.

The Power of Projects:
Meeting Contemporary Challenges in Early
Childhood Classrooms—Strategies and Solutions
JUDY HARRIS HELM & SALLEE BENEKE, Eds.

Bringing Learning to Life: The Reggio Approach
to Early Childhood Education
LOUISE BOYD CADWELL

The Colors of Learning: Integrating the Visual
Arts into the Early Childhood Curriculum
ROSEMARY ALTHOUSE, MARGARET H. JOHNSON,
& SHARON T. MITCHELL

A Matter of Trust: Connecting Teachers and
Learners in the Early Childhood Classroom
CAROLLEE HOWES & SHARON RITCHIE

Widening the Circle: Including Children with
Disabilities in Preschool Programs
SAMUEL L. ODOM, Ed.

Children with Special Needs:
Lessons for Early Childhood Professionals
MARJORIE J. KOSTELNIK, ESTHER ETSUKO ONAGA,
BARBARA ROHDE, & ALICE PHIPPS WHIREN

Developing Constructivist Early Childhood
Curriculum: Practical Principles and Activities
RHETA DeVRIES, BETTY ZAN,
CAROLYN HILDEBRANDT, REBECCA EDMIASTON,
& CHRISTINA SALES

Outdoor Play:
Teaching Strategies with Young Children
JANE PERRY

Embracing Identities in Early Childhood
Education: Diversity and Possibilities
SUSAN GRIESHABER & GAILE S. CANNELLA, Eds.

Bambini:
The Italian Approach to Infant/Toddler Care
LELLA GANDINI & CAROLYN POPE EDWARDS, Eds.

Educating and Caring for Very Young Children:
The Infant/Toddler Curriculum
DORIS BERGEN, REBECCA REID, & LOUIS TORELLI

Young Investigators:
The Project Approach in the Early Years
JUDY HARRIS HELM & LILIAN G. KATZ

Serious Players in the Primary Classroom:
Empowering Children Through Active Learning
Experiences, 2nd Edition
SELMA WASSERMANN

Telling a Different Story:
Teaching and Literacy in an Urban Preschool
CATHERINE WILSON

Young Children Reinvent Arithmetic:
Implications of Piaget's Theory, 2nd Edition
CONSTANCE KAMII

Supervision in Early Childhood Education:
A Developmental Perspective, 2nd Edition
JOSEPH J. CARUSO & M. TEMPLE FAWCETT

The Early Childhood Curriculum:
A Review of Current Research, 3rd Edition
CAROL SEEFELDT, Ed.

Leadership in Early Childhood:
The Pathway to Professionalism, 2nd Edition
JILLIAN RODD

Inside a Head Start Center:
Developing Policies from Practice
DEBORAH CEGLOWSKI

Uncommon Caring:
Learning from Men Who Teach Young Children
JAMES R. KING

Teaching and Learning in a Diverse World:
Multicultural Education for Young Children,
2nd Edition
PATRICIA G. RAMSEY

Windows on Learning:
Documenting Young Children's Work
JUDY HARRIS HELM, SALLEE BENEKE,
& KATHY STEINHEIMER

Bringing Reggio Emilia Home: An Innovative
Approach to Early Childhood Education
LOUISE BOYD CADWELL

Master Players: Learning from Children at Play
GRETCHEN REYNOLDS &
ELIZABETH JONES

Understanding Young Children's Behavior:
A Guide for Early Childhood Professionals
JILLIAN RODD

Understanding Quantitative and Qualitative
Research in Early Childhood Education
WILLIAM L. GOODWIN & LAURA D. GOODWIN

(Continued)

Early Childhood Education Series titles, continued

Diversity in the Classroom: New Approaches to
the Education of Young Children, 2nd Edition

FRANCES E. KENDALL

Developmentally Appropriate Practice in
"Real Life"

CAROL ANNE WIEN

Quality in Family Child Care and Relative Care

SUSAN KONTOS, CAROLLEE HOWES,
MARYBETH SHINN, & ELLEN GALINSKY

Using the Supportive Play Model: Individualized
Intervention in Early Childhood Practice

MARGARET K. SHERIDAN,
GILBERT M. FOLEY, & SARA H. RADLINSKI

The Full-Day Kindergarten:
A Dynamic Themes Curriculum, 2nd Edition

DORIS PRONIN FROMBERG

Assessment Methods for Infants and Toddlers:
Transdisciplinary Team Approaches

DORIS BERGEN

The Emotional Development of Young Children:
Building an Emotion-Centered Curriculum

MARION C. HYSON

Moral Classrooms, Moral Children: Creating a
Constructivist Atmosphere in Early Education

RHETA DeVRIES & BETTY ZAN

Diversity and Developmentally Appropriate
Practices

BRUCE L. MALLORY & REBECCA S. NEW, Eds.

Understanding Assessment and Evaluation in
Early Childhood Education

DOMINIC F. GULLO

Changing Teaching, Changing Schools:
Bringing Early Childhood Practice into Public
Education—Case Studies from the Kindergarten

FRANCES O'CONNELL RUST

Physical Knowledge in Preschool Education:
Implications of Piaget's Theory

CONSTANCE KAMII & RHETA DeVRIES

Caring for Other People's Children:
A Complete Guide to Family Day Care

FRANCES KEMPER ALSTON

Family Day Care: Current Research for
Informed Public Policy

DONALD L. PETERS & ALAN R. PENCE, Eds.

Reconceptualizing the Early Childhood
Curriculum: Beginning the Dialogue

SHIRLEY A. KESSLER & BETH BLUE SWADENER, Eds.

Ways of Assessing Children and Curriculum:
Stories of Early Childhood Practice

CELIA GENISHI, Ed.

The Play's the Thing:
Teachers' Roles in Children's Play

ELIZABETH JONES & GRETCHEN REYNOLDS

Scenes from Day Care

ELIZABETH BALLIETT PLATT

Raised in East Urban

CAROLINE ZINSSER

Play and the Social Context of Development in
Early Care and Education

BARBARA SCALES, MILLIE ALMY, AGELIKI
NICOLOPOULOU, & SUSAN ERVIN-TRIPP, Eds.

The Whole Language Kindergarten

SHIRLEY RAINES & ROBERT CANADY

Children's Play and Learning

EDGAR KLUGMAN & SARA SMILANSKY

Experimenting with the World:
John Dewey and the Early Childhood Classroom

HARRIET K. CUFFARO

New Perspectives in Early Childhood Teacher
Education: Bringing Practitioners into the Debate

STACIE G. GOFFIN
& DAVID E. DAY, Eds.

Young Children Continue to Reinvent
Arithmetic—2nd Grade

CONSTANCE KAMII

The Good Preschool Teacher

WILLIAM AYERS

A Child's Play Life: An Ethnographic Study

DIANA KELLY-BYRNE

The War Play Dilemma

NANCY CARLSSON-PAIGE
& DIANE E. LEVIN

The Piaget Handbook for Teachers and Parents

ROSEMARY PETERSON &
VICTORIA FELTON-COLLINS

Promoting Social and Moral Development in
Young Children

CAROLYN POPE EDWARDS

Today's Kindergarten

BERNARD SPODEK, Ed.

Visions of Childhood

JOHN CLEVERLEY
& D. C. PHILLIPS

Starting School

NANCY BALABAN

Ideas Influencing Early Childhood Education

EVELYN WEBER

The Joy of Movement in Early Childhood

SANDRA R. CURTIS

MAJOR TRENDS AND ISSUES IN EARLY CHILDHOOD EDUCATION

Challenges, Controversies, and Insights

SECOND EDITION

EDITED BY

JOAN PACKER ISENBERG
MARY RENCK JALONGO

FOREWORD BY SUE BREDEKAMP

TEACHERS
COLLEGE
PRESS

Teachers College, Columbia University
New York and London

Published by Teachers College Press, 1234 Amsterdam Avenue, New York, NY 10027

The principles of global education enumerated in Chapter 11 are adapted from *Educating the Global Village: Including the Young Child in the World*, 2nd ed., by L. B. Swiniarski, M.-L. Breitborde, & J.-A. Murphy. © 1999. Reprinted by permission of Pearson Education, Inc., Upper Saddle River, NJ.

Library of Congress Cataloging-in-Publication Data

Major trends and issues in early childhood education : challenges, controversies, and insights / edited by Joan Packer Isenberg, Mary Renck Jalongo ; foreword by Sue Bredekamp.—2nd ed.
    p. cm. — (Early childhood education series)
    Includes bibliographical references and index.
    ISBN 0-8077-4351-8 (cloth : alk. paper) — ISBN 0-8077-4350-X (pbk. : alk. paper)
    1. Early childhood education—United States.   2. Child development—United States.   3. Curriculum planning—United States.   4. Early childhood educators—Training of—United States.   I. Early childhood education series (Teachers College Press)

LB1139.25 .M353 2003
372.21—dc21   2002040927

ISBN 0-8077-4350-X (paper)
ISBN 0-8077-4351-8 (cloth)

Printed on acid-free paper

Manufactured in the United States of America

10 09 08 07 06 05 04 03   8 7 6 5 4 3 2 1

*For all the early childhood educators who
have dedicated their professional lives to
the care and education of the very young*

J.P.I.
M.R.J.

Contents

Foreword by Sue Bredekamp   ix
Acknowledgments   xiii

Introduction   1

PART I   Child and Family Issues   11

Chapter 1
Development Issues Affecting Children   13
C. Stephen White and Joan Packer Isenberg

Chapter 2
Young Children's Affirmation of Differences: Curriculum That Is
Multicultural and Developmentally Appropriate   30
Edwina Battle Vold

Chapter 3
Perspectives on Inclusion in Early Childhood Education   47
Doris Bergen

Chapter 4
Working with Families of Young Children   69
Kevin J. Swick

PART II   Curricular Trends and Issues Affecting Practice   81

Chapter 5
Developmental Appropriateness: New Contexts and Challenges   85
Shirley C. Raines and John M. Johnston

Chapter 6
Assessing and Reporting Young Children's Progress:
A Review of the Issues   97
Sue C. Wortham

Chapter 7
Shaking the Very Foundations of Emergent Literacy:
Book Reading Versus Phonemic Awareness   114
Lea M. McGee

Chapter 8
Sensitivity to the Social and Cultural Contexts of
the Play of Young Children   126
Fergus Hughes

Chapter 9
Educational Technology in the Early and Primary Years   136
Sudha Swaminathan and June L. Wright

PART III Policy and Professional Development Issues   151

Chapter 10
Counting the Cost of Caring: Intended and Unintended
Consequences of Early Childhood Policies   153
Frances O'Connell Rust

Chapter 11
Global Education: Why and When to Teach It?   164
Louise Boyle Swiniarski

Chapter 12
The Professional and Social Status of the Early
Childhood Educator   177
Doris Pronin Fromberg

Epilogue   193
About the Editors and the Contributors   195
Index   201

Foreword

This book is an important part of what has become a long tradition in the field of early childhood education—the thoughtful and critical examination of issues and controversies surrounding our practices, policies, and professional development. In my work in the field of early childhood education over the last 25 years, I have had the unique opportunity to observe and participate in the ongoing discussions about many of these issues at the national level, especially in the areas of developmentally appropriate practice, curriculum and assessment, and teacher preparation and development. Although much of this work remains controversial, what has been exhilarating for me as a professional has been the opportunity to engage in dialogue (sometimes heated, always challenging) about the most fundamental concerns facing those who work with young children today. Such dialogue with individuals from all the diverse perspectives represented in our field has given me the most wonderful opportunity for an early childhood professional—to continually learn more about children and teaching. What excites me about this book is that it offers those opportunities to new generations of professional leaders who will carry on the dialogues in the future.

Three important themes provide the conceptual organizers for this volume: context, continuity, and controversy. Just as development and learning occur in and are influenced by social and cultural contexts, so, too, do all the major questions confronting our field demand examination in relation to various contextual factors. The first section of this book explores these contextual issues in depth, especially the child, family, and cultural contexts, while every chapter in the book also contextualizes the issues for the reader. Contextual influences are always present, but usually implicit. However, any thoughtful analysis of critical issues must explicate the context within which beliefs, values, or even specific practices are deemed appropriate.

Of course, the "burning" issues of our day are not really new. Some of these debates—such as what and how to teach very young children—began in the 19th century and continue today in much the same form as they did when the Committee of Nineteen of the International Kindergarten Union was forced to issue three reports because it could not come to consensus on the kindergarten curriculum in the early 1900s. Too often, however, early childhood educators are ahistorical and present ideas or concepts as though they were being discovered for the first time. The National Association for the Education of Young Children (NAEYC) published a volume of history to honor its 75th anniversary to ensure that the field does not continue to be so ahistorical. NAEYC's book attempts to correct this often-repeated error by focusing on the theme of continuity in examining each issue.

Finally, as they should, the contributors to this book confront the controversies that continue to challenge our field. Because our work is so underfunded and undervalued, early childhood educators sometimes fear that if we do not present a united front about what is good for children, we will lose the little public support that we have been able to obtain. We have worked hard to promote the importance of high-quality care and education for young children and to set some standards to guide our professional practice. At times, we fear that any internal disagreement, especially if it becomes too public, will undermine our meager achievements. And yet professions have multiple responsibilities; they must be the standard-setters for their own members, while at the same time they must continually question their own practices and beliefs to ensure that the knowledge base continues to grow and develop. Just as young children must experience some disequilibrium to learn more complex cognitive concepts, so, too, early childhood professionals' understanding can be increased through exploration of disagreements or differences of opinions within the field. Such open discussion of controversy serves the important function of helping professionals socially construct solutions to problems or alternatives for ineffective practices or policies.

Understanding the contexts, continuities, and controversies of early childhood education is a particularly challenging task because of the diversity of our field. The number and types of settings in which early childhood educators work (far beyond the traditional public school kindergarten), the range and levels of professional preparation, and the crises of low salaries and high turnover make all the issues more complex. But future leaders of early childhood education must recognize that we are one profession and be aware of the ways in which the issues connect with and influence one another. Perhaps the most important aspect of continuity is between and among the many issues dissected in this book; making those connections is partially the responsibility of the reader.

Moreover, NAEYC developed a recruitment videotape as part of the *Career Encounters* series broadcast on cable and public television. The producers have a long history of producing such programs for career fields as diverse as podiatry, psychiatry, and engineering. To develop the script, they surveyed hundreds of early childhood educators for their views about their jobs. They were struck by something very different in the way early childhood educators describe their work compared with people in other careers. While all survey respondents cited the challenges of inadequate salaries and low status, all the respondents also expressed optimism about their chosen field. The potential of young children tends to make early childhood educators view their work as vitally important and themselves as capable of making a difference. One hopes that current and future leaders of the early childhood profession who read this book will also share that optimism about the future of our profession. The dialogue that will result as readers explore the issues and controversies of the past, present, and future will surely serve to make the world better for young children and their families.

—Sue Bredekamp
Director, Research Council for Professional Development

Acknowledgments

We would like to acknowledge the many people who worked on this, the completely revised and updated second edition of MAJOR TRENDS AND ISSUES IN EARLY CHILDHOOD: CHALLENGES, CONTROVERSIES, AND INSIGHTS. Thanks to all of the authors for their collective wisdom and for producing well-crafted chapters under very tight time constraints. Our appreciation also goes to Sue Bredekamp, who recognized the timeliness of this collection and whose Foreword offers a powerful statement about our profession and shared vision for the future of the field. Without the skillful guidance of Susan Liddicoat of Teachers College Press, who not only supported our proposal for the first edition but also urged us to consider a second edition, this book would not have become a reality. We wish to acknowledge the Early Childhood Education Series editor, Leslie Williams, for her reflections on what the authors had written and on our ways of framing their ideas. Lori Tate of Teachers College Press deserves recognition for her detailed and consistent editing of the original edition. We also want to thank our graduate students, who struggled long and hard with us over these issues in our graduate classes as well as the children, families, and teachers with whom we have worked over the years. They are the ones who enabled us to stay grounded in the realities of daily practice, and envisioning them as our readers no doubt played a major role in the success of the first edition.

Because writing a book places such heavy demands on many people, we would like to thank our families, friends, and colleagues for their unfailing support as we conceived, developed, and completed this book. To them, we extend our heartfelt appreciation. And to the teachers, children, and families living and learning in contemporary society, we hope that our book might play a small but significant role in improving the field that has been our first love as teachers, writers, and editors— the field of early childhood education.

Introduction

What enables an early childhood educator to attain the highest standards of practice as a caregiver, classroom teacher, or teacher educator? The National Association for the Education of Young Children's (1998) criteria for accreditation identified a constellation of traits. Among the abilities noted are such things as understanding the sociocultural, historical, and political forces that influence early childhood; critically examining alternative perspectives on issues in the field; applying theoretical and research knowledge to practice; and engaging in reflective inquiry that leads to deeper professional understandings of early childhood educators' role and code of ethics.

The advanced study of early childhood education ordinarily includes experiences and courses that are designed to offer a broad perspective on the field. Usually, these courses and seminars include the words *issues* or *trends* in their titles. In the past, undertaking this formal study of the field has often been approached as a survey, a quick overview that was admittedly superficial and sometimes overwhelming for the early childhood educator due to the complex nature of our profession. The implicit assumption of this approach is what Mary Belenky and her colleagues (1986) would refer to as "received knowing," the view that there are experts who "own" the knowledge and graciously bestow it upon others.

When we conceived of this book, we wanted to take a different stance on early childhood trends and issues, one that would welcome and embrace practitioners from diverse early childhood settings. We knew that while the vast majority of our readers would be able, quite literally, to put a face on each trend and issue by reflecting on their immediate or previous experiences with young children, some readers would be new to the field and need specific examples to better understand the underlying principles. Our book, we agreed, was intended to support both relative newcomers to the advanced study of early childhood education and more seasoned scholars in examining key dimensions of the field from multiple, collected perspectives. Additionally, we wanted our diverse readership to recognize that their individual enlightenment and collective power as early childhood educators was predicated not merely on how much informa-

1

tion they could absorb but also on their efforts to arrive at personally constructed meaning and participate in thoughtful lines of inquiry that would offer an enriched and enlarged perspective on their multifaceted roles. It was anticipated that our readers' ideas, experiences, theoretical orientations, and ethical principles would interact with those of their colleagues and that our book might play a role in stimulating thinking as readers engaged in "thinking along with" our authors and critically evaluating what each one of them had to say. Fostering such transactional processes was the essential purpose for the first edition and it continues to be the purpose for this second edition.

This slim volume has no pretensions about being an exhaustive review of the field, although it is replete with useful information. Rather, we asked our authors to draw on their experiences, to communicate their deeply felt commitment, and by so doing to enfranchise our readers in the larger community of early childhood professionals. We wanted to raise our readers' level of awareness that, taken as a field, early childhood education has highly revered traditions, is profoundly significant for society at large, poses perpetually challenging situations, and is characterized by dynamic growth and change. We also wanted to celebrate the fact that, as a profession, we can lay claim to a certain clarity of focus because most early childhood educators are firmly grounded in the concept of the "whole child"—education that affirms and balances the child's physical, social, emotional, cognitive, and aesthetic needs in learning experiences. As a result, early childhood educators have, generally speaking, resisted pressure to encourage them to become one-dimensional—to consider, for example, only basic skills or scores on tests. It is interesting to see other fields suddenly awaken to something that outstanding early childhood professionals have always emphasized—a learner-centered orientation that takes children's developmental needs and uniqueness as individuals into account. As this book will suggest, there is always much more that can and should be done to ensure that every young child is afforded the best possible educational opportunities, opportunities that will nurture his or her capacity to participate in a democratic society (Children's Defense Fund, 2001).

GOALS FOR THE BOOK

To further clarify and elaborate on our goals for this book, we turn to the metaphor of a lens. There are lenses that offer a sharper focus, lenses that expand our range of vision, and lenses that magnify details. Metaphorically speaking, the authors represented in this volume supply such lenses on the field of early childhood education by sharing the depth and breadth of their professional perspectives on various aspects of early childhood education as well as striving to provide an overall view of the "state of the art" in their particular areas of specialization. As editors, we are confident that these leaders in the field are sufficiently knowledgeable and insightful to expand and enlarge the vision of our readership. Like a young child on a sunshine-bright day who is hoisted onto an adult's shoulders to gain a better look at things and outfitted with small plastic sunglasses to reduce the glare, MAJOR TRENDS AND ISSUES IN EARLY CHILDHOOD EDUCATION: CHALLENGES, CONTROVERSIES, AND INSIGHTS is designed to offer our readers the multiple vantage points and clarity of vision represented by our authors. The substance of this volume is not intended to be prescriptive. Rather, our overarching goal is to invite a distinguished and diverse group of early childhood educators into the ongoing conversation about what we can do as a profession to meet the needs of all young children. If our book has succeeded in attaining the goals we originally set for it, then it will stimulate further interest, encourage readers to try out new lenses, and serve as an impetus to delve deeper into those aspects of the field that have the greatest personal and professional significance for each reader.

FRAMEWORK FOR THE BOOK

In order to provide a framework for this volume, we return to the key words in the book's title. Each author has identified *trends*: the general direction, course, or tendency of events, data, or ideas. If we return to the metaphor of the lens, trends can be likened to a wide-angle lens, for they simultaneously give a sense of where we have been, where we are now, and where we may be headed in the future. As part of reviewing these directions in the field, our authors typically find themselves revisiting the long-standing traditions in the field and referring to our historical roots as a profession. The trends in early childhood education influence future policies and practices, thereby setting directions for the way we live, learn, teach, and work. When considered in this way, trends represent the social, philosophical, political, technological, and economic realities of our world.

Additionally, each author has addressed *key issues*: significant points and matters of consequence that are worthy of discussion and resolution. As a lens, issues are comparable to a powerful set of binoculars, for although there are many possible things that we can look at with them, binoculars are used primarily for the purpose of focusing on something that rivets our attention and merits more careful scrutiny. Issues often provide the forum for public debate that has profound significance for policies, funding, and educational outcomes affecting young children, their families, and their teachers.

Because there are different perspectives on trends and issues, *challenges* and *controversies* emerge. By a *challenge*, we mean a difficult and complex task that taxes the resources and problem-solving abilities of those who hope to accomplish a worthwhile goal through comprehensive services for children and families. Challenges are comparable to the view through a kaleidoscope—there are such intricate and rapidly shifting patterns that it is exceedingly difficult to discern exactly what has happened even though it is right before our eyes. Ways of counteracting neglect and violence in children's lives are good examples of challenges. These things are pervasive in society, yet they are difficult to fully comprehend and resistant to our best problem-solving strategies. Each author in this volume explicitly states many of the challenges before us as a profession.

When professionals in the field are pulled in different directions, *controversies* inevitably emerge. By a *controversy*, we mean an area of disagreement that occurs between groups that hold opposing viewpoints. When we return to the analogy of the lens, we see that controversies are like distributing a professional camera operator's assortment of lenses to various groups and asking them to film the same reality. Some will be zooming in on small details, while others will pan the entire scene; some will see a smaller picture within a larger one; others will use various filters that soften harsh lines or cast things in a completely different light. When these individuals compare what they see, they may become convinced that the perceptions held by others are wrong. Seeing the same reality in a decidedly different way leads to comparable disputes within the field of early childhood education and often leads to divisiveness among various factions. Such controversies have undeniable implications for children, families, and teachers of young children as they work to achieve some shared vision of who we are as a profession, where we are headed, and why. Figure Int.1 summarizes the key terminology that serves as a structure for each chapter.

As early childhood educators examine trends, explore issues, meet challenges, and reflect on controversies, the best possible outcome would be the final key word of our title: *insight*. By *insight*, we mean a brilliant flash of understanding, an "aha!" that illuminates our thinking and enables us to see, in the full sense of that word, more clearly. This capacity to discern the true nature of a situation enables early childhood educators to arrive at a collection of best practices that are supported by re-

---

WHAT IS A TREND?

Definition: The general direction, course, or tendency of events, data, or ideas.

Metaphor: A wide-angle lens that offers a panoramic view of where the field has been, where it is now, and where it may be headed.

WHAT IS AN ISSUE?

Definition: Significant points and matters of consequence that are worthy of discussion and resolution.

Metaphor: A powerful set of binoculars used to focus on something that rivets attention and merits further scrutiny.

WHAT IS A CONTROVERSY?

Definition: An area of disagreement, often persistent, that occurs between groups with opposing viewpoints.

Metaphor: Distributing an assortment of camera lenses to various groups and asking them to film the same reality—each group is convinced that it knows what is "real," what "works," and what is "right."

WHAT IS A CHALLENGE?

Definition: A difficult and complex task that taxes the resources and problem-solving abilities of those who hope to accomplish significant goals in the service of young children and families.

Metaphor: The view from a kaleidoscope—intricate and rapidly shifting patterns make it difficult to comprehend what has happened, to fully understand what is occurring, and to decide what to do next.

FIGURE INT.1. Trends, issues, and controversies: Definitions and metaphors.

search and a careful consideration of the individual child's circumstances rather than engage in a futile quest for simple solutions.

We suggest that our readers think about those five key words—*trends, issues, challenges, controversies,* and *insights*—as a superstructure that encompasses all the work herein and unifies the entire volume. Although each author's voice is unique and each chapter is distinctive, readers will be able to recognize that the specific content of every chapter has been built on some combination of these five elements. Several specific questions that the authors used to "frame" their chapters can also be used by readers to guide their inquiry into other areas of the early childhood education field. Our questioning framework for the chapter readings is shown in Figure Int.2.

INTRODUCTION TO THE TRENDS AND ISSUES

- Why are these trends significant?
- Why are these issues of concern?

EXPLORATION OF THE TRENDS AND ISSUES

- What are the different trends and key struggles associated with this challenge or controversy?
- Why does this aspect of early childhood education generate discussion, debate, and controversy?
- How realistic are the proposed solutions?

THEORETICAL / HISTORICAL SOCIAL CONTEXT

- How is this contemporary problem rooted in social/historical traditions?
- How do these traditions influence its current interpretations?

APPLICATION, ANALYSIS, AND EVALUATION OF THE TRENDS AND ISSUES

- How do these trends and issues affect the individual early childhood practitioner? The profession as a whole?
- How do these trends and issues affect children and families?
- What do these trends and issues mean for the future of teaching and learning?
- What other questions does this controversial issue generate?
- What obstacles will we have to overcome in the future?
- What are the consequences of these trends, issues, challenges, and controversies for you, the reader, in your current professional role and setting?

FIGURE INT.2. Questioning framework for early childhood trends and issues.

PHILOSOPHICAL STANCE OF THE BOOK

Three themes run across the chapters in this volume. First of all, the authors represented here are scholar-practitioners. These are the voices of professionals who know early childhood education "from the inside out," individuals who are intimately acquainted with the realities of caring for and educating the very young. We hope that our authors' grounding in the traditions of the field, powerful ideas about its current status, and recommendations for the future will resonate within each one of our readers. Although some readers may see this scholar-practitioner stance as a limitation, we consider the fact that our authors speak clearly and directly to practitioners to be an important strength of the first edition and have continued with that goal in mind throughout the revision process for the second edition.

Second, because our authors know young children and understand child development, they hold all young learners in high esteem and recognize that children actively build their understandings of the world; therefore, readers will notice an undercurrent of constructivism, in the Piagetian sense of the word, throughout the book. Additionally, our authors share an appreciation for the Vygotskian notion that learning is fundamentally social in nature, that all of us—children, families, caregivers, classroom teachers, and teacher educators—learn from one another. This statement might seem obvious until our readers consider the full meaning of that assertion. Everyone knows that children learn from their teachers, but it literally turns education on its head to consider the other direction—the many ways in which teachers can and must learn from children and families. Likewise, most people assume that scholars have something of value to share with practitioners, but it is just as important for faculty to study alongside practitioners as equal partners. All of our authors stress the importance of human relationships through which learning occurs and, in light of that recognition, all the authors call in their unique voices for meaningful collaboration, establishing a sense of community, promoting educational equity, and reforming early childhood education in ways that put children's needs first.

Third, each author "lets readers in" on his or her efforts to arrive at shared meaning and common purposes about the field while simultaneously acknowledging that other meanings and purposes exist (Wein, 1995). To establish this tone, we asked authors to introduce their chapters with a personal/professional experience that could serve as a concrete example so that readers can begin by glimpsing the chapter's "take" on the topic. We identify these theoretical and philosophical underpinnings of the book not only on a chapter-by-chapter basis but also for the work as a whole at the outset. In this way, readers can determine for themselves how much of their own thinking is attributable to these influences and decide for themselves which of these lenses on the field are worth using or are sufficiently powerful to warrant modifying their customary point of view.

OVERVIEW OF THE CONTENTS

This book consists of twelve chapters grouped into three parts. As readers consider these main parts of the book, key questions emerge. For Part I, that question is: *How do early childhood educators optimize every young child's growth, development, and learning and, at the same time, respect and support the families in which diverse populations of young children live?* For Part II, the main question is: *What forces have defined the content and processes of early childhood education, shaped the settings in which it occurs, and influenced ideas about what counts as evidence of learning?* For Part III, the basic query is: *How does the larger social context influence public policy affecting children and families and the early childhood professional's role?*

Throughout these 12 chapters, the authors raise as many questions as they answer and invite readers to revisit our past traditions as we seek solutions to today's and tomorrow's dilemmas. The difficult issues presented are designed to spark discussions among our readers that will promote reflective practice.

Everyone associated with this project has worked to present a well-reasoned and carefully documented perspective on some of the major trends and significant issues facing the field of early childhood education. Yet we know that in a book such as this, we risk omitting an issue that some of our readers may think important, and if this is the case, we urge readers to make these issues part of their inquiry into the field. As co-editors, as co-authors, and as early childhood educators, it is our fervent hope that this work will encourage practitioners and teacher educators to enter into the dialogue in knowledgeable, skillful, and insightful ways as we work together in a profession that dedicates itself to the care and education of the very young.

REFERENCES

Belenky, M. F., Clinchy, B. M., Goldberger, N. R., & Tarule, J. M. (1986). *Women's ways of knowing: The development of self, voice, and mind*. New York: Basic Books.

Children's Defense Fund. (2001). *The state of America's children yearbook.* Washington, DC: Author.

National Association for the Education of Young Children. (1998). *Accreditation criteria and procedures of the National Academy of Early Childhood Programs.* Washington, DC: Author.

Wein, C. A. (1995). *Developmentally appropriate practice in "real life": Stories of teachers' practical knowledge.* New York: Teachers College Press.

PART I

CHILD AND FAMILY ISSUES

We begin Part I with a case that illustrates how child and family issues converge to exert a profound influence on young children's lives.

In contrast to several of his classmates, Jason cried not at the start of kindergarten or at the beginning of the schoolday but in October at the end of the schoolday. His teacher was sympathetic at first but eventually lost patience and complained that Jason's crying was "driving her crazy." In desperation, she resorted to the behavioristic approach recommended by a more experienced teacher, convinced that if she ignored the crying it would eventually disappear—but it did not. Clues to Jason's puzzling behavior began to emerge after a concerned neighbor reported the child's situation to Children and Youth Services. Jason's mother had abandoned the family during the summer, and his father, who had a demanding job and a long commute, suddenly had sole responsibility for the boy. Monday through Friday, 5-year-old Jason was a latchkey child who would get off the school bus, unlock the front door, and stay home alone until his father arrived around 7:00 P.M. When the social worker spoke with Jason, the kindergartener confided that he had been frightened by a television commercial for a "scary movie" and was terrified to stay by himself when it was dark outside. Reflecting on Jason's situation illustrates that child development and learning cannot be separated from the individual circumstances of the child and his or her family.

Some of the social ramifications of Jason's experiences include his difficult family situation, his relationship with teacher and peers, the influence of the media, and the role of social services. Additionally, there is a political side to Jason's situation. Some political questions to consider include: Why has the United States lagged behind other nations in providing a federally supported system of child care that would provide the high-quality after-school programming this child and family so desperately need? Why did the teacher defer so readily to the recommendation of another teacher, and why did she persist with it long after it proved to be unsuccessful? The history of early childhood education is another key influence that can be used to shed light on this particular situation. Child development theory, Maria Montessori's *Casi de bambini*, the first American kindergarten, and the Head Start program have all contributed in some way to early childhood educators' collective wisdom of practice.

As readers begin to consider the particular cases of children they know, these reflections lead to the question that undergirds Part I: *How do early childhood educators optimize every young child's growth, development, and learning and, at the same time, respect and support the families in which diverse populations of young children live?*

In Chapter 1, C. Stephen White and Joan Packer Isenberg address the topic of child development and teachers' duty to meet the needs of every child, regardless of the conditions each child confronts. The authors describe five major factors that jeopardize children's development and offer timely recommendations for practice.

Chapter 2, by Edwina Battle Vold, chronicles the history of multicultural education, provides a developmental sequence for young children's understandings about diversity, and describes the inevitable controversies that emerge as we attempt to meet the needs of youngsters in a pluralistic society. The author concludes by urging educators to become more culturally responsive teachers whose behavior reflects a genuine commitment to anti-bias.

In Chapter 3, Doris Bergen provides an overview of the distance we have traveled as a profession in meeting the special needs of young children. She sheds light on the historical, political, and social influences that have forged contemporary ideas about inclusion and encourages early childhood practitioners to consider inclusive practices as they currently exist as well as future directions for inclusion.

Chapter 4, by Kevin J. Swick, examines the roles of child, family, and early childhood educator in the context of the community. He argues for an empowerment perspective that emanates from a commitment to caring, authentic collaboration, meaningful communication, and high-quality programs that offer resources and support to contemporary American families.

Together, these four chapters remind us that early childhood education can never by decontextualized and does not occur in isolation. Rather, our work on behalf of young children is deeply woven into our own lives, the lives of the children in our care, and their families' lives both in and out of school.

Chapter 1

Development Issues Affecting Children

C. Stephen White

Joan Packer Isenberg

Lynette is a first-grader who lives with her single-parent mother. She generally arrives at school unclean, hungry, and with her hair hanging in her eyes. Although she has quite good intellectual skills, Lynette has difficulty establishing positive peer relationships. Consequently, she plays alone on the playground, is often the last to be selected for group work, and is sometimes the object of ridicule from her peers. Nonetheless, Lynette works hard to please her teachers and her peers. Although she reads above grade level, Lynette is rarely recognized for her intellectual capabilities. It seems that in school, Lynette can do little to create a favorable impression among her teacher or her peers.

Many children like Lynette arrive at school tired, unhealthy, or unduly stressed, yet they, like all children, must have their developmental needs met in order to thrive. Developmental needs are essential requirements that affect the "long-term implications of childhood events, not just their immediate consequences" (Garbarino, 1995, p. 156). Now, consider the following statistics about America's children:

- 13.5 million children live in poverty, a sharp increase since 1970 (Children's Defense Fund, 2001).
- 9 million children lack health care; 22% of children have not completed their needed vaccinations (Children's Defense Fund, 1995; Federal Interagency Forum on Child and Family Statistics, 2001).

- 20% of children ages 3–17 have one or more developmental, learning, or behavioral disorders (Zill & Schoenborn, 1990).
- An estimated 3 million children were reported as suspected victims of child abuse and neglect in 1997. Young children are at greatest risk, with infants representing the largest proportion of victims (Children's Defense Fund, 2001).

These data and Lynette's case clearly portray conditions that affect more children today than at any other time since the Great Depression (Garbarino, 1998). Even though some progress has been made on behalf of children—such as decreased infant mortality, early education programs for children born into poverty, and a national vaccination program for preschool children—data such as these continue to document an increase in the physical, behavioral, social, and learning problems of America's children and youth (Federal Interagency Forum on Child and Family Statistics, 2001; Garbarino, 1998). Such conditions pose serious threats to children's growth and development. Thus, teachers and caregivers must reexamine their roles and responsibilities to address the realities children bring to early childhood settings (Klein, 2001). Simultaneously, broad societal changes must be institutionalized to foster children's well-being both in the United States and throughout the world.

This chapter first identifies children's developmental needs and definitional debates related to child development and examines the historical traditions of the field of early childhood. Next, it addresses selected adverse and positive influences on children's development. The chapter concludes with suggestions to educators of young children about ways to meet these developmental challenges. The topics selected for this chapter, while not exhaustive, have relevance for the entire field of early childhood.

CHILDREN'S DEVELOPMENTAL NEEDS

What exactly do children need in order to develop optimally? At a minimum, all children have physical, social and emotional, and cognitive needs. Physical needs include food, clothing, shelter, and medical care. Basic social and emotional needs include a consistent and predictable relationship with an attentive and caring adult who has high social and moral expectations, strong peer acceptance, and "freedom from exploitation and discrimination in their communities" (Weissbourd, 1996, p. 8). Minimal cognitive needs include the ability to communicate thoughts and feelings, to process information in a meaningful way, to engage in constructive problem solving, and to experience success both at school and in the community (Case, Griffin, & Kelly, 2001; Weissbourd, 1996). Many children also need "special health, social, and educational services to deal with inherited and acquired ailments and disabilities" (Weissbourd, 1996, p. 8). How well early childhood professionals meet children's essential needs strongly influences how successful they will be as learners and as future citizens (Hyson & Molinaro, 2001; Peisner-Feinberg et al., 2000; Weikart, 1998).

Children who grow up with their basic physical and material needs met are likely to trust themselves and their community, possess a zest for life, and build on inner resourcefulness to participate in society, regardless of the obstacles they face. They are also more likely to develop a sense of confidence and competence in family, school, and community endeavors as a result of repeated, successful coping experiences (Bronfenbrenner, 1979; Brooks-Gunn, Britto, & Brady, 1999; Denham, 2001; Erikson, 1963; Vygotsky, 1978; Weissbourd, 1996).

On the other hand, children who grow up without having basic needs met are at a clear disadvantage for a healthy start in life (Brooks-Gunn et al., 1999; Denham, 2001; Children's Defense Fund, 2001). Many of these children exhibit particular behavioral and developmental characteristics (e.g., developmental disabilities, medical fragility, poor school performance), making them vulnerable to being able to function effectively as learners (Bradley et al., 1994; Denham, 1998).

DEFINING TERMS

Professionals across disciplines—social workers, teachers, parents, and policy makers—rely on their understandings of children's development to determine responsible policies and practices. Most agree that child development issues, while complex and fluid, are foundational and interdisciplinary. Beyond that, however, there is little agreement about developmental goals, strategies to optimize development, or ways to prepare children for an unpredictable future (Katz, 1996).

Development is often defined as dynamic change over time (Berk, 2002; Katz, 1996). Recent child development theory and research have called into question three long-standing notions associated with development. New data have challenged (1) the assumptions about developmental universals, making us increasingly aware of cultural influences on development; (2) the simplistic use of ages and stages to explain behavioral norms; and (3) theoretical dichotomies such as nature versus nurture to describe development (Berk, 2002; Case et al., 2001). These new data have reopened the definitional debate and are providing the context that is challenging and changing old views and assumptions that have influenced early childhood educators' beliefs and actions. This is a more difficult challenge than it was in the past, for not only is there more information about every aspect of development but that information is increasingly difficult to integrate.

Similarly, notions of resiliency have challenged early childhood educators' thinking. Resiliency is the ability to adapt to disappointment, setbacks, or obstacles in one's life by actively facing an obstacle or difficulty (Berk, 2002; DeGarmo & Forgatch, 1999; Quyen, et al., 1998).

The study of resiliency may be the most important research in child development in postmodern times, for it represents a shift in viewing children's development from one of remediation to one of primary prevention and from one of deficit to one of strength (Berk, 2002). While few dispute the resiliency paradigm, Weissbourd (1996) questions its unilateral acceptance. His assumption that everyone is vulnerable under the right set of conditions portrays resilient children as those "who have not yet encountered an environment that triggers their vulnerabilities" (p. 43). While this perspective challenges the prevailing resiliency paradigm, it neglects to account for those children who are succeeding in spite of adversity.

Thus, the explosion of new child development knowledge has prompted new insights into the complexity of development. Both past and present child development theory and research have deep roots in the traditions and history of early childhood as a distinct field.

HISTORICAL VIEWS OF DEVELOPMENT IN EARLY CHILDHOOD

Early leaders in the field have provided a strong tradition of care and education that has consistently guided the profession's thinking. The centrality of positive interaction experiences and nurturing environments to children's healthy development suggests one example of this long-standing tradition. Our roots begin in the 18th century with Rousseau's (1762/1947) empowering paradigmatic change from a utilitarian and adult view of children to one that affirmed their goodness and their need for supportive adults in their lives and for humane treatment. Later in history, Dewey's (1916) work centered on the belief that education is an integral part of life and that the school community offers children an opportunity to practice democratic principles in group living. While Dewey's principles are still advocated, they often conflict with current views of education for children and provide a possible reason for the tensions between schools and families and the school reform movement.

In the field of psychology, early child development theorists (Ainsworth, Bell, & Stayton 1974; Bowlby, 1969; Spitz, 1949) also found human relationships central to the care and education of children. Later, Piaget (1951) focused his theory on the inseparability of cognitive and affective development, while Erikson (1963) explained the early years as critical for healthy psychosocial development, establishing the traits of trust, autonomy, initiative, and industry. The current view of development as being highly influenced by the sociocultural context is exemplified by renewed interest in Vygotsky's (1978) work. For Vygotsky, the social context—individuals, family, school, and societal expectations—shapes the child's thinking and development. The scope of psychological theory and research continuously provokes reexamination of the assumptions early childhood educators hold regarding children's development.

From anthropology, Bronfenbrenner's (1979) ecological model of child development reminds us of the crucial relationship between the child and the immediate and surrounding environments. Moreover, Bronfenbrenner's belief in the bidirectionality of responses between adults and children gives children an equal role in shaping adults' behaviors.

From recent research in neurobiology, we have learned that brain development that takes place prenatally and in the first years of life is more extensive and vulnerable than previously believed and is influenced over time by the early environment and by early stress (Carnegie Corporation, 1994; Lindsey, 1999). In addition, the environment affects the number of brain cells, the number of connections among them, and the way in which these connections are wired. Consequently, parents and other adult caregivers are a vital component in providing good prenatal care, warm and loving attachments, and positive age-appropriate stimulation (Newberger, 1997).

Like their forebears in the field, contemporary early childhood professionals recognize and reinforce the early antecedents of healthy development and model the conviction that children are good and worthwhile, competent rather than helpless, and survivors rather than victims. Thus, child care, school, and family settings must be safe havens for children where life is organized and predictable, and every adult should hold realistic but high expectations for all children regardless of their backgrounds.

ADVERSE INFLUENCES ON CHILDREN'S DEVELOPMENT

As we enter the 21st century, many professionals are unaware of or unwilling to recognize the problems facing many of America's young children. These adversities, often termed *risk factors*, place children "at high risk of adverse outcomes when they become adolescents" (Schorr, 1988, p. xix). A 1994 report by the Carnegie Corporation warned that "poor quality child care, inadequate health care, and increasing poverty are creating a quiet crisis among children younger than three" (p. 4), while Kozol (1995) has advocated systemic change in public education.

Consider the case of the Clark family, a middle-class, two-parent, suburban family with no apparent problems. When Jennifer Clark, a housewife for many years, suddenly found herself faced with a divorce and little financial support for her two young children, she was forced to sell her home, move to a less costly area, and find employment. Now her children were living in a single-parent household, with a working mother, and in a neighborhood that is less safe and protected. As a result of their changing circumstances, the Clark children have more challenges to meet in their daily lives.

Such changes have profound consequences for children, yet there is much teachers can do to enable children to become successful learners and citizens and "partially immunize" them against the stresses and strains of their lives when multiple adverse influences interact (Grych & Fincham, 1997; McMillan & Reed, 1993).

Five major adversities—poverty, inadequate health and safety protection, violence, prenatal exposure to drugs, and substandard child care—and their influences on children's development will be delineated next.

Poverty

The risks from child poverty—including poor health, inadequate child care, developmental delays, and insufficient nutrition—pose serious threats to children's well-being. While poverty is defined as insufficient income, two pervasive myths abound about low-income families (Brooks-Gunn et al., 1999; McLoyd, 1998; Weissbourd, 1996).

The myth that all poor children are alike does not account for the diverse conditions children in poverty can experience "in the length of time they are poor, in the circumstances and quality of their families' lives, in the work patterns of their parents, in the circumstances of their communities, in the nature of their problem" (Weissbourd, 1996, p. 10).

The second myth, that poverty is more common among children of color than among White children, overlooks the fact that White children comprise the largest group of poor in America. However, a higher percentage of African American children are poor and are likely to remain so longer than White children (McLoyd, 1998).

Moreover, the costs of child poverty are both economic and social. Children who live in poverty, taken as a group, will cost billions of additional dollars in services to support special education, foster care, programs for teenage parents, and the criminal justice system (Children's Defense Fund, 2001). Almost all the adversities that lead to devastating outcomes are out of proportion among poor children, who are denied access to many products and services available to most advantaged Americans (McLoyd, 1998; Schorr, 1988).

Inadequate Health and Safety Protection

Access to health care is also an issue affecting children's development. In spite of this country's advanced health systems, there are still 11.9 million American children uninsured (Children's Defense Fund, 2001). Although immunization rates have increased dramatically since 1990, one-third of American children still are not immunized before their second birthday, leaving more than 1 million 2-year-olds vulnerable to a host of preventable diseases such as measles, tetanus, polio, and hepatitis B. Additionally, recent statistics reveal that 7 infants out of 100 are low-birthweight babies (less than 5.5 pounds), placing them at greater risk of infant death and disability, and 500,000 pregnant women are uninsured, risking inadequate prenatal care (Carnegie Corporation, 1994; Children's Defense Fund, 2001). These conditions seriously jeopardize children's physical growth, brain development, and ability to learn.

Despite increased societal attention to providing safe environments for children, efforts to protect children from harmful influences do not reach enough children in the early years, particularly infants and toddlers. Unprotected children may reside in unsafe neighborhoods and be supervised by baby-sitters who are unqualified or adults who abuse or neglect them (Lewit, 1992). These conditions are known antecedents to later unhealthy development and must be addressed at the policy level by communities and comprehensive school efforts to ensure young children's health and safety. Clearly, healthy children have a greater chance of growing into productive learners and citizens.

Violence

A third threat to children's healthy development, violence, has reached epidemic proportions in America (Children's Defense Fund, 2001; Garbarino, 1998). As the following figures detail, the toll is great:

- In 1997, 4,205 children were killed by gunfire in the United States. Homicide is the third leading cause of death among children ages 5 to 14 (Children's Defense Fund, 2001).

- The average cost of treating a child wounded by gunfire equals about a year of college education (Garbarino, 1995).
- More than half of fifth-graders in New Orleans reported they had been victims of some type of violence; 70% had witnessed weapons being used (NAEYC, 1994).

There are prevention measures that lessen the effect of all forms of violence on children's development. Because violence is often interconnected with other adverse factors that collectively inhibit children's development, it must be viewed as a broad social problem. Experts agree that violence prevention must not only include efforts to control violent behavior but also must address its root causes (e.g., poverty, repression, and absence of individual responsibility and family support) and risk factors (e.g., guns, media, drugs, incarceration, witnessing violent acts, and community deterioration) (Carnegie Corporation, 1994; Children's Defense Fund, 2001; NAEYC, 1994). Curbing violence requires a systemic approach that includes changes in families, neighborhoods, and schools and demands a critical mass of people willing to work together to change the structure and policies that frame children's lives.

Prenatal Exposure to Drugs

Prenatal exposure to drugs has contributed to a new and rapidly growing population of "crack children" who are entering the public schools at a rapid rate (Cornelius, Day, Richardson, & Taylor, 1999). Because crack is seldom the only drug used, a developing fetus may be exposed to a variety of substances. The profile of drug-exposed children is clear in the literature (Lewit, 1992; Thomas, 2000; Walker, Rosenberg, & Balaban-Fill, 1999). These children often suffer from cognitive defects (such as poor abstract reasoning and memory, poor judgment, and an inability to concentrate or process information) or several physical abnormalities (such as brain damage, deformed hearts, and missing limbs). Drug-exposed children may also exhibit behavioral problems such as hyperactivity, frequent tantrums, and the inability to cope with stressful events in their lives (Greer, 1990; Thomas, 2000). Those with profound to moderate effects from prenatal drug exposure are usually identified by age 6. However, many of these children do not receive preschool education and thus are not professionally diagnosed until first grade (Thomas, 2000).

Societal conditions such as poverty, substandard education, and violence, often associated with crack children, also influence children's development. The interaction of these social and physical factors may cause dysfunctions and social stigmas. Meeting the unique needs of prenatally drug-exposed children is particularly challenging to teachers in self-contained classrooms, for they often lack specialized training in instructional strategies. Consequently, they rely heavily on referrals for assessment and placement in special education settings.

Substandard Child Care

How young children are cared for and *who* cares for them and how they have been educated clearly affect child development. According to a recent study (Helburn, 1995), of the 5 million children in child care, most receive "poor to mediocre" care and one in eight is in a setting so poor that basic health and safety needs are jeopardized. Out of more than 400 child-care centers in four states, only one in seven was rated as good based on NAEYC accreditation criteria (e.g., providing children with close relationships with caring adults who focus on individual needs). Even worse, the children receiving the poorest-quality care were typically the very youngest—the infants and toddlers. These findings parallel similar findings related to quality child care (Galinsky, Bond, & Friedman, 1993; Kontos, Howes, Shinn, & Galinsky, 1995; Phillips, Mekos, Scarr, McCarney, & Abbott-Shim, 2000) and are integral to the current political debate about requiring welfare mothers to work.

Related to quality is the issue of cost. In the current political debate over putting welfare mothers to work, little thought has been given to its outcome—a dramatic increase in the need for more child care at the very time when federal funding is being reduced. The connection of cost of child care to its quality and outcomes serves as a potent reminder that high-quality child-care programs are indispensable in preparing children for better school performance and stronger self-esteem (Boyer, 1991; Hyson & Molinaro, 2001) and reducing later juvenile crime and delinquency (National Center for Youth Law, 1995). What are these positive influences and how can they be achieved?

POSITIVE INFLUENCES ON CHILDREN'S DEVELOPMENT

Children who grow up in environments with positive influences are likely to succeed even against the odds. Often termed *protective factors*, positive conditions include a combination of sustenance; significant relationships with available and caring adults; consistency and predictability in relationships, expectations, and limits; strong emotional ties within the family; regular acceptance and affirmation of actions; and a variety of stimulating materials in family and school settings (Berk, 2002; Bradley et al., 1994;

Hyson & Molinaro, 2001; Quyen et al., 1998). These psychological influences are likely to develop traits of self-efficacy, personal responsibility, optimism, and coping ability (Bradley et al., 1994; Denham, 1998; 2001).

Early childhood professionals are well positioned to provide positive conditions for all children. Most researchers agree that reaching children through quality early education programs is a proven strategy to help them achieve success in school and lead healthier, more productive lives. Many successful intervention programs for children of all ages (e.g., Accelerated Schools, Comer Schools, the Coalition of Essential Schools, Reading Recovery, and Success for All) are dispelling the myth that certain threatening influences are reasons to assume failure for any child (Berk, 2002; Children's Defense Fund, 2001; McLoyd, 1998; Weissbourd, 1996).

Why are children succeeding in these programs despite the many threats to their development? These programs incorporate factors known to influence development in a positive direction. They employ certified and caring adults who are knowledgeable and trained in best practices, who view themselves as facilitators, who are skilled in their ability to establish relationships built on mutual trust and care, and who approach children with an "open eye" to their needs (Hyson & Molinaro, 2001; Schorr, 1988). These programs also involve parents, community agencies, and educators in a collaborative endeavor for children's education and development (Knitzer & Cauthen, 2000).

Looking broadly at the effects of both adverse and positive influences on children's development gives insight into why some children succeed in schools while others do not. It also illuminates the many challenges early childhood professionals face in reeducating themselves to understand and take a proactive stance on the critical issues affecting children's development.

IMPLICATIONS AND RECOMMENDATIONS FOR CHILD DEVELOPMENT

It is essential for early childhood professionals to recognize the implications of the conditions affecting all children's development. Adults who strive to build children's adaptability view children as resources, not problems, and work to create environments that protect them from adverse risks rather than attempting to "fix" the children. The following five suggestions provide a starting point for successfully meeting these developmental challenges.

1. *Teach coping skills to children.* Early childhood professionals can help all children maximize their potential by fostering self-esteem and a

sense of efficacy. Developing nurturing relationships and focusing on children's strengths rather than labeling, blaming, and criticizing children's behavior foster children's belief in their abilities and rest on the core principles and traditions of early childhood education (Ashiabi, 2000; Berk, 2002; Denham, 1998). Early childhood curricula must enable children, despite disadvantages, to develop social competence, problem-solving skills, autonomy, adaptability, and a sense of purpose or future to maximize their healthy development. Conflict resolution, characterized by community building and social and moral problem solving, can be taught to teachers, parents, and children from diverse backgrounds through its inclusion in early childhood education programs and training (Ashiabi, 2000; Browning, Davis, & Resta, 2000; Wheeler, 1994). Strong early childhood programs also provide children with predictable environments so they can develop the "language skills, social competence, self-confidence, and ways of thinking that would help them discover how the world works . . . the attributes that help in the mastery of school tasks" (Schorr, 1988, p. 182).

2. *Institute reform in schools and programs that serve poor children.* According to Haberman (1994), current educational settings for children in poverty are hostile, prisonlike environments that differ dramatically from those experienced by advantaged children. Proponents of school reform have taken the position that all children can learn and that children's learning is more alike than different (Golbeck, 2001). Yet, just as in the past, schools continue to label poor children as special learners who need "direct instruction" and reinforce the myth that poor children cannot be expected to learn very much. This kind of labeling perpetuates a self-fulfilling prophecy for poor children (Brooks-Gunn et al., 1999; Weissbourd, 1996). Instead, early childhood professionals must teach to all children's strengths. Educators who ask "How do I make this child part of the curriculum?" rather than "How can I be expected to teach this child?" are beginning to reduce the barriers that are created for poor children by assuming a more holistic approach to teaching.

3. *Provide teachers and caregivers with access to resources that protect children's health and safety.* There is strong evidence that timely and appropriate environmental interventions by an interdisciplinary team of professionals—including health care professionals, teachers, social workers, and other caring adults—can minimize children's personal pain and distress (Carnegie Corporation, 1994; Children's Defense Fund, 2001). Teachers must be open to actively participating on these teams to develop better methods and strategies to identify children's special needs. Moreover, because schools and other early childhood

programs are the settings in which most children spend their days, teachers and caregivers must be knowledgeable about the communities and help families access those resources (Rhodes & Hennessy, 2001). Early childhood educators must work with other professionals dedicated to serving young children in order to ensure children's health and safety.

4. *Prepare future and practicing teachers to work effectively with children abused by violence and poverty.* Early childhood educators can help children deal with the effects of violence and poverty in their lives through the development of strong programs and curricula, responsible teacher preparation, professional development, and strong partnerships with parents (NAEYC, 1994). Cooperative, respectful, and egalitarian teachers and caregivers are generally the most successful in working with children facing multiple threats to development (Rhodes & Hennessy, 2001). Additionally, these successful teachers tend to be nonjudgmental in their interactions with children, to take a problem-solving approach to children's life events, to believe in their ability to influence children's development rather than fantasizing about rescuing them from their hostile environments, and to try to understand the views of all stakeholders in children's lives (e.g., parents, children, community members) as potential sources of important information. Perhaps most important, these teachers and caregivers have high expectations and efficacy beliefs for all children. Teacher preparation and staff development programs must revisit the portrait of successful teachers and align coursework, experiences, and training toward the development of these dispositions (Early & Winton, 2001; Isenberg, 2000).

5. *Develop teachers and administrators who can meet children's developmental needs while addressing academic standards.* Since the 1980s, the education reform movement has focused on upgrading academic content standards while, in some states, diminishing attention to the developmental considerations of young children's learning (Hyson & Molinaro, 2001). Although this trend is most evident in K–12 education, a move toward more formal education—such as teacher-directed instruction on predetermined skills in preschools and programs such as Head Start—has also occurred. As a result, some teachers believe that the development of the whole child (emotional, physical, and social as well as cognitive needs) is neglected and ignored (Adcock & Patton, 2002). Teachers and administrators need support in developing teaching techniques that simultaneously address mandated curriculum standards and the developmental needs of young children. They also need to demonstrate an expanded repertoire of ways to teach academic content such as alphabet letters. Professional organizations, along

with teacher preparation and staff development programs, should encourage the sharing of developmentally effective teaching strategies.

CONCLUSION

The ideas presented in this chapter are intended to stimulate thought, provoke discussion, and lead to better solutions to breaking down the barriers to children's optimal development. Even though many children continue to experience seemingly unabated adverse influences, early childhood educators must move beyond appalling statistics and alarming accounts of children's circumstances. Early childhood teachers and caregivers can, at the very least, exert a powerful positive influence on the lives of all children. Perhaps children like Lynette, in the opening case of this chapter, would benefit much more if their teachers adopt a model of learning that emphasizes comprehensive and coordinated services, provide an environment that encourages adaptability and affirmation, embrace an attitude that these children can be successful in school despite their vulnerability, and utilize a nonthreatening, supportive teaching style. Early childhood professionals, regardless of roles, must find ways to accept and nurture all children and provide the conditions necessary to optimize their healthy growth and development.

REFERENCES

Adcock, S. G., & Patton, M. M. (2002). Views of effective early childhood educators regarding systemic constraints that affect their teaching. *Journal of Research in Childhood Education, 15*(2), 194–208.

Ainsworth, M., Bell, S., & Stayton, D. (1974). Infant and mother attachment and social development. Socialization as a product of reciprocal responsiveness and stigmas. In M. P. Richards (Ed.), *The integration of a child into a social world* (pp. 99–135). New York: Cambridge University Press.

Ashiabi, G. (2000). Promoting the emotional development of preschoolers. *Early Childhood Education Journal, 28*(2), 79–84.

Berk, L. E. (2002). *Infants, children, and adolescents*. Boston: Allyn & Bacon.

Bowlby, J. (1969). *Attachment and loss* (Vol. 1). New York: Basic Books.

Boyer, E. L. (1991). *Ready to learn: A mandate for the nation*. New York: Carnegie Foundation for the Advancement of Learning.

Bradley, R. H., Whiteside, L., Mundfrom, D. J., Casey, P. H., Kelliher, K. J., & Pope, S. K. (1994). Early indications of resilience and their relation to experiences of low birthweight, premature children living in poverty. *Child Development, 65*(2), 346–360.

Bronfenbrenner, U. (1979). *The ecology of human development.* Cambridge, MA: Harvard University Press.

Brooks-Gunn, J., Britto, P. R., & Brady, C. (1999). Struggling to make ends meet: Poverty and child development. In M. E. Lamb (Ed.), *Parenting and child development in "nontraditional" families* (pp. 279–304). Mahwah, NJ: Erlbaum.

Browning, L., Davis, B., & Resta, V. (2000). What do you mean "Think before I act?": Conflict resolution with choices. *Journal of Research in Childhood Education, 14*(2), 232–238.

Carnegie Corporation of New York. (1994). *Starting points: Meeting the needs of our youngest children.* New York: Author.

Case, R., Griffin, S., & Kelly, W. M. (2001). Socioeconomic differences in children's early cognitive development and their readiness for schooling. In S. L. Golbeck (Ed.), *Psychological perspectives on early childhood education: Reframing dilemmas in research and practice* (pp. 37–63). Mahwah, NJ: Erlbaum.

Children's Defense Fund. (1995). *The state of America's children yearbook.* Washington, DC: Author.

Children's Defense Fund. (2001). *The state of America's children yearbook.* Washington, DC: Author.

Cornelius, M. D., Day, N. L., Richardson, G. A., & Taylor, P. M. (1999). Epidemiology of substance abuse during pregnancy. In P. J. Oh and R. E. Tarter (Eds.), *Sourcebook on substance abuse: Etiology, epidemiology, assessment, and treatment* (pp. 1–13). Boston: Allyn & Bacon.

DeGarmo, D. S., & Forgatch, M. S. (1999). Contexts as predictors of changing maternal parenting practices in diverse family structures: A social interactional perspective of risk and resilience. In E. M. Hetherington (Ed.), *Coping with divorce, single parenting, and remarriage: A risk and resiliency perspective* (pp. 227–252). Mahwah, NJ: Erlbaum.

Denham, S. A. (1998). *Emotional development in young children.* New York: Guilford.

Denham, S. A. (2001). Dealing with feelings: Foundations and consequences of young children's emotional competence. *Early Education & Development, 12*(1), 5–10.

Dewey, J. (1916). *Democracy and education.* New York: Macmillan.

Early, D. M., & Winton, P. J. (2001). Preparing the workforce: Early childhood teacher preparation at 2- and 4-year institutions of higher education. *Early Childhood Research Quarterly, 16*, 285–306.

Erikson, E. H. (1963). *Childhood and society.* New York: Norton.

Federal Interagency Forum on Child and Family Statistics. (2001). *America's children: Key national indicators of well-being.* Washington, DC: U.S. Government Printing Office.

Galinsky, E., Bond, J. T., & Friedman, D. E. (1993). *The changing American workforce: Highlights of the national study.* New York: Families and Work Institute.

Garbarino, J. (1995). *Raising children in a socially toxic environment*. San Francisco: Jossey-Bass.

Garbarino, J. (1998). Raising children in a socially toxic environment. *Child Care Information Exchange, 122*, 8–10.

Golbeck, S. L. (2001). Instructional models for early childhood: In search of a child-regulated/teacher-guided pedagogy. In S. L. Golbeck (Ed.), *Psychological perspectives on early childhood education: Reframing dilemmas in research and practice* (pp. 3–34). Mahwah, NJ: Erlbaum.

Greer, J. (1990). The drug babies. *Exceptional Children, 56*(5), 382–384.

Grych, J. H., & Fincham, F. D. (1997). Children's adaptation to divorce: From description to explanation. In S. A. Wolchik & I. N. Sandler (Eds.), *Handbook of children's coping: Linking theory to intervention* (pp. 159–193). New York: Plenum.

Haberman, M. (1994). Can teachers be educated to save students in a violent society? In D. R. Walling (Ed.), *Teachers as leaders: Perspectives on the professional development of teachers* (pp. 153–177). Bloomington, IN: Phi Delta Kappa.

Helburn, S. (Ed.). (1995). *Cost, quality, and child outcomes in child care centers*. Denver: University of Colorado, Economics Department.

Hyson, M. C., & Molinaro, J. (2001). Learning through feeling: Children's development, teachers' beliefs and relationships, and classroom practices. In S. L. Golbeck (Ed.), *Psychological perspectives on early childhood education: Reframing dilemmas in research and practice* (pp. 107–131). Mahwah, NJ: Erlbaum.

Isenberg, J. P. (2000). The state of the art in early childhood professional preparation. In D. Horm-Wingerd and M. Hyson, (Eds.), *New teachers for a new century: The future of early childhood professional preparation* (pp. 15–48). Jessup, MD: U.S. Department of Education.

Katz, L. G. (1996). Child development knowledge and teacher preparation: Confronting assumptions. *Early Childhood Research Quarterly, 11*(12), 135–146.

Klein, E. L. (2001). Children's perspectives on their experiences in early education and child-care settings. In S. L. Golbeck (Ed.), *Psychological perspectives on early childhood education: Reframing dilemmas in research and practice* (pp. 131–150). Mahwah, NJ: Erlbaum.

Knitzer, J., & Cauthen, N. K. (2000). Innovative strategies support children and families coping with welfare change. *Young Children, 55*(1), 49–51.

Kontos, S., Howes, C., Shinn, M., & Galinsky, E. (1995). *Quality in family child care and relative care*. New York: Teachers College Press.

Kozol, J. (1995). *Amazing grace: The lives of children and the conscience of a nation*. New York: Crown.

Lewit, E. M. (1992). *U.S. health care for children*. Los Altos, CA: Center for the Future of Children.

Lindsey, G. (1999). Brain research and implications for early childhood education. *Childhood Education, 75*(2), 97–100.

McLoyd, V. C. (1998). Children in poverty: Development, public policy, and practice. In W. Damon (Ed.), *Handbook of child psychology: Vol. 4. Child psychology in practice* (pp. 135–208). New York: Wiley.

McMillan, J. H., & Reed, D. R. (1993). *Defying the odds: A study of resilient at-risk students*. Richmond, VA: Metropolitan Educational Research Consortium.

National Association for the Education of Young Children (NAEYC). (1994). NAEYC position statement on violence in the lives of children. *Young Children, 48*(6), 80–84.

National Center for Youth Law. (1995). Links between early childhood services and juvenile justice. *Youth Law News, 16*(1).

Newberger, J. J. (1997). New brain development research—A wonderful window of opportunity to build public support for early childhood education! *Young Children, 52*(4), 4–9.

Peisner-Feinberg, E. S., Burchinal, M. R., Clifford, R. M., Cualkin, M. L., Howes, C., Kagan, S. L., et al. (2000). *The children of the cost, quality, and outcomes study go to school: Technical report.* Chapel Hill: University of North Carolina, Frank Porter Graham Child Development Center.

Phillips, D., Mekos, D., Scarr, S., McCarney, K., & Abbott-Shim, M. (2000). Within and beyond the classroom door: Assessing quality in child care centers. *Early Childhood Research Quarterly, 15*(5), 475–496.

Piaget, J. (1951). *The child's conception of the world.* Savage, MD: Littlefield Adams.

Quyen, G. T., Bird, H. R., Davies, M., Hoven, C., Cohen, P., Jensen, P. S., et al. (1998). Adverse life events and resilience. *Journal of the American Academy of Child and Adolescent Psychiatry, 37,* 1191–1200.

Rhodes, S., & Hennessy, E. (2001). The effects of specialized training on caregivers in early-years settings: An evaluation of the foundation course in playgroup practice. *Early Childhood Research Quarterly, 15*(5), 559–576.

Rousseau, J.-J. (1947). Émile, ou De l'éducation [Émile, or, On Education]. In O. E. Tellows and N. R. Tarrey (Eds.), *The age of enlightenment.* New York: Croft. (Original work published 1762)

Schorr, L., with Daniel Schorr. (1988). *Within our reach: Breaking the cycle of the disadvantaged.* New York: Anchor.

Spitz, R. (1949). The role of ecological factors in emotional development in infancy. *Child Development, 20,* 145–156.

Thomas, J. Y. (2000). Falling through the cracks. Crack-exposed children in the U.S. public schools: An educational policy issue. *Journal of Education Policy, 15*(5), 575–583.

Vygotsky, L. (1978). *Mind in society: The development of higher psychological processes.* Cambridge, MA: Harvard University.

Walker, A., Rosenberg, M., & Balaban-Fill, K. (1999). Neurodevelopmental and neurobehavioral sequelae of selected substances of abuse and psychiatric medications in utero. *Neurological Disorders: Developmental and Behavioral Sequelae, 8,* 845–867.

Weikart, D. P. (1998). Changing early childhood development through educational intervention. *Preventative Medicine, 27,* 233–237.

Weissbourd, B. (1996). *The myth of the vulnerable child*. Reading, MA: Addison-Wesley.

Wheeler, E. J. (1994). Peer conflict in the classroom: Drawing implications from research. *Childhood Education, 70*(5), 296–299.

Zill, N., & Schoenborn, C. A. (1990). Developmental learning and emotional problems: Health of our nation's children, United States, 1988 (*Advance Data No. 19*). Washington, DC: U.S. Department of Health and Human Services.

Chapter 2

Young Children's Affirmation of Differences: Curriculum That Is Multicultural and Developmentally Appropriate

EDWINA BATTLE VOLD

In summer 2001, our 5-year-old granddaughter and her sisters accompanied us to a birthday party for one of our colleagues. Upon our arrival, the 5-year-old looked out of the car window and saw many adults and children gathered outside on the lawn from countries such as Nigeria, Ghana, Kenya, along with African Americans and a few European Americans, all of whom had made connections through the local university. She then exclaimed: "Grandpa, they are all Black. We are White! What are we going to do?" To which the older granddaughter said, "Give me your hand, everything will be all right."

It was difficult at the time for my husband and me to know what our 5-year-old granddaughter was really thinking; however, we knew that her concerns and observations were real and influenced by her perceptions, categorizations, reasoning, and inferences. Her question and observations indicated to us that she was curious about a new experience and was actively seeking information to help her understand and make sense of her potentially widening world of new and different people. Her question— posed to her grandpa, who is also White, rather than to her grandma, who is African American—gave us an indication that she was seeking intervention and assurance from someone who was most like her that this new experience could be a positive one. Interestingly, that support came from her older sister, who took her hand and calmly led her into the midst of some new and different children who, they quickly discovered, were quite similar to them in age and behaviors.

Early childhood educators are cognizant of the fact that the ability and willingness to interact socially and emotionally with diverse groups is learned behavior. However, there are two questions that remain unanswered by many early childhood educators:

1. How and to what extent can early childhood educators and parents best prepare young children in their early years to accept and respect diversity?
2. What developmentally appropriate strategies can be used to modify children's attitudes and behaviors that already reflect biases and prejudices?

Using the scholarly work of teacher educators and researchers in early childhood education and multicultural education (Banks, 1997; Derman-Sparks & A.B.C. Task Force, 1989; Nieto, 1992; Saracho & Spodek, 1983; Sleeter & Grant, 1988; Vold, 1992), this chapter focuses on the questions raised regarding young children and diversity. First, I present a rationale for a curriculum on diversity and discuss its appropriateness for young children. Next, I describe the evolution of multicultural education and the sociopolitical context in which it developed. Then, I review the debates surrounding multicultural education and the controversies regarding children's readiness to deal with concepts of diversity. Finally, I highlight competencies needed by teachers and caregivers who are responsible for implementing a curriculum on diversity.

A CURRICULUM ON DIVERSITY

Curriculum, no matter what its content, affects students by initiating learning and by exposing students to experiences designed to help all children to attain skills and knowledge and to change values and feelings. Thus, curriculum becomes a systematic plan for exposing students to content and to processes of learning and living (Swartz & Robison, 1982).

Historically, early childhood educators have used varied approaches to help young children recognize and appreciate diversity. This diversity is not relegated to race alone but includes the varied social categories of gender, language, class, exceptionality, and religion. The varied approaches used are content- and process-oriented in their attempt to increase knowledge and social interaction skills and to change values and feelings about differences. The varied approaches fall within the educational purview of multicultural education. Broadly defined, multicultural education embodies the instructional methods used to generate children's cultural sensitivity through diversified curricula, instructional practices, and textual materials. It includes a diversified body of knowledge (Fereshter, 1995) and involves processes through which young children can begin to reconstruct the efficacy of the social and political systems they participate in including the classroom, families, and communities (Vold, 1992).

Multicultural educators have not advocated a single approach to multicultural education. Neither have early childhood educators advocated one approach. In response to issues reflective of different schools and their conceptual views of school and society, educators have designed varied approaches to multicultural education, as noted above. Sleeter and Grant's (1988) typology, or classification, of multicultural education approaches include:

1. Teaching the exceptional and the culturally different
2. Single-group studies
3. The human relations approach
4. The multicultural education approach
5. The education that is multicultural and social reconstructionist approach

Of the five approaches, the human relations approach is the model most frequently applied to early childhood settings according to Swadener, Arnold, Cahill, and Marsh (1995). This approach includes helping children communicate with, accept, and get along with people who are different from themselves; reducing or eliminating stereotypes; and helping children develop self-esteem and identity. The single-group studies approach is seldom used in early childhood programs; however, teaching the exceptional and culturally different approach, which promotes assimilationist principles, continues to be the primary curriculum model for Head Start programs. The education that is multicultural and social reconstructionist approach extends multiculturalism into the realm of social action and focuses at least as much on challenging social stratification as on celebrating human diversity and equal opportunity. *The Anti-Bias Curriculum: Tools for Empowering Young Children* (Derman-Sparks & the A.B.C. Task Force, 1989) was one of the first curricula for children in the preoperational stage to deal with anti-bias and the social reconstructionist perspective, a topic that is discussed later in this chapter.

The multicultural education typology of Banks (1988) is referred to as "levels of curriculum reform," although these levels emerge as varied approaches in schools and are based on the differing views of school and society of those who must implement the curriculum. They include:

1. The contributions approach to multicultural education, which focuses on heroes, holidays, and discrete cultural elements
2. The additive approach, which adds concepts, themes, and perspectives to the program without changing the structure of the content or processes
3. The transformation approach, which changes the structure of the curriculum to enable students to view concepts, issues, events, and themes from the perspective of diverse groups
4. The social action approach, which allows students, even in the preoperational stage, to make decisions on important issues and take actions to solve them

Too often, early childhood programs design curricula based on the contributions approach and/or the additive approach.

To summarize, the most salient features of any of the approaches to multicultural education when used in programs with children are as follows:

- Instructional strategies which are flexible and appropriate to the developmental levels of children
- Content which is unbiased, incorporating contributions of cultural groups
- Instructional materials that are free of bias, omissions and stereotypes and show individuals from different social/cultural categories portraying the full range of occupational and social roles
- Teachers and caregivers who have positive attitudes and behaviors toward cultural diversity and individual uniqueness (Grant, 1977, p. 30)

These features put more emphasis on process rather than content, allowing teachers more opportunities to emphasize cross-cultural interactions that assist children in dispelling stereotypes that they have accumulated in experiences outside the classroom.

APPROPRIATENESS FOR YOUNG CHILDREN

The appropriateness of a multicultural education curriculum for young children must take into account their levels of development in two areas: moral development (i.e., how children formulate values and beliefs) and cognitive development (i.e., how children process information). There is some concern regarding the moral, social, physical, and cognitive readiness of young children to deal with issues of diversity, but there seems to be general agreement on the part of teachers, parents, and caregivers that children are physically and socially able to deal with them. Thus, this part of the chapter focuses on the moral and cognitive readiness of young children to respond to diversity issues using the theory and research of Robert Coles, Lawrence Kohlberg, Jean Piaget, and Lev Vygotsky.

Moral Development

Moral development begins at infancy and continues throughout life. We know that young children in their early childhood years are in the process of developing values and beliefs that affect later judgments and behaviors toward themselves and others. In fact, children in early childhood are not only formulating values and beliefs but also altering feelings and attitudes that affect judgments about peers with whom they interact daily.

Moral development is about character development—learning the difference between right and wrong, having respect for oneself and others, and being empathic and caring toward other human beings (Muzi, 2000). According to Coles (1997), moral development is influenced by social and cultural forces outside the classroom. It develops as a response to moral experiences as they take place in a family or a classroom. Coles (1997) further states:

> We grow morally as a consequence of learning how to be with others, how to behave in this world, a learning prompted by taking to heart what we have seen and heard. The child is a witness; the child is an ever-attentive witness of grown-up morality—or lack thereof; the child looks and looks for cues as to how one ought to behave, and finds them galore as we parents and teachers go about our lives, making choices, addressing people, showing in action our rock-bottom assumptions, desires, and values, and thereby telling those young observers much more than we may realize. (p. 5)

Much of the research conducted during the twentieth century was based on the work of Lawrence Kohlberg (1984), who identified three levels of moral development, each containing two stages: the preconventional level, the conventional level, and the postconventional level. The preconventional morality stage, which is the stage of our 5-year-old grandchild and central to this chapter, is characterized by egocentrism, meaning that children regard what is and who is good or bad based on their needs being satisfied. This stage is also characterized by concern about whether or not punishment will result. In his earlier work, Kohlberg (1976) also stated that the preconventional stage is a time when children rely very heavily on adults for direction as to what is good and bad. They are obedient to adult authority and base their judgments and behaviors on models.

Cognitive Development

An intellectual process, cognitive development is both active and interactive. In fact, Anastasiow (1977) contends that successful teaching and parenting shortens children's trial-and-error learning experiences. When children are helped in their attempts to figure out the way the world works, learning is facilitated. Thus, direct experience is a crucial context for developing anti-bias concepts, such as the situation described in the opening scenario with our 5-year-old granddaughter (Piaget & Inhelder, 1969; Vygotsky, 1978). According to these theorists, not only does direct experience facilitate learning or cognitive development, but it is also the most effective way for children to learn. For example, from infancy to ages of 5, 6, and 7—Piaget's preoperational stage of cognitive development—young children need opportunities to explore and interact in varied experiences to construct meaning. It is through schemes—a major assumption of Piaget's theory in which unobservable mental knowledge is accumulated—that young children develop patterns of behavior and thinking that help them to construct language and meaning associated with objects, people, and things. These schemes can embody experiences with race, ethnicity, class, language, and exceptionalities. Through more and more direct experiences with diversity, young children can begin to refine their thoughts and behaviors about the differences they observe in others. Eventually young children are able to create larger systems of thought and operations that expand their world. This expansion of their world beyond what they know as "normal" allows learners to take risks and to continue to venture into new and different social interactions, as our granddaughter did in the opening story.

Vygotsky is best known as a cognitive psychologist with a sociocultural perspective. Like Piaget, Vygotsky regarded children as active learners, but unlike Piaget, he argued that sociocultural processes rather than cognitive processes are of paramount importance. Crucial to his theory is the belief that children can and do learn on their own; but through direct experiences and appropriate intervention by adults or other, more knowledgeable individuals, young children can learn even more and at a faster rate. This aspect of Vygotsky's theory is referred to as the zone of proximal development (ZPD). The sociocultural dimension of development is crucial to the questions raised in the beginning of the chapter with regard to intervention by parents and teachers and the ways in which to modify children's attitudes and behaviors that reflect biases and prejudices. According to Vygotsky, at any given point in development, there are tasks that individuals can do and concepts that they can understand, while at the same time, there are tasks and concepts that are beyond their capabilities. Between these extremes, there are things that can be learned and that can be accomplished with help, referred to as scaffolding. Providing that help in early childhood is often the role of the teacher or caregiver. In families, parents frequently play the key role of providing that support.

Kelvin Seifert (1993) offers some implications of the ZPD and the sociocultural perspective to teachers in early childhood settings and also to parents:

> [T]he ZPD has proven to be helpful in planning teaching strategies. It suggests the importance of active, sensitive involvement with tasks that children undertake, and reminds teachers of their role in making children's initial activities meaningful to children themselves. . . . Young children need adults, or at least other individuals more competent than themselves, to create zones of proximal development as children develop and learn. (p. 19)

Since young children in the preoperational stage of cognitive development and the preconventional stage of moral development are constantly learning new concepts, reconstructing old concepts into new knowledge and skills, and using these capabilities to alter their modes of thinking and feeling, early childhood educators must provide more organized experiences in which children can interact willingly with individuals and groups different from themselves. Both vicarious and real experiences provide young children with opportunities to explore and discover our multicultural world. In fact, such direct experiences help children begin to develop and progress to higher levels of cognition and moral judgment, which are necessary to effective participation in multicultural education approaches with an anti-bias and social reconstructionist perspective.

THE SOCIOCULTURAL EVOLUTION
OF MULTICULTURAL EDUCATION

Multicultural education evolved as an educational concept in the 1970s. For more than three decades, it has been a strategy used in schools to help students understand and respond to facts, attitudes, and behaviors of different groups with regard to race/ethnicity, class, exceptionalities, language, and gender. As an educational strategy, it represented a shift from the "melting-pot theory" to a recognition of "cultural pluralism." The melting-pot theory is sometimes referred to as "the melting-pot myth" because of its assumption that all cultures and all racial groups are expected to assimilate, resulting in a superior one-model American. On the other hand, "cultural pluralism," as of the 1970s, implied that all cultural, racial, and ethnic groups in American society have the right to mutually coexist and have the freedom to maintain their own identities and lifestyles within the confines of the dominant culture (Stent, Hazard, & Rivlin, 1973). The development of multicultural education, with its deemphasis on the melting-pot theory and its new emphasis on cultural pluralism and the sociocultural climate in which it evolved, is shown in Figure 2.1.

Following World War I, there was a push for assimilation and conformity. The myth of the melting pot was prominent in educational thought and practice and continues to prevail in the popular media and in some educational practices. Immigrants were encouraged to renounce their ancestry in favor of values and behaviors of the dominant European American groups of the United States. In the 1950s, intergroup education emerged, followed by ethnic studies education in the 1960s. This was a period when Black Americans and other people of color began to assert their identities in contrast to the expected behaviors before and after World War II. There was Black Power, Chicano Power, and Indian Power. In the midst of riots, racial tensions, and increased awareness of inequities in work, housing, and education, many people of color were exerting their ethnic awareness and pride. Schools responded with ethnic studies that became an addendum to the already-existent curriculum content. The educational curriculum from kindergarten to postsecondary school included studies of separate racial and ethnic groups, emphasizing what Boyer (1985) calls the four Fs: facts, foods, famous people, and festivals. The four Fs curriculum highlighted a few facts about famous people from minority groups that were excluded from the traditional curriculum. For example, it included celebrations of African American music, literature, and foods during Black History Month; celebrations of foods and festivals of Native Americans around Thanksgiving; and celebrations of the foods and music of Mexican Americans around Cinco de Mayo.

The 1970s brought about the actual birth of multicultural education and the beginning of educational change. Educators and theorists such as Banks and Banks (1997), Boyer (1985), Nieto (1992), and Ramsey, Vold, and Williams (1989) would agree that multicultural education is distinguished from its predecessors by its recognition and valuing of cultural pluralism. Multicultural education rejects the view that schools should seek to "melt away" cultural differences or the view that schools should tolerate differences. Christine Sleeter and Carl Grant, in a 1987 article in the *Harvard Educational Review*, delineate characteristics of a multicultural education approach that

PHASE	CHARACTERISTICS
The melting pot 1900–	Monocultural education dominated schools
	Orientation to the ideal of *E pluribus unum*
	Focus on assimilation
	Curriculum content/strategies drawn from classic disciplines (Western / European tradition)
The push toward Anglo conformity 1920–	Monocultural education dominated schools
	Focus on acculturation and similarity
	Curriculum drawn from classic disciplines and/or orientation toward preparation for citizenship and loyalty
Toward desegregation 1950–	Intergroup education promoted
	Pressure to eliminate the separate but equal doctrine
	Focus on racial balance and institutional change rather than curriculum
	Supreme Court ruling of *Brown v. Board of Education*
Toward ethnic revitalization 1965–	Ethnic studies education as separate courses
	Recognition of the validity of the minority and ethnic experiences; Head Start focuses on the culturally different for young children
	Curriculum content/strategies drawn from the history, traditions, and issues affecting particular ethnic/cultural groups
The recognition of cultural pluralism 1975–	Multicultural approach to education appears
	Diversity of cultural heritage seen as source of the nation's strength
	Anti-bias curriculum developed
	Differences and similarities emphasized
	Promotion of curriculum drawn from integration of multicultural perspectives throughout all subject areas
The affirmation of diversity 1990–1991	Focus on historically correct data about diverse groups in American society
	The disuniting of America debate continues
	Push to examine the identities and assumptions of White ethnic groups
	Link between multicultural education and critical pedagogy/culturally responsive teaching
	Empirical research on multicultural education programs

FIGURE 2.1. The evolution of multicultural education. *Source*: Adapted from Vold, 1989.

promotes cultural pluralism and social equality by reforming the school program for all students to make it reflect diversity. These reforms include school
staffing patterns that reflect the pluralistic nature of American society; unbiased curricula that incorporate the contributions of different social groups,
women, and the handicapped; the affirmation of the languages of non-
English-speaking minorities; and instructional materials that are appropriate and relevant for the students and which are integrated rather than supplementary. (p. 422)

Grant (1977), in an earlier work, added an action dimension and argued
that multicultural education should prepare students to challenge social-
structural inequality and promote cultural diversity. This was the beginning of the education that is multicultural and social reconstructionist
approach, which has as its goal dealing with social inequalities engendered
by racism, sexism, and classism.

It was during this period in the evolution of multicultural education
that early childhood educators began to design age-appropriate strategies
to help young children adjust to new school and child-care environments
with ease and develop a sense of belonging rather than feelings of displace-
ment. Presentations at early childhood conferences brought together concerned educators interested in cultural and language diversity. Workshops,
seminars, and discussion groups focused on working with children in culturally diverse communities and helping children in more monocultural communities—rural and urban—to become more sensitive to our multicultural
society. Educators at all levels, from early childhood educators to teacher
educators in early childhood education, were actively and collaboratively
seeking ways to help young children develop a strong sense of self, a sense
of belonging, and an appreciation for people different from themselves.

It was also during this period that Louise Derman-Sparks and the
Anti-Bias Curriculum (A.B.C.) team developed the Anti-Bias Curriculum,
which was published in 1989. It was their belief that the preschool years
form the foundation for children's development of a strong sense of self,
empathy, positive attitudes toward people different from themselves, and
social interaction skills. An underlying assumption of the Anti-Bias Curriculum is that institutional and interpersonal racism and other forms
of oppression in our society hinder healthy development of self-worth
and an appreciation of diversity. The curriculum focuses on helping
children learn how to become aware of the connection between power
and issues of race, language, and physical disabilities, as well as the relationship between a lack of knowledge and the presence of stereotypes
and biases.

According to Derman-Sparks (1998), there are four goals of the Anti-
Bias Curriculum that are interactive and build on one another:

1. To nurture each child's construction of a knowledgeable, confident self-concept and group identity
2. To promote each child's comfortable, empathic interaction with people from diverse backgrounds
3. To foster each child's critical thinking about bias
4. To cultivate each child's ability to stand up for him- or herself and for others in the face of biasing

Those early childhood educators and parents who use the Anti-Bias Curriculum find that a total environment is created to promote an understanding, respect, and affirmation of diversity.

In the latter part of the 1980s, educators such as Giroux (1988) and Nieto (1992) added another dimension to multicultural education. Some refer to it as critical thinking, and others as critical pedagogy. Scriven and Paul (1994) define critical thinking as

> [an] intellectually disciplined process of actively and skillfully conceptualizing, applying, analyzing, synthesizing, and evaluating information gathered from, or generated by, observation, experience, reflection, reasoning, or communication as a guide to belief and action. (p. 2)

Critical pedagogy then becomes a process of preparing individuals to make carefully thought-out judgments about the worth, accuracy, and value of the information gained from real and vicarious experiences. Nieto (1992) added critical pedagogy to her definition of multicultural education, which she characterizes as

> a process of comprehensive school reform and basic education for all students. It challenges and rejects racism and other forms of discrimination in schools and society and accepts and affirms the pluralism (ethnic, racial, linguistic, religious, economic, and gender, among others) that students, their communities, and teachers represent. Multicultural education permeates the curriculum and instructional strategies used in schools, as well as the interactions among teachers, students and parents, and the very way schools conceptualize the nature of teaching and learning. Because it uses critical pedagogy as its underlying philosophy and focuses on knowledge, reflection and action (praxis) as the basis for social change, multicultural education furthers the democratic principles of social justice. (p. 83)

Nieto sums up her description of multicultural education as a process that is—or should be—an anti-racist stance, a part of basic education important for all students, a way of promoting education for social justice, and a reflection of a critical pedagogy perspective.

After more than three decades of multicultural education and more than six decades of concern for civil and human rights in education and in society, educators are still struggling with the effective management of cultural diversity and provisions for equality in schooling. For multicultural education to become a reality in the 21st century, there must be a commitment to use our knowledge and research to promote diversity, reduce prejudice, and demand a democratic society with social justice and equality for all people. This is a goal and a practice that is best begun in the early years of childhood.

DEBATE AND CONTROVERSIES SURROUNDING MULTICULTURAL EDUCATION

The multicultural education movement has encountered much criticism since its inception in the early 1970s. Attempts to gain full acceptance have been hampered by confusion and debate over its various meanings, its philosophical basis, and its viability as a vehicle for bringing about equity in society. According to Banks (1986), this confusion and debate is to be expected because multicultural education

> deals with highly controversial and politicized issues such as racism and inequality. [It] is likely to be harshly criticized during its formative stages because it deals with serious problems in society and appears to many individuals and groups to challenge established institutions, norms and values. It is also likely to evoke strong emotions, feelings and highly polarized opinions; as it searches for its raison d'être, there is bound to be suspicion and criticism. (p. 222)

Conservative leaders, such as Arthur Schlesinger, Jr., E. D. Hirsch, Diane Ravitch, William Bennett, Thomas Sowell, and Lynnne Cheney, have been strong in their opposition to multicultural education. They resist the change to a more inclusive curriculum and see it as a divisive tool that reinforces and extends the already existing myths and stereotypes propagated about society's ethnic and racial groups (Campbell, 2000).

These conservative perspectives on multicultural education are not lost in the early childhood and child development arguments. The major debate among teachers and parents of young children concerns whether there is a lack of "developmental readiness" or cognitive capacity to deal with the content of multicultural education. This debate is fueled by arguments about young children's egocentrism and lack of understanding of history and time, which make it difficult for young children to avoid superficial or stereotypic conceptions (Swadener et al., 1995).

Conservative educators with and without backgrounds in early childhood education often assume that young children are unaware of differences relating to race, culture, ethnicity, and other characteristics and that they do not discriminate against those who are different from themselves (Wolpert, 1998). There are even debates about the focus on differences to the exclusion of similarities, which is seen as divisive. But, as Ramsey (1998) points out, children do notice human differences at an early age and these distinctions become part of the earliest constructions of their social world. Not only do children see differences; their ideas about them also begin to reflect the attitudes of significant adults at an early age.

Ramsey's findings echo the research reviewed in Joel Spring's (1995) *Intersection of Cultures*. He describes research findings that show that young children classify differences between people and are influenced by bias toward others:

> By the age of 2 children are aware of gender differences and begin to apply color names to skin color. Between ages 3 and 5, children try to figure out who they are by examining the differences in gender and skin color. By 4 or 5 years old, children engage in socially determined gender roles, and they give racial reasons for the selection of friends. (p. 92)

Despite the criticisms of multicultural education and the debates on its inappropriateness for young children, there is no doubt that the concerns and the healthy debates reflect our need as multicultural educators and early childhood educators to examine new and challenging ways to create environments that respond positively to the dynamics of changing demographics in and out of school classrooms. We know that education cannot solve all of society's problems with regard to biases concerning race, ethnicity, gender, language differences, and exceptionalities, but we believe that systemic curriculum changes that support our culturally pluralistic nature remain the potentially most important influence on attitudes of respect for and affirmation of differences.

IMPLICATIONS FOR TEACHERS OF YOUNG CHILDREN

Knowing how to respond appropriately to our 5-year-old granddaughter presented a challenge, but not an impossible task, because of our own background knowledge of diversity and children's development. We were aware that children can grow in their observation of the world and their differentiations of that world only through direct experiences (Piaget & Inhelder, 1969). We were also aware of the importance of adults serving as facilitators and interpretors of new experiences (Vygotsky, 1978). In addition, we truly believed that the preoperational stage is the period during which to expose young children to experiences that can expand their interaction skills beyond their own group.

Nieto (1992) challenges teachers of young children to become multicultural persons in their own right. She says the process may take many years because of our own schooling, which has generally been monocultural and focused on assimilation or conformity. And she says we have had few if any models for developing a multicultural perspective. The same strategies offered by Wolpert (1998) to help students address biases can also be used to challenge teachers and caregivers who want to create an anti-racist/anti-bias environment for young children. She recommends the following:

- Continuously reevaluate ways to integrate an anti-bias approach.
- Watch for bias that children encounter in the media and in their environment, and listen to their comments.
- Gather materials that contradict the stereotypes and make the invisible visible.
- Ask questions to develop critical thinking.
- Create opportunities for problem solving: what would you do if . . . ?
- Take action to protest bias. (p. 193)

Davidman and Davidman (1997) further challenge teachers of all children to remember that effective teaching is directly linked to multicultural education and that every classroom and school has the potential to be a multicultural setting. They further remind teachers and caregivers that a classroom or child-care center becomes a multicultural setting when students in that room experience a multicultural curriculum and that the multiculturalness of a setting is not determined by the type of students in the class; rather, it is created by the perspective and knowledge base of the teacher or caregiver.

CONCLUSION

The United States has always been a culturally diverse country. In the 21st century it will continue to become more diverse, multicultural, and multinational. Young children will have many more opportunities to interact with individuals and groups different from themselves. They will need to be appreciative of and knowledgeable about diverse traditions, dialects, languages, and customs to ensure that they not only tolerate but affirm differences. Our 5-year-old granddaughter, like many other 5-year-olds, exhibited many of the characteristics of young children in the preoperational stage, including obedience, avoidance of punishment, and fear of new and different things over which they have no control. Egocentric thought was also present; however, she also expressed a willingness to expand her experiences beyond her own world. She was fortunate to have adults and an older sister to provide the intervention and assurance that she needed to take that important step toward reducing prejudice and discrimination and learning ways to enlarge her circle of friends.

REFERENCES

Anastasiow, N. J. (1977). Developmental parameters of knowledge transmission. In M. Scott & S. Grimmett (Eds.), *Current issues in child development* (pp. 23–27). Washington, DC: National Association for the Education of Young Children.

Banks, J. A. (1986). Multicultural education and its critics: Britain and the United States. In S. Modgil, G. Verma, K. Mallick, & C. Modgil (Eds.), *Multicultural education: The interminable debate* (pp. 10–19). London: Falmer.

Banks, J. A. (1988). Approaches to multicultural reform. *Multicultural Leader*, *1*(2), 1–3.

Banks, J. A. (1997). Approaches to multicultural curriculum reform. In J. A. Banks & C. A. M. Banks (Eds.), *Multicultural education: Issues and perspectives* (3rd ed.). (pp. 229–250). Boston: Allyn & Bacon.

Banks, J. A., & Banks, C. A. M. (1997). *Multicultural education: Issues and perspectives* (3rd ed.). Boston: Allyn & Bacon.

Boyer, J. (1985). *Multicultural education: Product to process*. Manhattan, KS: Kansas State University Press.

Campbell, D. E. (2000). *Choosing democracy: A practical guide to multicultural education* (2nd ed.). Upper Saddle River, NJ: Prentice Hall.

Coles, R. (1997). *The moral intelligence of children*. New York: Random House.

Davidman, L., & Davidman, P. T. (1997). *Teaching with a multicultural perspective* (2nd ed.). New York: Longman.

Derman-Sparks, L. (1998). Activism and preschool children. In E. Lee, D. Menkart, & M. Okazawa-Rey (Eds.), *Beyond heroes and holidays: A practical guide to K–12 anti-racist, multicultural education and staff development* (pp. 188–192). Washington, DC: Network of Educators on America.

Derman-Sparks, L., & the A.B.C. Task Force. (1989). *The Anti-Bias Curriculum: Tools for empowering young children*. Washington, DC: National Association for the Education of Young Children.

Fereshter, M. H. (1995). Multicultural education in the United States: A historical review. *Multicultural Review*, *4*(2), 38–48.

Giroux, H. A. (1988). *Teachers as intellectuals: Toward a critical pedagogy of learning*. Granby, MA: Bergin & Garvey.

Grant, C. A. (1977). Anthropological foundations of education that is multicultural. In C. A. Grant (Ed.), *Multicultural education: Commitments, issues and applications*. Washington, DC: Association for Supervision and Curriculum Development.

Kohlberg, L. (1976). Moral stages and moralization: Cognitive developmental approaches. In R. Lickona (Ed.), *Moral development and behavior: Theory research and social issues* (pp. 247–320). New York: Holt, Rinehart, and Winston.

Kohlberg, L. (1984). *Essays in moral development: Vol 2. The psychology of moral development*. San Franscisco: Harper Row.

Muzi, M. J. (2000). *Child development through time and transition*. Upper Saddle River, NJ: Prentice Hall.

Nieto, S. (1992). *Affirming diversity: The socio-political context of multicultural education*. New York: Longman.

Piaget, J., & Inhelder, B. (1969). *The psychology of the child* (H. Weaver, Trans.). New York: Basic Books.

Ramsey, P. G. (1998). *Teaching and learning in a diverse world: Multicultural education for young children* (2nd ed.). New York: Teachers College Press.

Ramsey, P. G., Vold, E., & Williams, L. R. (1989). *Multicultural education: A source book*. New York: Garland.

Saracho, O. N., & Spodek, B. (1983). *Understanding the multicultural experience in early childhood education*. Washington, DC. National Association for the Education of Young Children.

Scriven, M., & Paul, R. (1994). *Defining critical thinking*. Draft statement for the National Council for Excellence in Critical Thinking Instruction, Sonoma State University, Rohnert Park, CA.

Seifert, K. L. (1993). Cognitive development and early childhood education. In B. Spodek (Ed.), *Handbook of research on the education of young children* (pp. 9–21). New York: Macmillan.

Sleeter, C. E., & Grant, C. A. (1987). An analysis of multicultural education in the United States. *Harvard Educational Review, 57*, 421–444.

Sleeter, C. E., & Grant, C. A. (1988). *Making choices for multicultural education: Five approaches to race, class and gender*. Columbus, OH: Merrill.

Spring, J. (1995). *The intersection of cultures: Multicultural education in the United States*. New York: McGraw-Hill.

Stent, M. D., Hazard, W. R., & Rivlin, H. (1973). *Cultural pluralism education: A mandate for change*. New York: Appleton-Century-Crofts.

Swadner, B. B., Arnold, M. S., Cahill, B., & Marsh, M. M. (1995). Cultural and gender identity in early childhood: Anti-bias, culturally inclusive pedagogy with young learners. In C. A. Grant (Ed.), *Educating for diversity: An anthology of multicultural voice* (pp. 381–402). Boston: Allyn & Bacon.

Swartz S., & Robison, J. F. (1982). *Designing curriculum for early childhood*. Boston: Allyn & Bacon.

Vold, E. B. (1989). The evolution of multicultural education: A socio-political perspective. In P. G. Ramsey, E. B. Vold, & L. R. Williams (Eds.), *Multicultural education: A source book* (pp. 3–42). New York: Garland.

Vold, E. B. (1992). Reading and writing: A multicultural perspective. In E. B. Vold (Ed.), *Multicultural education in early childhood classrooms* (pp. 30–51). Washington, DC: National Education Association.

Vygotsky. L. S. (1978). *Mind in society*. Cambridge, MA: Harvard University Press.

Wolpert, E. (1998). Redefining the norm: Early childhood anti-bias strategies. In E. Lee, D. Menkart, & M. Okazawa-Rey (Eds.), *Beyond heroes and holidays: A practical guide to K–12 anti-racist, multicultural education and staff development* (pp. 194–205). Washington, DC: Network of Educators on America.

Chapter 3

Perspectives on Inclusion in Early Childhood Education

DORIS BERGEN

In the second-grade classroom that was Dee's first teaching assignment, there were four children with special needs, only one of whom was "identified." This child had a physical handicap that required her to wear braces. The three other children were a child with a learning disability that affected his symbolic memory and reading skill, one who was intellectually gifted but socially isolated, and one whose disruptive behavior required constant monitoring. Although Dee's early childhood education program had not included preparation for working with children with special needs, it had prepared her well for providing a developmentally appropriate classroom. Thus, she used that skill to make adaptations to meet the needs of these children. Dee's second teaching assignment was in a preschool, and, at various times during her years of employment, she had children with mental retardation, hearing impairment, juvenile diabetes, celiac disease, Legg-Perthes disease, seizures, attention-deficit/hyperactivity disorder, and language delays. She initially identified some of the children's problems, gained information from parents, and helped her staff learn to work with these children. When she served as director of preschool programs, she assisted her staff in adapting teaching for children with Down syndrome, visual impairment, autism, disfigurement from facial burns, language delays, neurological impairments, and problems resulting from abuse and neglect. She also conferred with related service personnel, such as speech therapists and pediatricians, as well as with parents. She recently supervised a toddler program of "reverse inclusion," in which a number of typically developing children were enrolled with children who were at risk for developmental delay. This collaborative, interdisciplinary program with a human services agency included professionals from a wide range of disciplines, as well as students preparing for these disciplines.

Although this set of experiences may seem like a vision of an early childhood educator of the future, it is actually a part of this author's biography and, no doubt, similar to experiences of many early childhood educators in the past. The idea of including children with disabilities in their programs is not a new concept for early childhood educators, many of whom have always included children with special needs in their programs. Because these educators emphasize developmentally appropriate learning, child choice and control, and facilitated peer interaction, they have usually been successful in managing such classrooms even though the label "inclusion" was not applied to them until recently.

Why has the issue of inclusion continued to be problematic for early childhood educators and intervention specialists? What conditions in the present environment have made inclusion both a positive opportunity and a subject of concern? This chapter addresses issues surrounding the emphasis on inclusion of children with disabilities in early childhood settings, presents differing viewpoints concerning the challenges and opportunities of inclusion within the historical/theoretical/social context of this movement, describes recent research about effects of inclusive programs, and discusses problems in implementing inclusion as well as suggestions for removing barriers to effective inclusion.

DIVERSE VIEWPOINTS ON THE MEANING OF INCLUSION

It is a rare early childhood educator or special educator who would not agree that all children can learn and that they should have the opportunity to learn to their highest potential. Both the proponents and opponents of full inclusion believe that all children should be in environments that maximize their learning opportunities. They differ about what that environment should be like and how it can be achieved. The debate is not as vociferous in early childhood as it is among those who teach older children, but the basic differences in viewpoint are expressed by teachers and parents at all levels.

As is the case with many newly advocated practices, the meaning of the term *inclusion* is often ambiguous and varied. There are also contrasting opinions as to when, how, and even *if* it should be the preferred practice for meeting the needs of children previously served in separate programs. The most far-reaching model, in terms of effects on both children and teachers, is that of "full inclusion." Full inclusion has all children, no matter what their disability, present in the regular education classroom (or, for very young children, in a child-care setting) with both special and regular educators sharing joint responsibility in a team-teaching or teaching-consulting model that adapts the curriculum to meet the needs of all learners.

At the opposite end of the continuum from full inclusion is the completely self-contained special education classroom, which has been the model commonly used to serve the needs of school-age children with disabilities. (Younger children are often not served at all.) On the continuum between full inclusion and no inclusion are models that incorporate special education children in regular education for various time periods less than the full day, involve the regular and special educator in varied balanced or unbalanced role responsibilities, and include or exclude children with severe or multiple disabilities. Guralnick (2001) has outlined five major models called inclusion presently in operation for preschool-age children:

1. Full—all children in the same class
2. Cluster—grafting a special education class onto a regular education class at the same site
3. Reverse—adding a group of typically developing children to a special education class
4. Social—having interaction for playtime and other less academic parts of the day (i.e., a type of "mainstreaming")
5. Dual—with children enrolled part of the day in each type of class

This chapter centers on the debate between advocates for "full" inclusion and those who favor any of the "partial/optional" inclusion models because this is the area where the debate is presently focused. Few educators are presently advocating the old model of completely separate education for children with disabilities.

The Full-Inclusion Argument

Full-inclusion advocates believe that a "separate but equal opportunity" approach does not give children with disabilities the best forum for reaching their potential achievement levels (Sailor, 2002; Shapiro, Loeb, & Bowermaster, 1993; Van Dyke, Stallings, & Colley, 1995). They are particularly concerned that children with severe disabilities need to be in integrated settings in order to give them "normalized" experiences so that they can learn the social interaction skills to prepare them for inclusion in the broader society (Gartner & Lipsky, 1987). They believe these children will improve their self-concept and gain in cognitive skills by being surrounded by peer models of achievement. They cite research evidence that special "pull-out" programs have had little effect on improving the performance of children with disabilities (e.g., Deno, Maruyama, Espin, & Cohen, 1990). Further, they believe that by being in the regular classroom, even children with severe disabilities will interact with peers and be able to form friendships (Hamre-Nietupski, Hendrickson, Nietupski, & Sasso, 1993). The importance of friendship development is stressed in a number of inclusion models (Bergen, 1993; Odom, 2002), but until recently research on such friendship development has been sparse.

The advocates see full inclusion as also benefiting typical children by helping them lose their fears and stereotypic thinking about persons with disabilities, which will have long-term benefits for society as a whole (Covert, 1995). Although there have been no long-term studies of this hypothesis, proponents believe that having experiences with people of diverse cultural, socioeconomic, and disability conditions result in all children learning attitudes and behaviors that will make them good citizens of a diverse society. In a recent survey of parents who children were in "reverse-inclusion" settings, parents of both typical children and children with disabilities gave strong support for inclusion and 94% said they would place their child in such a setting again (Rafferty, Boettcher, & Griffin, 2001).

Proponents do not believe that inclusion will prevent typical children from continuing to learn at their highest potential. Some research evidence seems to bear this out; children who are typically developing appear to do as well in inclusive as in noninclusive settings (Buysse & Bailey, 1993). In fact, proponents say an added benefit of inclusion is that children who are at risk for school failure but who don't presently "qualify" for special education services can have their learning needs met more effectively when an individualized rather than a "standard curriculum applied to all" approach is prevalent (Stainback & Stainback, 1991). While the claims for the benefits of inclusion are worthy, there is not yet a strong research base for the claims; the mandates of P.L. 94-142 were based primarily on "ideological, theoretical, and legal grounds, not on empirical evidence" (Guralnik, 2001, p. 4).

In order for the full-inclusion model to work, proponents agree that a rethinking of present regular education methods of instruction and staffing patterns is needed. They support curricular reforms and team-teaching approaches, although they think the regular education teacher should take ultimate responsibility for all children in the class (Jenkins, Pious, & Jewell, 1990). They do not suggest a reduction in special education personnel, however, because having a sufficient number of special education intervention specialists who are skilled in fostering adaptations to meet individualized needs is essential for the model to be effective. They believe that, with such changes in regular classroom structure, all children can benefit. For those children with severe disabilities, the addition of individual child aides may be necessary so that they can function well in the inclusion classroom, but these individual child aides must also work as part of the integrated team. Thus, in order to make inclusion most effective, proponents believe that major structural changes in educational practice are needed.

The Partial-/Optional-Inclusion Argument

Most opposition to a full-inclusion approach comes from people who want to maintain the present continuum of options, which include special education self-contained classrooms, resource rooms that provide assistance on an as-needed basis, and other "mainstream" options, as well as the full-inclusion option. Their argument is based on two types of concern, one of which is related to the social skill/self-concept dimension and one to academic achievement goals. Proponents of the range-of-options view include parents who have been especially concerned about children with moderate to severe disabilities. In a recent survey of parents of such children, Palmer, Fuller, Arora, and Nelson (2001) found that 39% of the parent respondents disagreed or strongly disagreed that full inclusion is a good model for students with severe disabilities and 45% disagreed or strongly disagreed that this model would be good for their child. The reasons they gave were either that the disabilities were too severe to be handled in a regular classroom or that the present school situation was not capable of handling such children. Particular concerns were expressed for children with specific intensive needs, such as those arising from autism, hearing or vision impairments, or complex health problems.

Others see full inclusion as problematic for children with mild or moderate needs, such as learning disabilities or mild developmental delays. They are not sanguine that the ideal classroom envisioned by full-inclusion proponents will be available for most children (Mather & Roberts, 1994) and fear that there will be a return to conditions of the past, when many children who needed learning assistance were overlooked in the "standard curriculum for all" classroom. This concern about academic achievement—that children with mild or moderate disabilities may be overlooked in a classroom geared to meet typical children's needs—is of particular concern because such children are more likely to be in inclusion settings than are children with intensive needs (Buysse, Bailey, Smith, & Simeonsson, 1994). Because of concerns that the regular classroom will not really change, these proponents of partial inclusion believe that children with mild disabilities may not be able to achieve as well in full-inclusion settings, and they cite research showing support for this view (e.g., Mather & Roberts, 1994). Joining this argument are those concerned about gifted children, whose needs have also been often overlooked in the regular classroom (Zigmond et al., 1995).

In regard to the social and self-concept dimension, the range-of-option advocates assert that while labeling and segregating children may not be conducive to social skill or self-concept improvement, there is little indication that having all children in the regular classroom will solve this problem. They cite research showing mixed results or even negative effects of inclusion when children lack social skills, because such children may be ignored or even rejected by peers (Guralnik, 2001; Odom et al., 2002; Roberts, Pratt, & Leach, 1991). Even preschool children are aware that they must make adaptations when interacting with their peers with disabilities, and although some studies show that peer social interactions increase, there is little evidence of strong friendship development (Buysse & Bailey, 1993). Friendship development must be a specifically structured goal, and adult facilitation of peer interactions must occur if friendships are to develop (Bergen, 1993; Odom et al., 2002).

Further, proponents of partial/optional inclusion assert that if children with disabilities have repeated failure doing academic tasks, they will not develop a positive self-concept (Dickman, 1994). They stress that teachers in inclusion settings must be especially skillful in adapting curriculum and instructional methods for these children to be successful in academic work. Because effective full-inclusion models require more adults (and more highly skilled adults) in the educational environment, they are also more expensive to implement. The advocates of partial or optional inclusion believe they are more realistic about what models can be embraced given teacher skill levels and the personnel resources of most schools.

Many of the objections to full inclusion that have been expressed arise from such practical concerns rather than from value issues. That is, although both teachers and parents have a generally positive view of the need for inclusion and support its goals, they also identify problems in implementing these models (Peck, Carlson, & Helmstetter, 1992; Semmel, Abernathy, Butera, & Lesar, 1991). While most would agree that the goals of inclusion are ones they support, they may disagree on what environment might be best for which children with which types of disabilities, how and by whom placement decisions should be made, and how the costs of providing such environments can be borne by schools. These issues are even more problematic for the infant/toddler population of children with disabilities because the options are fewer.

Inclusion Arguments and Early Childhood Practices

The arguments opposing full inclusion make presumptions about regular classroom environments and teaching styles that may not or may not be accurate for early childhood and early childhood intervention settings. Regular education classrooms at the primary level may still primarily use an approach of whole-group instruction and individual workbook use that does not differentiate among children on the basis of their needs (Baker & Zigmond, 1990). Classrooms at preschool and kindergarten levels are more likely to meet individual needs with activity choices, opportunities for peer interaction, and adaptations for learning. With recent emphasis at the state and national level on academic readiness and preparation for proficiency tests, however, even many preschools have changed their emphasis.

Early intervention classrooms, funded to serve children identified with disabilities, usually combine a developmentally appropriate curriculum with specific attention to children's individual needs. They have been good examples of individualized approaches, but some of these classrooms are disappearing as the emphasis on full inclusion in non–special education environments (i.e., natural environments) is stressed. In the past, when proponents of full inclusion described the preferred environment for effective full inclusion, their description was quite similar to what occurred in "traditional" kindergarten and preschool classrooms. Unfortunately, the present "academic drift" occurring in these classrooms because of pressure from later-grade proficiency testing policies may also hinder the move to effective inclusion.

In general, however, early childhood educators and early childhood intervention specialists share similar educational goals and recommended practices, making it possible for them to work well together in team approaches (Bergen, 1994a). For example, both groups use a team of staff members, individualize children's learning experiences, stress social skill development, and include curriculum opportunities for children to use a range of learning modalities. The majority of early educators do support the value of inclusion and are willing to make the transition to inclusion as long as support services are available.

Because early educators have often had other staff members in their classrooms, when they move to inclusive classrooms, they are usually more accepting of having special educators and other resource personnel, such as physical therapists, observing and working with the children and of incorporating teacher aides who can assist children with severe impairments or behavioral problems. Most child-care and preschool programs still do not have an early childhood intervention specialist available to act as a team member or consultant on a regular basis, however (Wolery et al., 1994). In 1997, fewer than half of NAEYC-accredited programs had access to services of early childhood intervention specialists (McDonnell, Brownell, & Wolery, 1997). Some personnel preparation programs are preparing dual license/certified teachers who will have skills to meet the educational needs both of children who are typical and who have disabilities. At the preschool level, mandated publicly funded programs have usually served only children with disabilities, although some of them include children who are at risk for developmental delay. Many of these are using reverse-inclusion models that incorporate typical children in their classrooms. The Head Start program has long had a mandate to include a portion of children with special needs in each class, and many private preschool and child-care programs also have accepted such children, but usually without the support of special educators or related personnel services.

Implementing inclusion is often a different matter for teachers in early childhood classrooms at the kindergarten and primary grade levels, because the teachers' structural constraints, personnel resources, and instructional methods differ. For example, teachers rarely have even one other adult in the classroom even though there may be 25 to 30 children in the class. Moreover, there has been increasing pressure on these teachers to focus on getting every child in the class to meet a certain level of performance, regardless of their special needs, learning modalities, or developmental status. Thus, although individual teachers may wholeheartedly embrace a developmentally appropriate philosophy, they may still be subjected to external pressures from state-mandated proficiency tests beginning at primary level and the subsequent directives from administrators to meet standard test score criteria. The problems they face in implementing an effective inclusive classroom are therefore more similar to those of teachers of older children. Although primary teachers may see the same potential benefits from inclusion that parents and teachers of preschool children have noted, they must resolve these concerns in regard to academic achievement and have the support of the educational system in order to have effective inclusion classrooms.

CONTEXTS OF THE INCLUSION DEBATE

If many of these arguments seem familiar, it may be because the contro-versy over inclusion, by whatever name it is called, is not a new one. These viewpoints are rooted in historical and political grounds and are strongly influenced by the social value structure of American society, which sends conflicting messages to parents, teachers, and children.

Historical/Political Context

Before the 1960s, there was little focus on special education except for children with severe sensory, motor, or cognitive problems. Educational service was either lacking or given in public institutional settings or privately funded special day facilities. When the Education of All Handi-capped Act was passed in 1975 (P.L. 94-142), it signaled a major para-digm shift in thinking because the law mandated that all children with disabilities were to be identified and educated and "to the maximum ex-tent appropriate, . . . educated with children who are not handicapped" (89 Stat 781). An individual educational plan (IEP) was required as well as supplementary services to meet IEP objectives. The usual placements made to meet the mandates of the law were in separate classrooms within existing school buildings. Even this "inclusion" in the same building was initially considered a potentially traumatic change because, before that time, children with disabilities were rarely even seen by typical children. Until 1986, special education placements were primarily in these self-contained settings staffed with teachers trained to work specifically with children identified as having particular types of disabilities, although there was some mainstreaming into a few regular classes (e.g., art, music). States and local districts varied greatly in the ways they implemented the law.

In 1986, the effectiveness of these separate special education class-rooms or resource rooms was questioned in a report by the assistant sec-retary of the Office of Special Education and Rehabilitative Services, Madeleine Will (1986). She proposed a Regular Education Initiative to remove categorical labels and return children with disabilities to regu-lar classrooms. Her views were advocated by theorists and researchers (e.g., Gartner & Lipsky, 1987; Reynolds, Wang, & Walberg, 1987), as well as parents and teachers in advocacy organizations (e.g., the Association for Persons with Severe Handicaps [TASH]). The term *inclusion* arose from proponents of the Regular Education Initiative who strongly advo-cated merger of the two systems (regular and special) (e.g., Stainback &

Stainback, 1992). Fuch and Fuch (1994) stated, "Increasingly, special education reform is symbolized by the term inclusive schools" (p. 299).

In the 1986 law extending identification and service to preschoolers, toddlers, and infants (P.L. 99-457) and its subsequent reauthorizations (Individuals with Disabilities Education Act [IDEA] of 1990 [P.L. 101.476]; the IDEA amendments of 1991 [P.L. 102-119] and 1997 [P.L. 105-117]), requirements for least restrictive environments were maintained. The least restrictive environment for infants and toddlers was interpreted to mean the home (i.e., the natural environment), with appropriate group-care environments left undefined. Although these amendments required public schools to be responsible for the education of children aged 3 to 5 who had disabilities or were at risk, each state determined the extent and types of risk included. The vast majority of preschool programs were segregated because funding was provided only for children with identified disabilities. The requirement in the 1997 amendment that requires providers to give reasons why children with disabilities are not placed in inclusive environments has affected the viability of segregated preschool programs. In addition, child-care settings as well as the home are being recognized as "natural environments" for infants and toddlers. According to Smith and Rapport (2001):

> Changes in state funding models, state policy around service delivery, and the need to provide early intervention in alternative environments have threatened the existence of many programs that are designed to provide early intervention in specialized environments. (p. 63)

This decentralization of services is posing new challenges for inclusive early intervention.

In a review of the status of inclusion at the beginning of the 21st century, Guralnik (2001) states, "We are far from achieving the goal of universal access to inclusive programs, irrespective of the forms that these inclusive programs may take" (p. 8).

Social Value Context

Three concepts in the social value context of American society have also influenced the debate over inclusion: (1) development as achievement, (2) fair competition, and (3) diversity. The first of these assumes that children's attainment of higher developmental stages is a measure of their achievement (Feinman, 1991). Although the emphasis on social/emotional or cognitive/language domains has alternately waxed and waned (Raver & Zigler, 1991), the idea that developmental progress reflects children's achievement is a pervasive value, and it is reflected in terms—such as *developmental milestones*, *developmental delay*, and *readiness*—that imply children must strive to achieve developmental goals to be prepared for the next level of challenge (Bergen, 1994b). It is also the rationale upon which recommendations both to include *and not to include* children with disabilities are often based because each group of advocates asserts that its model best promotes such achievement.

The second value—fair competition—has not been a concern of preschool teachers, but it affects the thinking of kindergarten and primary teachers because curriculum adaptations for children with disabilities are difficult to reconcile with the requirement to rate children's performance on comparative standards. Although not discussing inclusion per se, Bricker (1989) provides some insight into this dilemma. He describes the balancing of excellence and equity as a dilemma all teachers face because American social goals include both excellence and equity and these are often in conflict when teachers must make decisions. For example, teacher concern about fairness is often difficult to reconcile with decisions required in an inclusion classroom to give some children special assistance, additional time, or adaptations of the curriculum that may result in the lowering of standards. As emphasis on meeting proficiency standards by third or fourth grade has mounted, this issue of equality of work and fairness of grading has become even more relevant.

The third value that affects inclusion practice is diversity. Because the U.S. population now comprises a wide range of cultural and ethnic groups, most educators value diversity through inclusion as a positive step. However, there are others who are ambivalent about embracing diversity, and this has affected children with disabilities in two ways. First, because of family, cultural, or religious values, the acceptance of children who are "different" may vary among children's peers (and even among educators). Second, much has been written about misidentification of children due to cultural/ethnic or socioeconomic factors (Bergen & Mosley-Howard, 1994). Inclusion can increase the valuing of diversity, but careful planning is needed to ensure that the experience does not result in a reinforcement of stereotypes and a reaction against inclusion as a viable educational model.

All these contextual influences may affect commitment to inclusion models, but there are also a number of systemic, resource, and practice issues that must be addressed if the promise of the model is to be realized.

IMPLICATIONS FOR PRACTICE

A number of practical problems and barriers have prevented inclusion models from being effectively implemented. If early childhood educators are to make inclusion goals a reality, they will need to join with other educators and parents to address these issues.

Problems and Suggestions Related to Professional Preparation

 Problem. Few practicing regular education teachers or administrators have been prepared to work with nontypical children of any type (i.e., those with disabilities or those with special giftedness/talents).

Suggestion. Most higher education programs preparing preservice early childhood students are now including some content related to development of children with disabilities, methods of curricular adaptation, and, most important, attitudinal perspectives needed for success as a teacher in inclusion settings. In some cases, state licensure law requires that regular early childhood teachers be competent to teach children with a range of exceptionalities (e.g., Ohio). Some universities have combined programs in early childhood and early childhood intervention, but this emphasis is not universal even in preservice programs. There is still a great need for in-depth and sustained inservice initiatives for presently employed regular education teachers and administrators if the inclusion models being implemented are to be successful.

Problem. Special education teachers have typically not had sufficient preparation in regular education curricula and methods or in knowing how to serve as consultants and models for regular education teachers. Often practicum and student-teaching field sites that are termed "inclusive" show little evidence of a true teaming relationship between regular and special educators.

Suggestion. Personnel preparation programs for early childhood intervention specialists are now including more regular education knowledge and skill preparation in students' programs and preparing them for a consultative role. To be effective in consulting and teaming roles, students must have field experiences in settings where integrative adaptation skills can be practiced and special educators model intervention specialist roles. Such field sites must be deliberately developed through university and school–district partnerships.

Problem. Related services personnel (e.g., speech pathologists, physical therapists) continue to have distinctly separate and noncollaborative preparation programs, resulting in their holding the perspective of their own professional discipline, which generally supports separated rather than integrated services. Moreover, they are often not available for inclusion programs, especially at the preschool level (McDonnell et al., 1997).

Suggestion. Higher education institutions must chart new ground in providing interdisciplinary programs for preparing professionals whose work roles will require working together. Such changes must alter the historically established practices of these professions (McWilliam, 1995). Given the constraints of accrediting agencies, this will not be an easy task; however, these preparation programs should interface with regular and special education preparation if inclusive initiatives requiring team approaches are to be effective.

Problem. Few professionals now in teaching, administration, or related services roles have had systematic training in how to work effectively as part of a team, resulting in ad hoc approaches to teaming and poorly functioning teams whose members lack knowledge and skills about team approaches.

Suggestion. An absolutely essential focus in personnel preparation programs must be on content, including effective team approaches, practice in working in team situations, and observation of varied team interactions. Many university programs now address these issues at least minimally, and some devote courses to this topic. Because few university faculty have engaged in team teaching or other team activity themselves, however, they need to develop the ability to model effective team approaches to students, and they may need help in learning how to do this.

Problems and Suggestions Related to Personnel Resources

Problem. The personnel resources of many regular education programs/ schools do not permit staffing patterns that can exemplify the team models recommended by inclusion advocates.

Suggestion. Preschools and primary schools must have a sufficient number of adults available (including special educators, related services personnel, and teacher aides) to make the inclusion model be truly individualized. Regular educators cannot take the responsibility for the learning of all children when the personnel support services that are needed are not in place, especially when they are also being asked to increase children's academic performance. In regular education preschools and in child-care programs, which typically have approximately 20 children and at least one aide per class, the need is primarily for adults with special education expertise who can serve in team-teaching and consulting roles. In regular kindergarten–primary units, when the size of classes continue to be 25 to 30 children, the need is for either additional personnel (including early childhood intervention specialists) and/or smaller class size. In all settings, the roles taken by related services personnel need to be clarified and methods by which they can best assist the regular teachers should be made explicit.

Problem. The common practice of programs/school districts that encourages regular teacher "volunteers" to take most of the children with disabilities into their classrooms—and that has been questioned on both legal and value grounds (Giangreco, Dennis, Cloninger, Edelman, & Schattman, 1993)—results in unequal distribution of such children and greater responsibility for some teachers.

Suggestion. All teachers should be prepared to include children with disabilities in their classrooms, be expected to make their best efforts to adapt instruction, and be given the appropriate supports they need. Sufficient special educators and related services personnel should be on the school teams so that they can provide individualized support for children in every classroom. Whether children with disabilities should be distributed evenly throughout all classrooms or clustered in classrooms when there are insufficient special education personnel to have them actively involved in every classroom has been a matter of debate. Some types of clustering models might be useful. However, this decision should be based on child needs, not on the lack of personnel or the resistance of personnel.

Problem. The teaching role of special educators is often marginalized because regular educators are not used to a team approach and because special educators are so overwhelmed with paperwork, caseload numbers, and meetings that they may not have time to perform the role they were trained to do (Marlowe, 2001).

Suggestion. A focus of team discussions should be on developing teaming approaches that utilize the expertise of all members of the teams and provide the individualized instruction that all children who need learning assistance must have. In such sessions, special educators must address their feeling of loss of control over children's instruction that the self-contained special education classroom provided them. Both regular and special educators must explore alternative roles and devise methods that enable the special educator to contribute fully in the regular class environment. Marlowe (2001) suggests hiring paralegals to do paperwork so that special educators can work in the classroom. In early childhood, personnel preparation is increasingly moving to a model that gives teachers both early childhood and special education expertise; thus, there may eventually be teams in which all team members hold both perspectives. However, unless administrative tasks can be reduced to a smaller portion of time, special educators cannot perform the intervention specialist role for which they are being trained.

Problem. Because of financial constraints on most programs and school districts, choices about personnel usually lean toward the least expensive options, which often results in the hiring of untrained aides rather than of behavior specialists or other professional special education consultants.

Suggestion. Programs/school districts should evaluate the cost-effectiveness of having a number of specialists who can give many teachers assistance in analyzing their environments and choosing methods to accommodate such children in the classroom rather than immediately opting for less expensive untrained aides to take care of the "problem" child. These specialists could help teachers to change the environment, adapt curriculum, or learn new management strategies that could be useful for all children.

When aides are definitely needed to work with specific children, they should not be viewed as a means for keeping a "separated service" within the regular classroom for this child. Instead, the aides should be given ongoing training and mentoring in order to become effective team members who interact with all children. They could also be trained to do routine paperwork tasks, thus freeing the professional staff to be with children in the regular classroom. It is necessary for administrators and teachers, working together, to develop creative solutions that make the most of the adult personnel who are available, incorporate parent and other volunteers, and test alternative staffing patterns that draw on specific team resources—all while continuing to promote the "ideal" staff configurations to school boards, parents, and community decision makers. Whether the move to inclusion will result in "cheaper" special education services as regular educators take over the teaching of children with disabilities has been a matter of debate. In order to work well, inclusion may require a substantial *additional* financial commitment. The goal is to have services that are better for both typical and special-needs children because there is general agreement that present practices can be improved.

Problems and Suggestions Related to Organizational Systems and Structures

In their review of current conditions, Smith and Rapport (2001) conclude that since the time of the federal mandates there has been "little progress in early childhood inclusion related to policy development" (p. 64). A few of the problems related to policies affecting organizational structure and function are discussed here.

Problem. Time schedules of schools are not conducive to interdisciplinary team approaches, and when team planning time is provided, effective use of such time is not encouraged or monitored.

Suggestion. Because time for team planning is rarely sufficient in the daily or weekly schedule, creative solutions to enable teachers to plan together should be explored. This problem has been increasingly recognized by schools, and many of them are now using a variety of methods to increase the team planning time available. The efficient use of planning time can be addressed by training personnel in teaming strategies, at both the preservice and inservice level, and developing a planning and reporting system that documents effective use of the time. Many teams need mentoring so that specific planning for integrating curriculum and adapting instruction, rather than just rehashing individual children's problems, is accomplished during the team planning time. Effective use of team planning time is presently one of the greatest inservice needs.

Problem. Administrators lack clear guidelines on assessment and placement policies related to what is the "least restrictive environment" for various children and how that can best be determined, resulting in decisions often being based on parental or teacher/administrator preference rather than on a full ecologically based assessment.

Suggestion. Following Will's (1986) contention that problems may be in environments rather than in children, the preferred model of assessment should include a team assessment conducted in the regular classroom environment, noting what supports can be given or adaptations made by the teacher or other team members to make that experience successful for the child. After this effort has been made, if that environment does not promote a positive learning experience for the child, then alternative settings for some portion of the day (e.g., resource room, self-contained classroom) may be provided or the regular education environment may be revised. This approach begins at the least restrictive end of the continuum and moves to a more restrictive environment, as necessary, but always based on the best needs of the child (not the needs of the parent or teacher or administrator). Likewise, decisions as to whether children with disabilities or with special gifts/talents should be clustered should be based on which type of environment will result in greater learning opportunities for the children.

Problem. A particular concern of reverse-inclusion preschool programs is that state funding for typical 3- to 5-year-old children is minimal or nonexistent for typical young children, thus requiring parents of these children to pay for the inclusion program while state funding pays for the children with disabilities. There are also questions about the value of such programs, since they embed the typical children within the special education program rather than the recommended converse. As noted earlier, these programs were developed because the funding stream made these a possible way to serve infants, toddlers, and preschoolers; however, as greater emphasis is placed on natural environments and full inclusion, the ability of these programs to be inclusive is being questioned.

Suggestion. A variety of creative solutions have been used to include typical children in early childhood programs when no public funds exist for serving typical preschoolers. Although a few states now mandate preschool availability for all 4-year-olds (e.g., Georgia), often the best inclusive option is still the reverse-inclusion option. Until the movement to inclusion is truly inclusive, with a public financial commitment to provide the best of educational opportunities for all children, not just those with disabilities, the promise of inclusion at the preschool level will be only partially realized. As more and more very young children are placed in child-care settings, this problem becomes even more crucial. O'Brien (2001) suggests that there can be benefits to young children with disabilities when they are included in child-care programs that have appropriate support services. However, she stresses that "quality child care cannot be achieved without additional funding from a source other than young children's parents" (p. 245). Until such time as early education is available for all young children, the reverse-inclusion model will probably remain one of the better options for infants, toddlers, and preschoolers.

 Problem. With the mandates for academic achievement that schools face, the issue of fairness in regard to adaptations of academic work for children with disabilities is problematic.

Suggestion. Because this has been a recurring dilemma of American society, it is not a problem that is easily solved. What is needed, however, is a commitment among all parties to discuss this problem openly, with attention to all perspectives, and to reach a consensus, at least for each program/school district, as to how adaptations and evaluations of performance will be handled for children who have disabilities or are gifted with special talents. "Typical" whole-group instruction models will need to change to ones that support every child's learning on an individual basis (Gee, 2002). Professionals in special education and early childhood special education have a perspective on this issue that should be heard because their philosophy and experience with developmentally appropriate practice and individualization of curriculum can help inform the debate. The dilemma of excellence and equity, however, will to continue to be of concern to most educators.

Problem. Research evidence indicates that the mere presence of diverse children in a classroom does not automatically result in an increase in social skills, greater breadth of friendship and social acceptance, or more empathy and tolerance for those different from oneself. The inclusion goals of greater social development by children with disabilities and greater social integration of these children have not been found to exist in most studies (Buysse & Bailey, 1993; Guralnik, 1994).

Suggestion. The models of social acceptance provided by teachers and other adults and their facilitative efforts to encourage social skill development are essential for this important goal of inclusion to be achieved. Because lack of social acceptance is something many children face, not only those with disabilities, this social goal must be one that teachers, administrators, and parents actively promote, both within the classroom and in the broader society. Activities that engage children in cooperative learning, assist them in gaining empathy and respect for all people, and allow them to practice social skills on a daily basis must be embedded in the classroom environment if this goal of inclusion (and of our society) is to be realized (Odom et al., 2002). More research that specifically examines the efforts made toward social goals in varied types of inclusion programs is needed.

FUTURE OF INCLUSIVE TEACHING AND LEARNING

The fears of those who oppose inclusion (especially full inclusion) are that these models will not result in better educational opportunity, movement to more effective teaching strategies, or increased valuing of diversity in our society. During periods of "educational reform," it is often difficult to predict what the future of the implemented changes will be and whether they will be judged to have resulted in deep or only surface changes in the structures, personnel and resource allocations, values, and learning progress of those involved. At times it appears that these questions were all answered by Dewey (1944/1966), who saw "education for democracy" as the vehicle for change and the provider of opportunities for all children in our democratic society. As the experiences of the author attest, it has always been possible to have inclusive classrooms in early childhood, at least at the preschool level, but these were usually ad hoc efforts without the support services, personnel expertise, and methodological innovations that have been developed in recent years.

Because of the basic agreement between early childhood philosophy and practice and the goals of inclusion, however, it may be that early childhood educators are in the best position to demonstrate that these goals can be substantively and validly demonstrated to be effective. Although the research base is not yet clear on the question of inclusion effectiveness, reports of preschool teachers and parents have generally been very positive. With the models from Head Start, early intervention reverse inclusion, and both public and private preschool inclusion efforts, much is being learned about the practices that work best at the preschool level. It remains to be seen whether the early childhood system of values and methods exemplified at the preschool level can transform present kindergarten and primary schools in ways that make the goal of inclusion a reality.

Both regular early childhood and early childhood special education have much to learn from each other, but, because they already share many common values and methods, the chances for inclusion to be effective is strongest at this educational age level. They believe that all children, whatever their disabilities or gifts, must have the opportunity to learn through a range of modalities and to have a team of excellently trained educators to assist them. They also believe that, if typical children have the opportunity to play and work with children with disabilities (and vice versa) during their early childhood years, they will carry those experiences with them into their upper-age-level school experiences and be more accepting of diversity throughout their lives. Keeping alive the dream of a diverse society that includes and values all people and that gives everyone the opportunity to learn at their highest potential may rest in the hands those educators who take responsibility for the learning of all of the children in inclusive environments and demonstrate effective methods of inclusion practice. Ultimately the realization of that dream will be in the hands of the children who experience such optimum learning in an inclusive environment.

REFERENCES

Baker, J. M., & Zigmond, N. (1990). Are regular education classes equipped to accommodate students with learning disabilities? *Exceptional Children*, 56(6), 515–526.

Bergen, D. (1993). Teaching strategies: Facilitating friendship development in inclusion classrooms. *Childhood Education*, 69(4), 234–236.

Bergen, D. (1994a). Teaching strategies: Developing the art and science of team teaching. *Childhood Education*, 70(5), 300–301.

Bergen, D. (1994b). *Assessment of infants and toddlers: Transdisciplinary team approaches*. New York: Teachers College Press.

Bergen, D., & Mosley-Howard, S. (1994). Assessment perspectives for culturally diverse young children. In D. Bergen, *Assessment of infants and toddlers: Transdisciplinary team approaches* (pp. 190–206). New York: Teachers College Press.

Bricker, D. C. (1989). *Classroom life as civic education: Individual achievement and student cooperation in schools*. New York: Teachers College Press.

Buysse, V., & Bailey, D. B. (1993). Behavioral and developmental outcomes in young children with disabilities in integrated and segregated settings: A review of comparative studies. *Journal of Special Education*, 26, 434–461.

Buysse, V., Bailey, D. B., Smith, T. M., & Simeonsson, R. J. (1994). The relationship between child characteristics and placement in specialized versus inclusive early childhood programs. *Topics in Early Childhood Special Education*, 14, 419–435.

Covert, S. (1995). Elementary school inclusion that works. *Counterpoint*, 15(4), 1, 4.

Deno, S., Maruyama, G., Espin, C., & Cohen, C. (1990). Educating students with mild disabilities in general education classrooms: Minnesota alternatives. *Exceptional Children*, 57(2), 150–161.

Dewey, J. (1966). *Democracy and education*. New York: Free Press. (Original work published 1944)

Dickman, G. E. (1994). Inclusion: A storm sometimes brings relief. *Perspectives*, 20(4), 3–6.

Education of All Handicapped Act of 1975 (PL. 94-142). 89 Stat. 773.

Education of All Handicapped Act Amendments of 1986 (PL. 99-457). 20 U.S.C. §§ 1400–1485.

Feinman, S. (1991). Bringing babies back into the social world. In M. Lewis & S. Feinman (Eds.), *Genesis of Behavior: Vol. 6. Social influences and socialization in infancy* (pp. 281–326). New York: Plenum.

Fuch, S., & Fuch, L. S. (1994). Inclusive schools movement and the radicalization of special education reform. *Exceptional Children*, 60(4), 294–309.

Gartner, A., & Lipsky, D. K. (1987). Beyond special education: Toward a quality system for all students. *Harvard Educational Review, 57*(4), 367–395.

Gee, K. (2002). Looking closely at instructional approaches: Honoring and challenging all youth in inclusive schools. In W. Sailor (Ed.), *Whole-school success and inclusive education* (pp. 123–144). New York: Teachers College Press.

Giangreco, M. F., Dennis, R., Cloninger, C., Edelman, S., & Schattman, R. (1993). "I've counted Jon": Transformational experiences of teachers educating students with disabilities. *Exceptional Children, 59*(4), 359–372.

Guralnick, M. J. (1994). Mothers' perceptions of the benefits and drawbacks of early childhood mainstreaming. *Journal of Early Intervention, 18*(2), 168–183.

Guralnick, M. J. (2001). A framework for change in early childhood inclusion. In M. J. Guralnick (Ed.), *Early childhood inclusion: Focus on change* (pp. 3–38). Baltimore: Brookes.

Hamre-Nietupski, S., Hendrickson, J., Nietupski, J., & Sasso, G. (1993). Perceptions of teachers of students with moderate, severe, or profound disabilities on facilitating friendships with nondisabled peers. *Education and Training in Mental Retardation, 28*(2), 111–127.

Individuals with Disabilities Education Act of 1990 (PL. 101-476). 20 U.S.C. §§ 1400 et seq.

Individuals with Disabilities Education Act of 1991. (PL. 102-119). 20 U.S.C. §§ 1400 et seq.

Individuals with Disabilities Education Act of 1997. (PL. 105-17). 20 U.S.C. §§ 1400 et seq.

Jenkins, J. R., Pious, C. G., & Jewell, M. (1990). Special education and the regular education initiative: Basic assumptions. *Exceptional Children, 56*(6), 479–491.

Marlowe, B. (October, 2001). Inclusion threatened by poor teaching conditions and practices. *CEC Today*, p. 14.

Mather, N., & Roberts, R. (1994, Fall). The return of students with learning disabilities to regular classrooms. *Perspectives on Inclusion*, pp. 6–12.

McDonnell, A. P., Brownell, K., & Wolery, M. (1997). Teaching experience and specialist support: A survey of preschool teachers employed in programs accredited by NAEYC. *Topics in Early Childhood Special Education, 17*, 263–285.

McWilliam, R. A. (1995). Integration of therapy and consultative special education: A continuum in early intervention. *Infants and Young Children, 7*, 29–38.

O'Brien, M.(2001). Inclusive child care for infants and toddlers: A natural environment for all children. In M. J. Guralnick (Ed.), *Early childhood inclusion: Focus on change* (pp. 229–252). Baltimore: Brookes.

Odom, S. L. (Ed.). (2002). Social relationships of children with disabilities and their peers in inclusive preschool classrooms. *Widening the circle: Including children with disabilities in preschool programs* (pp. 61–80). New York: Teachers College Press.

Odom, S. L., Zercher, C., Marquart, J., Li, S., Sandall, S. R., & Wolfberg, P. (2002). In S. L. Odom (Ed.), *Widening the circle: Including children with disabilities in preschool programs* (pp. 61–80). New York: Teachers College Press.

Palmer, D. S., Fuller, K., Arora, T., & Nelson, M. (2001). Taking sides: Parent views on inclusion for their children with severe disabilities. *Exceptional Children, 67*(4), 467–484.

Peck, C. A., Carlson, P., & Helmstetter, E. (1992). Parent and teacher perceptions of outcomes for typically developing children enrolled in integrated early childhood programs: A statewide survey. *Journal of Early Intervention, 16*(1), 53–63.

Rafferty, Y., Boettcher, C., & Griffin, K. W. (2001). Benefits and risks of reverse inclusion for preschoolers with and without disabilities: Parents' perspectives. *Journal of Early Intervention, 24*(4), 266–286.

Raver, C. C., & Zigler, E. F. (1991). Three steps forward, two steps back: Head Start and the measurement of social competence. *Young Children, 46*(4), 3–8.

Reynolds, M. C., Wang, M. C., & Walberg, H. J. (1987). The necessary restructuring of special and regular education. *Exceptional Children, 53*(5), 391–398.

Roberts, C., Pratt, C., & Leach, D. (1991). Classroom and playground interaction of students with and without disabilities. *Exceptional Children, 57*(3), 212–224.

Sailor, W. (Ed.). (2002). *Whole-school success and inclusive education.* New York: Teachers College Press.

Semmel, M. I., Abernathy, T. V., Butera, G., & Lesar, S. (1991). Teachers' perceptions of the regular education initiative. *Exceptional Children, 58*(1), 9–24.

Shapiro, J. P., Loeb, P., & Bowermaster, D. (1993, December 13). Separate and unequal. *U.S. News & World Report,* pp. 46–60.

Smith, B. J., & Rapport, M. J. K. (2001). Public policy in early childhood inclusion: Necessary but not sufficient. In M. J. Guralnick (Ed.), *Early childhood inclusion: Focus on change* (pp. 49–68). Baltimore: Brookes.

Stainback, S., & Stainback, W. (Eds.). (1991). *Curriculum considerations in inclusive classrooms: Facilitating learning for all students.* Baltimore: Brookes.

Stainback, S., & Stainback, W. (1992). Schools as inclusive communities. In W. Stainback & S. Stainback, *Controversial issues confronting special education* (pp. 29–43). Needham Heights, MA: Allyn & Bacon.

Van Dyke, R., Stallings, M. A., & Colley, K. (1995). How to build an inclusive school community: A success story. *Phi Delta Kappan, 76*(6), 475–479.

Will, M. C. (1986). Educating children with learning problems: A shared responsibility. *Exceptional Children, 52,* 411–415.

Wolery, M., Martin, C. G., Schroeder, C., Huffman, K, Venn, M. L., Holcombe, A., Brookfield, J., & Fleming, L. A. (1994). Employment of educators in preschool mainstreaming: A survey of general early educators. *Journal of Early Intervention, 18*(1), 64–77.

Zigmond, N., Jenkins, J., Fuch, L. S., Deno, S., Fuchs, D., Baker, J. N., Jenkins, L., & Couthino, M. (1995). Special education in restructured schools: Findings from three multi-year studies. *Phi Delta Kappan, 76*(7), 531–540.

Chapter 4

Working with Families of Young Children

Kevin J. Swick

Every facet of early learning programs and practices is interrelated with parent and family dynamics. Two examples of different parent and family situations help to set the stage for our exploration of the work of early childhood educators with families of young children:

Jean is very active in her children's school. She recalls the positive memories she has of her parents' involvement in her education. In a journal entry she recently made, Jean observed that "being in helping roles seems so natural, it is just part of our lives."

Fred struggles to carry out his parenting roles. He is so engaged in work and just does not see himself in the nurturing role. He often refers to the negative treatment he received in childhood as possibly influencing his workaholic tendencies: "I guess I just never had any good memories of my relations with dad." Fred says that his new involvement with his son's teacher is really helping him see himself in new roles, "I am excited—maybe I can be a better father."

This chapter examines the rationale for family involvement in children's education, briefly notes historical perspectives on family issues, articulates the value of an empowerment perspective, presents strategies and perspectives for empowering families, and proposes key ways to strengthen families and to promote strong family–school partnerships. The final part of the chapter presents recommendations for practice.

THE IMPORTANCE OF STRONG FAMILIES

It is generally acknowledged that strong families positively impact every facet of life. Families have the potential to provide the foundation for a healthier and more harmonious society.

The impact of family is seen in multiple relations: mother–infant relations, marital dynamics, parent–teacher relations, intergenerational family issues, and various other relationships. Certainly the attachment of children and parents to each other is one of the most important functions of families (Swick, 1987). Family relationships are about bonding with each other in ways that strengthen everyone.

Family bonding is also vital to the development of parental self-esteem and identity (Fraiberg, 1977). Parents and other adult family members have opportunities to make a difference in the life of another human being. Kotre (1999) defines generativity as "a desire to invest one's substance in forms of life and work that will outlive the self" (p. 11). The process of becoming generative is critical to how parents develop a framework for nurturing and supporting their children.

Family provides children with their initial and in many cases their most powerful learning arrangement (Pipher, 1996). The dimensions of this influence include family members' modeling of behaviors and dispositions, the way family members relate to each person, and the kinds of learning opportunities family members provide as children grow and develop.

What children consistently observe in the behavior of significant adults is very influential in their continuing development of a schema to use in understanding their life experiences (Swick, 2001). Children who benefit from seeing and interacting with loving and nurturing parents and family are also likely to develop caring behaviors (Kitzrow, 1998). As Leavitt (1994) explains, the process of learning social behaviors is an intimate journey that is closely linked to children's early experiences.

Children need and indeed thrive on opportunities to grow and learn when they are nurturing and challenging (Swick, 2001). Children need avenues to show, try out, and further develop their talents and skills. This is especially true of their development of decency and caring (Hoffman, 2000).

Healthy family involvement both within the family system and in relation to family–school activities validates parents' and teachers' attempts to mentor and guide children (Swick, 1991; Ryan, Adams, Gullotta, Weissberg, & Hampton, 1995). Teachers note that such partnerships increase children's involvement in school and strengthen their sense of the value of education (Epstein, 1991).

HISTORICAL CONTEXT FOR WORKING WITH FAMILIES

Today's families have changed as a result of many societal events. Yet a consistent theme in the family literature is that of strengthening family–school–community connections (Swick, 1993). Parental involvement is thus a continuing thread in the mosaic of family development throughout history.

Further, the social revolution of the past 50 years has created changes in the way that families organize, function, and interrelate with themselves and others in the community (Schorr, 1997). Family organizational patterns are more diversified, responding to the societal stress resulting from increased social, economic, and educational expectations. Today, for example, in many families parents and children spend less time together than in the past and yet have increased the time they spend in individual and educational pursuits (Heymann, 2000).

With the diversification of the types of families, role change and confusion have also influenced family functioning. Unfortunately, as Elkind (1994) notes, in the rapidly changing conditions of today's families, role stressors have created situations in which children take on far too many adult roles. Also, in situations in which families lose their balance, child and spouse abuse as well as other dysfunctions become prevalent. Thus, a major challenge for early childhood educators involves relating in effective and supportive ways with families who are at risk for chronic problems.

Families At Risk for Chronic Problems

Families who are in continuous distress eventually burn out. Dimidjian (1989) has discussed this process, and Swick and Graves (1993) summarize the key point:

> The most alarming attribute of high-risk families is the "ecology of despair" that so often prevails. Taken in isolation, particular risk features, such as poverty or illiteracy, can be effectively mediated. Yet when these risks are embedded in a system that is characterized by despair and cynicism the potential for a culture of despair is quite high. (p. 44; see also Dimidjian, 1989)

The most damaging impact of the combined influences of risk factors comes from the attributes they typically foster (Kerr & Bowen, 1988; Magid & McKelvey, 1987; Ryan et al., 1995):

- A belief system that is predominantly fatalistic
- A context that often creates a very low sense of control

- An array of behaviors that indicate low self-esteem
- Relationship systems that are closed and unresponsive
- Behavioral syndromes that include rigid, passive–aggressive cycles of family interaction
- A cognitive structure that is impulsive and nonreflective

During the early childhood years, the key risk factors for families are poverty, ineffective parenting, inadequate home learning ecologies, illiteracy, poor health care, malnutrition, lack of job skills, abuse, and chemical addictions (Swick & Graves, 1993). Each of these risk factors negatively influences family dynamics and often leads to the emergence of other risk areas.

For example, *poverty* alone can often be managed through the use of appropriate social and economic supports that can help families become more skillful at handling their needs. On the other hand, it can set into motion a pattern of living that fosters other risk factors such as abuse, illiteracy, and alcohol and drug abuse.

Above all other factors, *"ineffective parenting* is the most serious risk confronting families during the early childhood years" (Swick & Graves, 1993, p. 27). Often, ineffective parents have themselves been victims of child abuse, neglect, and a general lack of family and community support. This cycle of neglect and ineptness can generate a series of related problems for children and families.

A final example of risk factors is *health care.* Poor prenatal health care is associated with low birthweight and other problems at birth and during the early years (Thompson & Hupp, 1992). Further, these early health care problems seem to stimulate a series of long-term health problems. Poor nutrition, low self-esteem, chronic poor health, and poor school performance are interrelated with poor health care (Thornton, 2001).

EMPOWERING PARENTS AND FAMILIES

Empowerment is defined as a process that strengthens people in their efforts to increase their mastery over the various stressors and situations relevant to their effective life functioning (Dunst, Trivette, & Deal, 1988). The concept of empowerment is embedded in the work of numerous scholars who have focused on various dimensions of strengthening people. Maslow's (1968) work is foundational in this sense. Swick and Graves (1993) point out that people's ability to grow and learn enables them to be contributing members of society.

Erikson's (1959) concepts of psychosocial development further enhance our understanding of empowerment. If individuals can negotiate the different facets of their psychosocial development successfully, they are then strengthened to become generative in their relations with others.

Another key is Bronfenbrenner's (1979) ecological perspective, which emphasizes the dynamic interactions of the systems that affect parents, children, and families. The idea that parenting and family life occur developmentally within *ecological systems* broadens our scope for understanding the many nuances of parenting and family life. For example, the infant's need to develop trust is certainly actualized within the primary relationship system of the family, and yet it is also strongly influenced by happenings in the broader context of society.

Significant to this ecological view is the way people perceive the personal impact of their involvement. Thus, one of the challenges to early childhood educators is to create conditions that support the development of nurturing and caring in parents and families. Insights from the field of family studies help us construct meaningful ways to meet this challenge. Four premises from the seminal work of Minuchin (1984) offer guidance: (1) Behavior takes place in a systems context; (2) individual development is intimately interrelated with the family's development; (3) family development is systematic; and (4) events that influence any family member have some direct or indirect influence on the entire family system.

The work of Bronfenbrenner (1979, 1986), Powell (1989), Comer and Haynes (1991), and Swick (1997) suggest that three key elements provide a foundation for empowering parents and families:

1. *Early childhood educators and families need to be intimately involved as partners in planning and nurturing healthy environments.* Beginning with the earliest years of the child's life, parents and educators should be interacting and collaborating with each other to create healthy places for everyone.
2. *Through the creation of dynamic school–family partnerships, a family-centered "curriculum for caring" should emerge.* Such a curriculum needs to address the issues involved in those attributes that promote human competence.
3. *The work of families is too critical to be left in the family domain.* A community effort at understanding and supporting families is an absolute necessity.

It is of major importance that early childhood education professionals adopt healthy and nurturing approaches to working with families. Swick and Graves (1993) suggest that the following research-based insights should guide our work with families:

- Realize that parents and families are more compatible and comfortable with helpers who are sensitive to and understanding of their unique situations.
- Be worthy of parents' and families' trust. Questions like the following help us check our level of trust with families. In their interactions with us, families often ask, Does this person really care about us? Is this person skilled in being an effective helper? Does this person have integrity?
- Build mutuality and self-confidence in parents. This sense of mutual concern and help is key to effective family involvement.
- Involve parents and families in the decision-making aspects of the program.

PROMOTING RESPONSIVE PARTNERSHIPS WITH PARENTS AND FAMILIES

Too often professionals see parents as a necessary part of the program but fail to see the very active role that parents can play in helping to shape and refine the program (Couchenour & Chrisman, 2000). A major challenge to achieving meaningful parent and family involvement has been the lack of conceptual and practical strategies to help professionals and parents develop the needed perspectives and skills (Powell, 1989).

Another challenge to supporting the development of strong parent and family involvement is parental fears and a lack of understanding on how to best pursue such involvement (Swick, 1993). Often parents feel uncomfortable in being assertive in their involvement in schools, particularly if their own school experiences as children were frustrating or negative. Powell (1989) found that parents often reported feeling isolated from the school because of these fears. They felt that in most cases teachers preferred that they remain passive. Yet early childhood teachers report that they want active, involved parents and families.

Overall, communication is the key to meeting all other challenges (Swick, 1991). Parents and teachers agree that their lack of communication skills often causes difficulties in shaping healthy parent–teacher and family–school partnerships. In many cases the professional is challenged by the cultural and related social differences that families may bring to the relationship process. Interestingly, both parents and teachers mention the three key barriers to effective communications with each other:

(1) lack of regular interaction and contact times, (2) failure to listen effectively, and (3) lack of follow-up and responsiveness to needed changes in the relationship (Couchenour & Chrisman, 2000).

In response to these challenges, early childhood professionals should emphasize the following strategies:

1. Maintain a positive attitude toward relating to the needs and strengths of all parents and families (Swick, 1994).
2. Plan and implement a variety of parent/family-friendly strategies that engage parents and families as active and meaningful partners (Couchenour & Chrisman, 2000).
3. Provide staff and parents with continuing education on strategies for strengthening their partnership (Swick, 1997).
4. Continually refine and strengthen your communication skills and dispositions (Swick, 1991).
5. Provide parents with opportunities to further strengthen their communication skills (Powell, 1989).
6. Maintain places in the school that are especially designed to meet parent and family needs and that encourage parents and families to be totally involved in all aspects of the school's program (Comer & Haynes, 1991).
7. Provide interpreters and other needed supports to respond to the needs of bilingual families (Lynch & Hanson, 1998).
8. Engage families and early childhood educators in multicultural learning (Gonzalez-Mena, 1997).

Encouraging a "Parents as Leaders" Approach

Early childhood educators have a long history of creating conditions that empower parents and families. Parents are needed more than ever in guiding and nurturing children and young people. Many early childhood education programs are promoting a "parents as leaders" philosophy in order to encourage parents to be effective problem solvers and nurturers of their children (File, 2001).

The benefits of parents as leaders have been highlighted in several studies, with emphasis on the following needs (Bronfenbrenner, 1979; Powell, 1989; Swick, Grafwallner, Cockey, & Barton, 1998): validating parents as capable caregivers; strengthening parent leadership skills; helping parents form social networks; increasing parent and child efficacy; expanding family resources; and increasing teacher and school efficacy. A brief description of one parent-leadership program is noted as follows.

Swick and colleagues (1998) describe the HOST (Helping One Student at a Time) parent-leadership program of a school district in Maryland: The use of parent leaders was the central element of the program. Fifteen HOST parents (two at each of seven schools and one in the remaining school) were recruited based on their interest and past involvement as leaders at the schools. They were also viewed positively by parents in the community.

Parent leadership adds greatly to the empowerment of parents and families. Some of the key outcomes of this Maryland effort were parents' increased self-confidence, acquisition of new skills, and opportunities to see how they could positively impact the lives of others (Swick et al., 1998).

Implications of Strong Families

Above all else, families can validate and strengthen schools in ways that enhance the status and functioning of teachers, staff, and children alike (Swick, 1991, 1994). Empowering families is indeed an investment in strengthening our communities (Bronfenbrenner, 1979, 1986). Families can positively affect the community in four primary ways: (1) modeling healthy lifestyles, (2) contributing to the social and economic sustenance of the community, (3) participating in the governance process, and (4) providing the key social system for renewing our social and spiritual lives (Pipher, 1996; Swick, 2001). Examples of how this impact works through modeling and through governing are as follows:

- *Modeling*. What happens in families eventually becomes a "model" for the entire community. For example, when families join together to do community service on a continuing basis, they set the model for the community (Pipher, 1996).
- *Governing*. Empowered families tend to be more civic-minded and more engaged in the governing processes. Two dimensions of parent and family involvement in community governance are especially important to note (Wuthnow, 1995): (1) parent and family interest in seeing their children live in safe and loving communities, and (2) parent and family desire to make a difference in the lives of all children in the community.

A key challenge for families, parents, and communities is to create a sense of community—to see themselves as a part of something valuable and to strive to create harmony between the individual and the community (Pipher, 1996). Empowering families to be more caring and nurturing in their child rearing is paramount to achieving the needed balance between individual growth and community empowerment. Five goals each of us must seek to nurture in families, schools, and communities during early childhood are:

1. A sense of caring and nurturance
2. Places of security, joy, stimulation, and continuity
3. Opportunities for children and families to have time together
4. Places for meaningful work
5. Opportunities and support for shared learning

RECOMMENDATIONS FOR PRACTICE

Some recommendations for practice that early childhood professionals should integrate into their work with families are as follows:

1. Gain knowledge and skills and utilize an empowerment approach in your work with families.
2. Utilize a variety of family involvement strategies to reach families who typically do not get involved in their children's education.
3. Develop and use family-strengthening strategies that help families in high-risk situations to resolve or prevent problems that may reduce their effectiveness.
4. Learn about and apply a strong "parents as leaders" philosophy in all your work with families.
5. Educate and involve the entire community in the family empowerment process.

REFERENCES

Bronfenbrenner, U. (1979). *The ecology of human development*. Cambridge, MA: Harvard University Press.

Bronfenbrenner, U. (1986). Ecology of the family as a context for human development: Research perspectives. *Developmental Psychology, 22*, 723–742.

Children's Defense Fund. (2000). *A status report on children—2000*. Washington, DC: Author.

Comer, J., & Haynes, M. (1991). Parent involvement in schools: An ecological approach. *Elementary School Journal, 91*(3), 271–278.

Couchenour, D., & Chrisman, K. (2000). *Families, schools, and communities: Together for young children*. Albany, NY: Delmar.

Dimidjian, V. (1989). *Early childhood at risk*. Washington, DC: National Education Association.

Dunst, C., Trivette, C., & Deal, A. (1988). *Enabling and empowering families: Principles and practices.* Lexington, MA: Lexington Books.

Elkind, D. (1994). *Ties that stress: The new family imbalance.* Cambridge, MA: Harvard University Press.

Epstein, J. (1991). Paths to partnership: What can we learn from federal, state, district, and school initiatives? *Phi Delta Kappan, 67,* 442–446.

Erikson, E. (1959). *Identity and the life cycle.* New York: Norton.

File, N. (2001). Family–professional partnerships: Practice that matches philosophy. *Young Children, 56*(4), 70–74.

Fraiberg, S. (1977). *Every child's birthright: In defense of mothering.* New York: Basic Books.

Gonzalez-Mena, J. (1997). *Multicultural issues in child care* (2nd ed.). Mountain View, CA: Mayfield.

Heymann, J. (2000). *The widening gap: Why America's working families are in jeopardy and what can be done about it.* New York: Basic Books.

Hoffman, M. (2000). *Empathy and moral development: Implications for caring and justice.* New York: Cambridge University Press.

Kerr, M., & Bowen, M. (1988). *Family evaluation.* New York: Norton.

Kitzrow, M. (1998). An overview of current psychological theory and research on altruism and prosocial behavior. In R. Bringle & D. Duffy (Eds.), *With service in mind: Concepts and models for service-learning in psychology* (pp. 11–29). Washington, DC: American Association for Higher Education.

Kotre, J. (1999). *Make it count: How to generate a legacy that gives meaning to your life.* New York: Free Press.

Leavitt, R. (1994). *Power and emotion in infant–toddler day care.* Albany: State University of New York Press.

Lynch, E., & Hanson, M. (1998). *Developing cross-cultural competence: A guide for working with children and their families* (2nd ed.). Baltimore: Brookes.

Magid, K., & McKelvey, C. (1987). *High risk: Children without a conscience.* New York: Bantam.

Maslow, A. (1968). *Toward a psychology of being.* New York: Van Nostrand.

Minuchin, S. (1984). *Family kaleidoscope.* Cambridge, MA: Harvard University Press.

Pipher, M. (1996). *The shelter of each other: Rebuilding our families.* New York: Ballantine.

Powell, D. (1989). *Families and early childhood programs.* Washington, DC: National Association for the Education of Young Children.

Ryan, B., Adams, G., Gullotta, T., Weissberg, R., & Hampton, R. (Eds.). (1995). *The family–school connection: Theory, research, and practice.* Thousand Oaks, CA: Sage.

Schorr, L. (1997). *Common purpose: Strengthening families and neighborhoods to rebuild America.* New York: Anchor/Doubleday.

Swick, K. (1987). *Perspectives on families.* Champaign, IL: Stipes.

Swick, K. (1991). *Teacher–parent partnerships to enhance school success in early childhood education.* Washington, DC: National Education Association.

Swick, K. (1993). *Strengthening parents and families during the early childhood years.* Champaign, IL: Stipes.

Swick, K. (1994). Family involvement: An empowerment perspective. *Dimensions of Early Childhood, 22,* 10–14.

Swick, K. (1997). A family–school approach for nurturing caring in young children. *Early Childhood Education Journal, 25*(2), 151–154.

Swick, K. (2001). Nurturing decency through caring and serving during the early childhood years. *Early Childhood Education Journal, 29*(2), 131–137.

Swick, K., Grafwallner, R., Cockey, M., & Barton, P. (1998). Parents as leaders in nurturing family–school involvement. *Contemporary Education, 70*(1), 47–50.

Swick, K., & Graves, S. (1993). *Empowering at-risk families during the early childhood years.* Washington, DC: National Education Association.

Thompson, T., & Hupp, C. (1992). *Saving children at risk: Poverty and disabilities.* Newbury Park, CA: Sage.

Thornton, A. (Ed.). (2001). *The well-being of children and families: Research and data needs.* Ann Arbor: University of Michigan Press.

Wuthnow, R. (1995). *Learning to care: Elementary kindness in an age of indifference.* New York: Oxford University Press.

PART II

CURRICULAR TRENDS AND ISSUES AFFECTING PRACTICE

A perpetually challenging question raised by early childhood educators throughout history is the one that we have used to frame Part II: *What forces have defined the content and processes of early childhood education, shaped the settings in which it occurs, and influenced ideas about what counts as evidence of learning?* We turn to the case of a child we know to illuminate this issue as well as to underscore the need to consider the link between child development and learning.

Bonnie is a second-grader who has a rare and poorly understood disease that afflicts approximately 250 children in the United States. Although an aggressive regimen of radiation and chemotherapy leaves Bonnie feeling ill, she expresses concern about missing school frequently and wants desperately to keep up with her peers, who are "learning to do cursive writing." Her illness causes her to be absent from school frequently, although it is not categorized as sufficiently debilitating for Bonnie to qualify for a teacher to visit her at home and help with schoolwork. In this dramatic case, it would be inhumane for a teacher to ignore Bonnie's physical condition and pile on the homework in the interest of "covering" a set of second-grade curricula. The goal of pushing Bonnie to keep pace with her peers diminishes in importance in light of her situation. Yet in less dramatic cases, this emphasis on academic learning to the virtual disregard of growth and development frequently occurs in classrooms.

There are many ways of conceptualizing curriculum. The word has its origins in the Latin *currere*, meaning "path" or "road." That pathway can go in many different directions. Most educators of the very young recognize that they are "learning how to learn" and focus on process as well as content. Yet as children enter the primary grades, the more traditional emphasis on content frequently takes over and creates developmental discontinuity between preschool programs and curricula in the primary grades. An even more important point about the curricular road early childhood educators select for their students is that what a teacher believes he or she is teaching and what the children are actually learning may not always be consistent. There is also a "hidden curriculum"—all the things that children learn about by observing adults and peers in action rather than from the lesson plan. Discrepancies between and among what is actually learned, what is taught, and what is evaluated make the field of curriculum in general and the early childhood curriculum in particular a perpetually challenging one.

The four chapters in Part II confront curricular issues—the heart and soul of teachers' daily practice. Each of these chapters reflects current controversies surrounding reform in an era of educational change. The uncertainty and uneasiness in our profession have resulted in movements and countermovements to rectify past educational ills. Be it the new focus on academic standards or federal legislation, such as the "No Child Left Behind Act", such initiatives have undeniable and far-reaching implications for the field of early childhood.

In Chapter 5, Shirley C. Raines and John M. Johnston explain developmentally appropriate practice and describe the impact that this construct has had on ideas about effective practice. The authors enable readers to see the enduring connections between our understandings about how young children develop and the curricula we design, as well as the ongoing debate about the nature of those connections.

Chapter 6 deals with assessment, the point of friction for many early childhood practitioners who are being pressured into making increases in children's standardized test scores a top priority. Sue C. Wortham reviews major trends and contemporary issues in early childhood assessment, including the controversy over standardized testing and the issues that emerge when evaluating the progress of young children with cultural differences, language differences, or disabilities. She provides a balanced perspective on reporting on and evaluating young children's progress and for using an array of methods to document what children think, know, feel, and can do.

Early childhood is a period of life that is teeming with literacy learning, and in Chapter 7 Lea M. McGee directly addresses the intense controversy surrounding the various approaches to fostering literacy growth in emergent and early readers. She captures the essence of the debate and provides research-based recommendations, based on emergent and early literacy research, that offer clear guidance to practitioners.

In Chapter 8, Fergus Hughes examines variations in commitment to young children's play across caregivers, across cultures, and within cultures. Additionally, he explains how gender affects children's play behavior. Chapter 8 concludes with a critique of the misleading work–play dichotomy and a call for establishing a climate of acceptance for children's play in early childhood programs.

The final chapter of Part II continues the examination of curricular issues and focuses on integrating technology into the early childhood curriculum.

Sudha Swaminathan and June L. Wright detail the debate about using computers with the very young and argue for careful selection of high-tech materials. They conclude their chapter with a look at the promise that technological advances hold for making materials more accessible, interactive, and capable of matching a wide range of abilities in children.

Together, the four chapters of Part II analyze early childhood curriculum from the standpoint of what early childhood professionals know about ways of educating young children, assessing children's progress, promoting growth in literacy, valuing play in the curriculum, and making the most of educational technology.

Chapter 5

Developmental Appropriateness: New Contexts and Challenges

SHIRLEY C. RAINES

JOHN M. JOHNSTON

In a bold stroke representing the profession's best thinking, the 1987 publication of the National Association for the Education of Young Children's position statement on *Developmentally Appropriate Practice in Early Childhood Programs Serving Children from Birth Through Age Eight* (Bredekamp, 1987) irrevocably changed the thinking and discourse about practices in early childhood programs. Since its recent entry into the professional education lexicon, the term *developmentally appropriate practices* (DAP) and the concept it represents have been adopted and used extensively by educators, policy makers, and businesses. Both the concept and the term have affected early childhood program practices; national, state, and local policies for curriculum and assessment; marketing of commercial early childhood materials and programs; and standards for early childhood educator preparation. Perhaps most importantly, new conversations are occurring among early childhood professionals about how to promote optimal growth, learning, and development of all young children.

This chapter (1) traces the evolution of the concept of developmentally appropriate practice, identifying new challenges arising from the changing contexts of contemporary early childhood education; (2) reviews the evolving knowledge base for developmentally appropriate practice; (3) samples how DAP principles are reflected in emerging curriculum trends; and (4) examines selected recurring issues and challenges regarding the concept of developmentally appropriate practice.

EVOLUTION OF THE DEVELOPMENTAL APPROPRIATENESS POSITION STATEMENT AND GUIDELINES

The first NAEYC position statement on DAP represented "the early childhood profession's consensus definition of developmentally appropriate practice in early childhood programs" (Bredekamp, 1987 p. iv) and was defined in terms of two dimensions: age appropriateness and individual appropriateness. Developed primarily to provide a clearer definition for use in NAEYC's National Academy of Early Childhood Programs accreditation system, the 1987 DAP guidelines were also responding to trends such as (1) more formal academic instruction of young children; (2) the "pushdown" into prekindergarten of narrowly defined academic skills, teaching practices, and materials from the public school curriculum; and, (3) testing, retention, and placement practices that assigned greater proportions of children to transition classes, retained them in grade, or denied them enrollment. With increasing numbers of infants and toddlers in group programs and an emerging knowledge base about early childhood development, learning, and teaching, there was a need for more clarity about practice.

Effects of Defining Developmentally Appropriate Practice

The first position statement and accompanying guidelines for DAP have resulted in important changes in early childhood practice and policy and, more important, new inquiries about how to best meet the development needs of all young children. Grounded in a coherent knowledge-based framework of theory, research, and best practices, the DAP framework and principles have been distributed and adopted widely in this country and abroad. DAP guidelines have had substantial impact on early childhood curricula, policies, and practices. In addition, they have been integrated into state and national teacher education programs and program accreditation standards (Ratcliff, Cruz, & McCarthy, 1999). Other educational organizations' position papers have also been influenced by the DAP position statement and guidelines (e.g., International Reading Association [IRA], National Council of Teachers of English, National Council of Teachers of Mathematics, Division for Early Childhood of the Council for Exceptional Children, Association of Teacher Educators, and the National Board for Professional Teaching Standards).

A decade of efforts to implement the 1987 DAP position and guidelines resulted in new knowledge and insights about early childhood programs, teaching, and learning. However, frequent misinterpretation, misrepresentation, and commercial co-opting of the concept of developmentally appropriate practices revealed the need for further clarification (Bredekamp & Copple, 1997). The 1987 DAP guidelines also precipitated critiques and challenges from the field regarding the appropriateness of theoretical and research foundations and the need for a broader more sensitive sociocultural perspective. Questions were also raised about the either/or, appropriate-versus-inappropriate approach to the DAP guidelines, their relevance to young children with exceptional educational needs, and the teacher's role as decision maker and curriculum developer (Bredekamp & Copple, 1997; Fleer, 1995; Mallory & New, 1994). As Bredekamp and Copple (1997) wrote in the preface to the revised DAP guidelines,

> Perhaps the most important contribution of the 1987 developmentally appropriate practice position statement was that it created an opportunity for increased conversation within and outside our field about our early childhood practice. (p. v)

DAP Redefined: The 1997 Position Statement and Guidelines

In July 1996 the NAEYC governing board adopted a revised DAP position statement. According to Bredekamp and Copple (1997):

> *Developmentally appropriate practices* result from the process of professionals making decisions about the well-being and education of children based on at least three important kinds of information or knowledge: (a) what is known about child development and learning; (b) what is known about the strengths, interest, and needs of each individual child in the group; and (c) knowledge of the social and cultural contexts in which children live. (p. 9)

The new position will be challenged as the trend toward children's entering early childhood programs at younger ages continues, as demand increases for out-of-home child care (Bredekamp & Copple, 1997), and as the number of state-funded prekindergarten programs continues to increase ("Quality Counts," 2002). Increasingly, programs serving young children must accommodate challenging disabilities and medical conditions (Council for Exceptional Children, 2000; Division for Early Childhood of the Council for Exceptional Children, 2000a). Further, the demographics of early childhood are changing significantly, with programs facing rapidly increasing ethnic, racial, and linguistic diversity of children served.

REFINING THE KNOWLEDGE BASE FOR DEVELOPMENTALLY APPROPRIATE PRACTICES

An expanding knowledge base—including theories, research, best practices, and standards—forms a central contextual feature for DAP today. Refining this knowledge base has generated an underlying set of principles—reliable generalizations—to inform decisions about early childhood practice (Bredekamp & Copple, 1997) that help to frame issues and address controversies and challenges.

Developmentally appropriate practice draws heavily on a family of theoretical perspectives that focus on the whole child (Goffin & Wilson, 2001). Essential theorists whose work undergirds DAP include Dewey (1916), Piaget (1952), Erikson (1963), Vygotsky (1978), Rogoff (1990), and Gardner (1993). For a more complete discussion of the theoretical foundation, readers are referred to these sources.

Research and Developmentally Appropriate Practice

Research on early childhood development, teaching–learning practices, and programs provides a further foundation for developmentally appropriate practices. Dunn and Kontos (1997) reviewed research on DAP and socioemotional and cognitive development. They noted that, overall, research supports DAP and that, in general, child-initiated environments were associated with higher levels of cognitive functioning, increased motivation, and less stress. They concluded that while DAP creates a classroom climate that contributes to healthy emotional development, the relationship between DAP and social development is less clear. Charlesworth (1998a) reviewed research related to DAP in relation to a number of variables, including stress; achievement; and racial, ethnic, and economic equity. Her review examined equity in participation in different types of activity and the education of culturally and linguistically diverse children. She concluded that research generally supports the DAP principles for all children in our diverse society. The knowledge base for DAP is further buttressed by long-term follow-up studies from programs that continue to reveal the importance of high-quality early childhood experiences for youngsters in homes, schools, and communities (cf. Campbell, Pungello, Miller-Johnson, Burchinal, & Ramey, 2001; Peisner-Feinberg et al., 2000).

Further, National Research Council committees have published comprehensive reviews of research focused on preventing reading difficulties in young children (Snow, Burns, & Griffin, 1998), the science of learning (Bransford, Brown & Cocking, 1999), integrated child development knowledge (Shonkoff & Phillips, 2000), and early childhood teaching, learning, and content (Bowman, Donovan, & Burns, 2000). These reports perform an important function, as illustrated by Bowman and colleagues (2000):

> A central purpose of the study is to help move the public discussion of these issues away from ideology and toward evidence, so that educators, parents, and policy makers will be able to make better decisions about programs for the education and care of young children. (p. 30)

Of particular importance to the 1997 DAP redefinition, these reports review research concerning diverse populations (e.g., children living in poverty, children with limited English proficiency, and children with disabilities) and strive to develop implications for practice in early childhood education programs and the training of early childhood teachers and childcare professionals.

Descriptions of Best Practices

An important component of the knowledge base for DAP includes the collective experience of early childhood teachers. This knowledge base is represented in teachers' descriptions of teaching practices reported in refereed professional journals such as *Young Children*, *Childhood Education*, and *Young Exceptional Children*. In addition, most professional associations in specialized content areas also publish refereed professional journals that include descriptions of best practice; for example, in literacy (*The Reading Teacher*), math (*The Arithmetic Teacher*), social studies (*Social Studies and the Young Learner*), and science (*Science and Children*). Our professional knowledge base for best practices is further supported by teachers who present their practice in books describing their efforts to teach in ways consistent with DAP principles (cf. Fisher, 1998; Lehrer & Shauble, 2002).

Standards for Professional Practice

Finally, standards represent the field's efforts to specify benchmark levels of knowledge, skills, and dispositions teachers should demonstrate in their practice. Since its introduction, the 1987 NAEYC DAP position statement and guidelines have had a direct impact on standards for teacher performance and teaching–learning practices at local, state, and national levels. National standards for the preparation of beginning early childhood teachers (Division for Early Childhood of the Council for Exceptional Children, 2000b; National Association for the Education of Young Children, 2001) and highly accomplished teachers (National Board for Professional Teaching Standards, 2001) are aligned with DAP principles and guidelines. Much in the same way, DAP principles have been incorporated into content-area position statements, teaching standards, and best practices.

CURRICULAR TRENDS

Beyond early childhood, other key professional organizations representing content areas are also calling for curricular reform. Consistent with DAP principles and guidelines, curriculum integration is an emerging focus of many curriculum reform efforts. For example, the Getty Center for Education in the Arts (1999) argues for comprehensive arts education that is integrated across the curriculum and includes experiences in art production, art history, art criticism, and aesthetics. In *Expectations of Excellence*, the curriculum standards for social studies, the National Council for the Social Studies (1994) takes the position that social studies teaching and learning are powerful when they are integrative. The National Council of Teachers of Mathematics (2000) standards support integration of mathematics as young children understand, organize, analyze, make connections, and represent their experiences in literacy, art, music, movement, science, and social studies (Copely, 2000). The *National Science Education Standards* (National Research Council, 1996) illustrate, for example, that as children engage in science inquiry, they will use mathematics as they count and measure and will use literacy knowledge and skills as they record observations in charts, graphs, drawing, and writing. *Learning to Read and Write: Developmentally Appropriate Practices for Young Children*, a joint position statement of IRA (1998) and NAEYC, makes clear that early literacy is developed in the context of experiences in all content areas. There is increasing evidence that subject-matter professional organizations are paying more attention to both content and process goals for children during the early childhood years. Similarly, these organizations are taking positions that recognize the developmental appropriateness of curriculum integration in early childhood teaching and learning.

RECURRING ISSUES

While there are a number of tensions around developmentally appropriate curriculum practices, two are particularly significant for current practice. Although there is an emerging emphasis on curriculum integration, paradoxically, at the same time, preschool, kindergarten, and primary grade programs are being subjected to increasing federal and state pressure for accountability and for standards-based reform. These demands are being accompanied by wider use of high-stakes testing and a more standardized and subject-centered curriculum—particularly in reading and mathematics—that is often accompanied by highly scripted teaching lessons. These trends continue unabated.

The movement toward national standards and national and state-mandated testing is seen by many as conflicting with developmentally appropriate prekindergarten through primary grade practices requiring active, engaged, hands-on learning. The trend toward integrated curriculum and increased use of thematic, unit, and project approaches means that early childhood administrators and teachers must incorporate systematic strategies for gathering evidence that can document children's attainment of knowledge and skills specified in standards. New standards for beginning and accomplished early childhood teachers also call for teachers to demonstrate the ability to systematically collect information about the knowledge, skills, and dispositions young children develop and to reflect on this information as they assess children and plan further teaching and learning experiences (NAEYC, 2001; National Board for Professional Teaching Standards, 2001).

A second and hotly debated issue in early childhood education today centers on the question: Is developmentally appropriate practice for everyone? Following publication of the 1987 DAP position and guidelines, criticism was aimed at reliance on Piaget's developmental theory as the conceptual base and the lack of a sociocultural perspective. Critics called for a broader foundation for DAP that included cultural, historical, and political theory and, in particular, questioned the applicability of DAP to children from diverse cultures or children with special educational needs (Charlesworth, 1998a; Lubeck, 1998a). Though the 1997 DAP guideline revision focused more on the strengths and needs of culturally and linguistically diverse children, the debate continues (Charlesworth, 1998b; Grieshaber & Cannella, 2001; Lubeck, 1998a, 1998b). Charlesworth argues from a child-centered perspective and interprets research as supporting DAP principles for all children in America's increasingly diverse society. She calls for constructive dialogue with families when DAP principles clash with a child's culture. In contrast, using a sociocultural framework, Lubeck, Grieshaber and Cannella, and others argue from a postmodern, critical theory perspective that views decisions about young children and their educational experiences as culturally situated and thus reflecting varying interpretations of appropriate educational goals and strategies. These critics further challenge the knowledge base for DAP as based primarily on positivist science and take the position that "there is no acknowledgment of competing discourses, contradictory results or different ways of imagining what is possible. Despite some caveats and additions, the [DAP] guidelines continue to be based on a seemingly objective science that provides firm grounding for making generalizations" (Lubeck, 1998a, p. 286). Lubeck (1998b) and others (Cannella & Grieshaber, 2001; Mallory, 1998; New, 1999) stress the importance of sustained conversations among parents, teachers, and community members as essential starting points in negotiating educational goals for children.

CHALLENGES

As the early childhood education field encounters new challenges, we must not lose sight of the meaning of developmentally appropriate practice and the intended purposes of the NAEYC position statement:

> The position statement defines developmentally appropriate practice as the outcome of a process of teacher decision making that draws on at least three critical, interrelated bodies of knowledge: (1) what teachers know about how children develop and learn; (2) what teachers know about the individual children in their group; and (3) knowledge of the social and cultural context in which those children live and learn. (Bredekamp & Copple, 1997, p. vii)

The primary purpose of the DAP position is to support program accreditation for early childhood centers and schools through the NAEYC National Academy of Early Childhood Programs (NAEYC, 1998). A second and broader purpose is to provide guidance for teachers, administrators, teacher educators, and policy makers as they respond to issues related to early childhood curriculum content and standards; testing, evaluation, and accountability; and teacher education, licensure, and continuing professional development.

While the DAP position was developed primarily to raise the quality of curriculum and program practices for all young children, much work remains. As Dunn and Kontos (1997) reported, developmentally appropriate practices are still not the norm in early childhood education programs. The overarching challenge now is how early childhood educators can form coalitions with parents and policy makers to address funding and regulation issues for early childhood programs.

One significant challenge is how the DAP position and guidelines can be used to effect changes in local, state, and national policies to ensure that all children, including those with disabilities and other special learning and developmental needs, have access to meaningful and contextually relevant curriculum. With new legislation, such as the federal No Child Left Behind Act of 2001 (the reauthorization of the Elementary and Secondary Education Act), which mandates that every state must set clear and high standards for what children in each grade should know and be able to do in the core academic subjects of reading, math, and science, early childhood educators must be better prepared to meet high standards while providing contextually relevant learning experiences.

Second, in addition to having a significant impact on early childhood curriculum, the No Child Left Behind Act requires all states to measure each child's progress toward those standards with tests aligned with those higher standards. In the face of a political climate supporting greater school accountability, the immediate challenge facing early childhood educators is how to advocate for positive changes in policy and practice to help ensure assessment practices that are authentic and meaningful for all young children and their families.

Finally, given the centrality of the teacher's role as defined in the DAP position and guidelines, how can we promote public awareness and debate about standards that on the one hand require some early childhood teachers to complete a rigorous baccalaureate or postbaccalaureate professional preparation program in early childhood teacher education and hold a specialized early childhood teaching license, and, on the other hand, require of many other early childhood teachers only a high school diploma or the equivalent, with no licensure requirement? Given that developmentally appropriate practices result from the process of teacher decision making, a critical challenge is how to establish an infrastructure of policy and adequate resources to ensure that all children are taught by high-quality teachers. While the No Child Left Behind Act mandates a well-prepared teacher in every classroom by 2005, this legislation addresses only K–12 education and does not extend to the thousands of young children in prekindergarten and child-care programs.

These and other challenges will require early childhood professionals who understand and are committed to the guidelines and principles for developmentally appropriate practice to participate proactively in local, state, and national arenas to work in partnership with parents and policy makers. Perhaps the biggest challenge for all early childhood professionals is to remain lifelong learners, given the constantly changing context and knowledge base for early childhood education and the newer trends and issues facing professionals and young children today and in the future.

REFERENCES

Bowman, B., Donovan, S., & Burns, S. (Eds.). (2000). *Eager to learn: Educating our preschoolers*. Washington, DC: National Academy Press.

Bransford, J., Brown, A., & Cocking, R. (1999). *How people learn: Brain, mind, experience, and school*. Washington, DC: National Academy Press.

Bredekamp, S. (Ed.). (1987). *Developmentally appropriate practice in early childhood programs serving children from birth through age 8*. Washington, DC: National Association for the Education of Young Children.

Bredekamp, S., & Copple, C. (Eds.). (1997). *Developmentally appropriate practice in early childhood programs* (rev. ed.). Washington, DC: National Association for the Education of Young Children.

Campbell, F. A., Pungello, E. P., Miller-Johnson, S., Burchinal, M., & Ramey, C. T. (2001). The development of cognitive and academic abilities: Growth curves from an early childhood educational experiment. *Developmental Psychology, 37*(2), 231–242.

Cannella, G., & Grieshaber, S. (2001). Conclusion: Identities and possibilities. In S. Grieshaber & G. Cannella (Eds.), *Embracing identities in early childhood education: Diversity and possibilities* (pp. 173–180). New York: Teachers College Press.

Charlesworth, R. (1998a). Developmentally appropriate practice is for everyone. *Childhood Education, 74*(5), 274–282.

Charlesworth, R. (1998b). Response to Sally Lubeck's "Is developmentally appropriate practice for everyone?" *Childhood Education, 74*(5), 293–298.

Copely, J. (2000). *The young child and mathematics*. Washington, DC: National Association for the Education of Young Children.

Council for Exceptional Children. (2000). *Bright futures for exceptional learners: An action agenda to achieve quality conditions for teaching and learning*. Arlington, VA: Author.

Dewey, J. (1916). *Democracy and education: An introduction to the philosophy of education*. New York: Macmillan.

Division for Early Childhood of the Council for Exceptional Children. (2000a). *DEC position statement on goal one of America 2000: All children will start school ready to learn*. Denver, CO: Author.

Division for Early Childhood of the Council for Exceptional Children. (2000b). *Personnel standards for early education and early intervention: Guidelines for licensure in early childhood special education*. Denver, CO: Author.

Dunn, L. & Kontos, S. (1997). Research in review: What have we learned about developmentally appropriate practice? *Young Children, 52*(5), 4–13.

Erikson, E. (1963). *Childhood and society*. New York: Norton.

Fisher, B. (1998). *Joyful learning in kindergarten* (rev. ed.). Portsmouth, NH: Heinemann.

Fleer, M. (Ed.). (1995). *DAPcentrisim: Challenging developmentally appropriate practice*. Watson, ACT: Australian Early Childhood Association.

Gardner, H. (1993). *Multiple intelligences*. New York: Basic Books.

Getty Center for Education in the Arts. (1999). *A guide for learning and teaching in art.* Los Angeles: Author.

Goffin, S., & Wilson, C. (2001). *Curriculum models and early childhood education: Appraising the relationship* (2nd ed.). Upper Saddle River, NJ: Merrill/ Prentice Hall.

Grieshaber, S., & Cannella, G. (Eds.). (2001). *Embracing identities in early childhood education: Diversity and possibilities.* New York: Teachers College Press.

International Reading Association (IRA) & National Association for the Education of Young Children (NAEYC). (1998). *Learning to read and write: Developmentally appropriate practices for young children.* Newark, DE, and Washington, DC: Authors.

Lehrer, R., & Shauble, L.(2002). *Investigating real data in the classroom: Expanding children's understanding of math and science.* New York: Teachers College Press.

Lubeck, S. (1998a). Is developmentally appropriate practice for everyone? *Childhood Education, 74*(5), 283–292.

Lubeck, S. (1998b). Is DAP for everyone? A response. *Childhood Education, 74*(5), 299–301.

Mallory, B. (1998). Educating young children with developmental differences: Principles of inclusive practice. In C. Seefeldt & A. Galper (Eds.), *Continuing issues in early childhood education* (2nd ed.) (pp. 213–237). Columbus, OH: Merrill.

Mallory, B., & New, R. (1994). *Diversity and developmentally appropriate practices: Challenges for early childhood education.* New York: Teachers College Press.

National Association for the Education of Young Children (NAEYC). (1998). *Accreditation criteria & procedures of the National Association for the Education of Young Children.* Washington, DC: Author.

National Association for the Education of Young Children (NAEYC). (2001). *NAEYC standards for early childhood professional preparation: Baccalaureate or initial licensure level.* Washington, DC: Author.

National Board for Professional Teaching Standards. (2001). *NBPTS early childhood generalist standards* (2nd ed.). Arlington, VA: Author.

National Council for the Social Studies. (1994). *Expectations of excellence: Curriculum standards for social studies.* Washington, DC: Author.

National Council of Teachers of Mathematics. (2000). *Principles and standards for school mathematics.* Reston, VA: Author.

National Research Council. (1996). *National science education standards.* Washington, DC: National Academy Press.

New, R. (1999). What should children learn? Making choices and taking chances. *Early Childhood Research and Practice* [On-line], *1*(2). Available: http:// ecrp.uiuc.edu/v1n2/new.html

Peisner-Feinberg, E., Burchinal, M., Clifford, R., Culkin, M., Howes, C., Kagan, S., Yazejian, N., Byler, P., Rustici, J., & Zelazo, J. (2000). *The children of the cost, quality, and outcomes study go to school: Technical report.* Chapel

Hill, NC: Frank Porter Graham Child Development Center, University of North Carolina at Chapel Hill.

Piaget, J. (1952). *The origins of intelligence in children*. New York: International Universities Press.

Quality Counts 2002: Building blocks for success [Special issue]. (2002, January 10). *Education Week, 22*(1).

Ratcliff, N., Cruz, J., & McCarthy, J. (1999). *Early childhood teacher education licensure patterns and curriculum guidelines: A state-by-state analysis.* Washington, DC: Council for Professional Recognition.

Rogoff, B. (1990). *Apprenticeship in thinking: Cognitive development in social context.* New York: Oxford University Press.

Shonkoff, J., & Phillips, D. (Eds.). (2000). *From neurons to neighborhoods: The science of early child development.* Washington, DC: National Academy Press.

Snow, C., Burns, M., & Griffin, P. (Eds.). (1998). *Preventing reading difficulties in young children.* Washington, DC: National Academy Press.

Vygotsky, L. (1978). *Mind in society: The development of higher psychological processes.* Cambridge, MA: Harvard University Press.

Chapter 6

Assessing and Reporting Young Children's Progress: A Review of the Issues

SUE C. WORTHAM

Denzel is sitting in the hallway of Silver Lake Elementary School. He is 4 years old and has been brought to the school by his mother for screening tests for the prekindergarten class. Earlier Denzel worked with a teacher who asked him questions about pictures and gave him tasks to do with blocks and shapes of several sizes and colors. He was asked to cut with scissors and copy designs on a piece of paper with a large pencil. Now Denzel is waiting with his mother for a vision and hearing examination by the school nurse. Denzel is uneasy because the school looks very big and the halls are very long. His mother reassures him, but she, too, is anxious about the meaning of the tasks Denzel was asked to do and whether he did well. While they wait for the nurse to call Denzel's name, they look at a book together.

Although Denzel and his mother might have been confused and unsure about the purpose of the screening tasks and vision and hearing examinations he experienced prior to enrolling in a prekindergarten class, he had probably been assessed many times in his young life. The initial assessment of a child's physical status and subsequent developmental progress begins before birth and continues through frequent examinations during the first days, weeks, and months of the first year. As the young child enters the preschool years, developmental assessments for more purposes are added, and when the child enters kindergarten and the primary grades, assessment broadens to include progress in learning and achievement.

In this chapter we examine the purposes for and methods of assessing young children's progress. Because there is dissonance between ideals of how young children should be assessed and current practices used, issues in assessment are central to the overall discussion. The issues are significant and give rise to the following salient questions about assessment of young children: What is assessment of young children's progress? Who are the young children who are addressed in assessment? Why are young children assessed? Why is the assessment of young children an issue, and how can assessment be used inappropriately? How should young children's progress be assessed and reported? What strategies can be used when assessment of young children is indicated? Finally, the chapter addresses perspectives of quality assessment of the young child's progress and draws implications for future teaching and learning.

WHAT IS ASSESSMENT OF YOUNG CHILDREN'S PROGRESS?

There are various perspectives of the meaning of assessment of young children's progress. The National Association for the Education of Young Children and the National Association of Early Childhood Specialists in State Departments of Education took the perspectives of conducting assessment for the purposes of reporting to parents and planning for instruction (NAEYC & NAECS/SDE, 1992). In their position paper, they proposed the following definition of assessment:

> Assessment is the process of observing, recording, and otherwise documenting the work children do and how they do it, as a basis for a variety of educational decisions that affect the child, including planning for groups and individual children and communicating with parents. Assessment encompasses the many forms of evaluation available to educational decision-making. (p. 10)

Goodwin and Goodwin (1993) discussed measurement in broader terms:

> Measurement is defined here as the process of determining through observation, testing, or other means, an individual's traits or behaviors, a program's characteristics, or the properties of some other entity, and then assigning a number rating, score, or label to that determination. It usually involves numbers, scales, constructs, reliability, and validity. This definition includes many measuring devices other than paper-and-pencil tests such as observation systems and nonreactive measures. (p. 441)

This description of measurement includes standardized tests as a part of the assessment process of the young child, one of the issues or concerns about assessment that is discussed later.

Shepard (1994) separated the definition of *assessment* into two categories, testing and assessment. Although she acknowledged that both terms mean the same thing, she preferred to define *tests* as the traditional standardized measures and *assessment* as developmentally appropriate procedures that are used.

It seems clear, then, that even the terms used in regard to assessment can be subject to individual interpretation. Is a physical examination of a child similar to a written examination in school? Can a child be measured for both physical growth and achievement in learning? Currently, *assessment* tends to be used as an umbrella term for all types of measurement and evaluation. Therefore, for the purposes of this chapter, the term *assessment* will be defined broadly enough to encompass all its purposes. In this context, assessment includes all the strategies used to measure development and learning that affect decisions that are made and planning that is conducted on behalf of young children.

Who Are the Young Children Addressed in Assessment?

All young children are addressed in the "who" of assessment. When early childhood professionals describe the importance of understanding how best to assess young children, they must be inclusive in describing the population. The types of assessments used and the purposes for such assessments depend on children's individual characteristics and backgrounds. Young children are diverse in development, culture, language, abilities, and life experiences. All these factors affect the nature and course of development and learning that influence the child's status and needs at a particular time. Our interest in and concerns for assessment must include the possibilities for diversity that inform how and why assessments are conducted. The population addressed in assessment in this chapter includes young children from birth through age 8, the years of early childhood.

Why Are Young Children Assessed?

Jacob is 2 years old. Although he seems very intelligent and is curious about everything in his environment, he speaks very little. His parents are concerned and anxious about his delay in language development. They asked the pediatrician about Jacob at his 2-year checkup. After the physician asked questions about Jacob's speech, he agreed with the parents that Jacob needed to be further evaluated. Because Jacob has had many respiratory infections, the pediatrician referred him for a hearing assessment. The results showed that Jacob had some hearing loss that was affecting his language development. Jacob was put under the care of the hearing specialist for further diagnosis and treatment.

Depending on individual characteristics and diversities, young children are assessed for many purposes. Taking the broader perspective of development and learning described earlier, it is proposed here that assessment serves the following purposes, especially for infants and toddlers:

- To monitor the course of physical, language, cognitive, and socio-emotional development
- To identify and serve infants and young children who are at risk to ensure healthy development and successful later learning
- To identify and serve infants and young children who have a disabling condition that would respond to early intervention (Wortham, 2001)

Assessment in the early weeks, months, and years of life is conducted to evaluate or measure the course of the young child's development. Early indicators that a child's development is not progressing normally provide the opportunity to use intervention services and programs to address the child's needs. Assessment should help determine whether a child needs to be placed in a particular program, can benefit from a particular program, or needs a specialized or individualized program. The child's progress in a program would be assessed as well as the appropriateness of programs and strategies. Thus, children who are born prematurely, suffer trauma during the birth process, present a disability such as mental retardation, or encounter an experience that results in injury are assessed to determine whether they are at risk for development and later learning. Young children in the preschool years might also be assessed for other risk factors, such as language differences, family instability resulting in poor social skills, or a lack of experiences needed for cognitive development.

There are a variety of preschool and early elementary programs available to serve young children. The uses for assessment cited above facilitate the identification, program planning, and program evaluation for all types of young children in all types of early childhood programs. Although assessment has a necessary role in these programs, there are also concerns about that role. We address these concerns in the next section.

WHY IS THE ASSESSMENT OF YOUNG CHILDREN AN ISSUE?

Anabella entered kindergarten after Christmas. Her parents moved into the community when her father was able to obtain work in a local restaurant. In April the kindergarten children were adminis-tered a readiness test to determine whether they were to be placed in kindergarten again or promoted to first grade. Although Anabella's score on the test was just below the mean, her teacher recommended that Anabella repeat kindergarten. Anabella's parents were very concerned. They felt that Anabella should go to first grade with her peers. The school believed that Anabella was not ready for first grade based on test results and would benefit from the additional time in kindergarten. Should the results of one test determine Anabella's placement?

The Use of Standardized Tests with Young Children

The increased use of standardized testing at all levels has been an issue in American education for many decades (Shepard, 2000; Wesson, 2001). However, the use of tests with children in preschool and early elemen-tary classrooms has been of particular concern to early childhood profes-sionals (Meisels, 2000). As in Anabella's case, standardized tests are most controversial when they are used to deny children entry to early child-hood classrooms, to place children in special education programs, to place children in transitional classrooms, or to retain them. The misuse or misap-plication of test results for these purposes has been questioned strongly by early childhood specialists as well as by experts in measurement (Goodwin & Goodwin, 1993, 1997; Kohn, 2001; Perrone, 1990, 1991; Shepard, 1994, 2000; Shepard & Graue, 1993; Wesson, 2001). The efficacy of screening tests for school readiness and the use of standardized tests for retention and placement have long been questioned by early childhood specialists (Foster, 1993; Meisels, 2000; Meisels, Steele, & Quinn-Leering, 1993; Pierson & Connell, 1992; Shepard & Graue, 1993). Longitudinal studies of retention found that retention practices also were not effective and do not benefit children (Allington & McGill-Franzen, 1995). Although these practices are now less popular than in the 1980s and 1990s, they still per-sist in some school districts and states (NAECS/SDE, 2000; Smith, 1999). Retention, particularly, has gained favor in the wake of new standards for accountability within school reform.

One issue is the difficulty of designing valid and reliable instruments because of the rapid developmental changes in young children. In addition, reliability or dependability of test scores is poor when young children are administered tests in groups. On the other hand, individual testing involves a major time commitment on the part of staff members. Another criticism is that the standardized tests developed for young children measure only cognitive elements, thus neglecting other areas such as social competence, self-esteem, and creativity (Goodwin & Goodwin, 1997; Katz, 1985).

Testing Young Children with Cultural and Language Differences

Early childhood specialists believe it is inappropriate to use standardized tests with young children for the reasons just discussed. There is also a question as to how appropriate our tests and assessment strategies are when one considers the diversity in young children attending early childhood programs. The growing number of children from low-income families and the influx of people from other countries, especially Southeast Asia and Central and South America, raise important questions about the fairness of existing tests for children who are school-disadvantaged and linguistically and culturally diverse. These dramatic changes in diversity indicate the need for alternative assessment strategies for young children (Goodwin & Goodwin, 1997; Kohn, 2001). Moreover, assessment of young children from families that are culturally and linguistically diverse must include many dimensions of diversity. It is not useful to proceed with an assessment that is culturally fair for populations in general, because there are many variations within communities and cultures that must be considered. Even when the assessor and the children being assessed share the same culture and language, there might be differences in cultural perceptions and language use between the assessor and the children being assessed (Barrera, 1996). Many types of information, including the child's background and the use of assessments, must be combined to determine a picture of the child that is reflective of individual, group, and family cultural characteristics.

Testing Young Children with Disabilities

The use of standardized tests with infants and young children with disabilities cannot be avoided. Identification of developmental delays and disabling conditions is important if early intervention is to be provided (Meisels et al., 1993). Nevertheless, Greenspan, Meisels, and the ZERO TO THREE Work Group (1996) believe assessments used with infants and young children with disabilities have been borrowed from assessment methodology used with older children and do not provide meaningful developmental information. These developmental psychologists propose that assessment should be based on current understanding of development and should use structured tests as one part of an integrated approach based on multiple sources of information. Play-based assessment is one major source of information among multiple strategies (Bergen, 1997; Fewell & Glick, 1998). During play, children can demonstrate skills and abilities that might not be apparent in other forms of assessment (Fewell & Rich, 1987; Segal & Webber, 1996). Observation of the child's interactions with trusted caregivers is another useful assessment strategy.

There are many challenges in conducting appropriate assessment with very young children as well as children entering preschool, kindergarten, and elementary school. In the next section, we look at current thinking on how young children should be assessed.

HOW SHOULD YOUNG CHILDREN'S PROGRESS BE ASSESSED?

Remember Denzel, whom you met in the opening scenario?

> Denzel has spent the past 9 months in the prekindergarten pro-
> gram at Silver Lake Elementary School. The initial assessment
> prior to the beginning of school and his fear about the school are
> long forgotten. He has had a happy year with many friends at
> school and has enjoyed having his mother as a helper in his room
> often during the year. Denzel and his mother are proud of what he
> has learned. Denzel has a portfolio of materials that document
> what he has learned. In addition, Denzel's teacher has records of
> other assessments she has conducted with Denzel and the other
> students during the year. She has compared Denzel's progress with
> the assessment results at the beginning of the year. This informa-
> tion will be forwarded to Denzel's kindergarten teacher next year.
> During the last week of school, Denzel and his mother visit the
> kindergarten classroom during an open house held in the evening.
> They get acquainted with the kindergarten teacher and study
> displays of work and projects completed by the kindergarten
> students this year. Both Denzel and his mother feel comfortable
> that kindergarten will be another good year, and they look forward
> to the beginning of school in the fall.

Regardless of how one defines *assessment*, it should benefit the child (Wiggins, 1993, 1998). The previous discussion on issues in early childhood testing and assessment remind us that some current practices do *not* benefit the child or are detrimental to the child. We now have guidelines on how to address issues of assessment to meet the unique challenges of measuring all young children. The National Early Childhood Assessments Resource Group was organized to establish principles and recommendations. The following principles were developed by that group (National Education Goals Panel, 1998):

1. Assessment should bring about benefits for children. Assessments should be tailored to a specific purpose and should be reliable, valid, and fair for that purpose.
2. Assessment policies should be designed recognizing that reliability and validity of assessments increase with children's age.
3. Assessments should be age-appropriate in both content and the method of data collection.
4. Assessments should be linguistically appropriate, recognizing that to some extent all assessments are measures of language.
5. Parents should be a valued source of assessment information, as well as an audience for assessment results. (pp. 4–5)

These principles directly address the concerns and issues discussed earlier and provide a framework for designing quality assessments. There are many assessment strategies that are appropriate for the developmental levels of children in early childhood that have been a part of the teacher's repertoire for many decades. Early childhood teachers have long known that they need to learn about the child in the context of the child's activities. In order to meet the criteria of the principles of assessment proposed by the National Early Childhood Assessment Resource Group and other specialists in early childhood assessment, a comprehensive system of assessment must be developed. Such a system provides the teacher with a variety of tools to better understand and plan for young children. The components of a comprehensive plan for using appropriate assessments are addressed in the following sections.

Appropriate Uses of Standardized Testing

A comprehensive assessment system includes the use of standardized tests when appropriate. As discussed previously, standardized tests such as screening instruments are used to identify and serve infants and young children with disabling conditions or who are at risk for developmental delay. Standardized tests are also used to identify children for preschool intervention programs such as bilingual programs and classes for children at risk for success in school. In these cases, standardized tests are one part of the screening and assessment process to identify children who will benefit from intervention programs prior to entry into kindergarten or who need additional, individual assistance in the primary grades.

Teacher Assessment Strategies

Although school districts often use informal tests or evaluation strategies developed by local teachers or staff members, teachers have devised their own assessments to measure development and learning. These strategies include observation, checklists, and rating scales.

One of the most useful ways to understand the individual characteristics of young children is through observation. As pointed out earlier, developmental progress is more likely to be noted from children's behavior in play or other natural activities than from a designed assessment or instrument. This is true for all domains of development (Segal & Webber, 1996; Wortham, 2001). Because young children learn best through active involvement with their environment, evaluation of learning may be assessed most appropriately by observation of the child during periods of activity. Observation records can be used to plan instruction, to report progress in various areas of development, and to monitor mastery of preschool curriculum objectives.

Checklists and rating scales are used at all levels of development and learning from infancy through secondary schools. A checklist is a list of developmental characteristics or learning objectives that can be used to record progress or mastery. Rating scales are similar to checklists but provide for assessment on a continuum. Whereas checklist items are rated with a negative or positive response, rating scales can be used when a range of criteria are needed to acquire accurate information (e.g., never, seldom, sometimes, usually). Some checklists and rating scales are standardized, while others are locally developed by a teacher, school district, or other agency and are not standardized.

Authentic and Performance Assessment

In the last two decades, there has been a new emphasis on a different approach to assessment. Traditional formal methods of measuring learning have focused on assessing the child's knowledge or skills. Performance assessments, however, require more in that they measure not only what the child knows, but also what the child can do or how the child can use the knowledge in a meaningful application (Herman, Aschbacher, & Winters, 1992; Pierson & Beck, 1993; Wiggins, 1993, 1998). Moreover, performance assessment includes completion of a task in a realistic context. While the terms *authentic* and *performance* are frequently used interchangeably, authentic assessment can be interpreted as having some connection to the real world and being an application of learning (Bergen, 1994; Ratcliff, 2001/2002). Performance assessment refers to the child's demonstrating in some way what has been learned and how that learning can be useful.

Advocates of authentic or performance assessment propose that authentic achievement must accompany authentic assessment. Neill (1997) describes this relationship:

> Assessment to enhance student learning must be integrated with, not separate from curriculum and instruction. . . . Schools need to ensure that development of "authentic instruction," which involves modes of teaching that foster understanding of rich content and encourage students' positive engagement with the world. (p. 35)

Thus, if we are to use authentic or performance assessment to understand how children can apply or use what they have learned, the learning activities they are provided must also be meaningful and related to real-world experiences. Performance-based assessments are particularly useful with young children because developmental progress as well as learning can be measured. In addition, performance assessments allow the teacher to observe the processes the child uses to learn. (Meisels et al., 1993).

There are many strategies that can be used to facilitate the child's demonstration of progress and learning, including the following:

- *Work samples.* Work samples are the types of assessment data most commonly thought of in terms of portfolio collections. Teachers are familiar with collecting samples of children's work. In the context of performance-based assessment, there is a specific purpose for the samples selected (Barbour & Desjean-Perrotta, 1998; Grace & Shores, 1992; Meisels, 1993).
- *Interviews.* Seefeldt (1993) suggested that interviews can be used to assess what children understand about concepts. A teacher can conduct an informal interview while children are working in centers, initiating it when noticing that relevant behaviors are occurring. In contrast, a structured interview involves prior planning on the teacher's part with specific questioning to elicit the child's thought (Engel, 1990). A third type of interview, the diagnostic interview, is conducted to determine why a child is experiencing difficulty in learning a concept.
- *Games.* Teachers can design games for specific learning objectives so that children demonstrate their thought processes in showing what they have learned. Teachers observe the children as they are engaged in the game and study how the children employ games strategies (Kamii & Rosenblum, 1990).

- *Portfolios*. Portfolios facilitate authentic assessment by providing a method of organizing various types of materials into a collection that can be used to evaluate the child's progress. Portfolios can be organized in many ways and can be collections of the child's work selected by the teacher, the child, or the teacher and child together. Depending on the type of curriculum and instruction in the classroom, the portfolio can be organized by developmental domain, by content area, or by integrated curriculum units or projects. The goals and objectives for the curriculum serve as the foundation for assessment as a framework for the portfolio contents (Barbour & Desjean-Perrotta, 1998; Glazer, 1993; Wortham, 1998, 2001).

HOW SHOULD YOUNG CHILDREN'S PROGRESS BE REPORTED?

Given that we should have a comprehensive system of assessment, how should we report young children's progress? How do we include both standardized, traditional teacher assessment strategies and authentic or performance assessments when reporting the child's developmental growth and learning? All of the strategies discussed in this chapter have a role in reporting a continuum of development and learning, information about the whole child, diagnostic information that allows the teacher to adjust instruction and activities, and, most important, examples of what the child has done to demonstrate understanding (Wortham, 2001).

The major function of reporting the child's progress is to communicate information about the child to the parents. To develop a quality approach to reporting progress, the assessment system should include documentation of the results of authentic assessments, a vehicle for interpreting the collected data from all types of assessments, and an effective method for communicating with parents. It is suggested that portfolios and narrative reports are effective strategies to use for reporting children's progress to parents.

As described in the previous section, portfolios facilitate the collection of information and materials relative to the child's assessment. The content of a teacher-and-child portfolio can include a section for work selected by the child, a section for work selected by the teacher, and a section for teacher assessment records such as observations, reports, checklists and rating scales, and other documentation of the child's progress.

Before the child's progress can be reported to parents, an evaluation or interpretation must be made of the material and data that have been collected. The evaluation of assessment data should be connected to specific criteria established for assessment of learning goals, and performance should be compared to this standard. The standards that are developed must be both appropriate for the child's level of development and consistent with the teacher's curriculum.

The combined assessments are used to develop a profile of the child. The profile includes conclusions about the child's progress and reports information about the child's strengths and weaknesses, achievements, and instructional needs. Evaluation can include process and product assessments. The teacher conducts frequent process assessments with the child, discussing portfolio materials and progress that has been made. Product evaluation includes review of portfolio materials to sum up a student's progress prior to sharing the evaluation with parents in a conference (Farr, 1993; Wortham, 1998, 2001). The portfolio serves as the resource for the teacher, child, and parents to discuss the child's evaluation through a review of portfolio contents.

A written report of the child's evaluation can be used with the portfolio as a reporting tool or as a separate alternative to report progress. Including all assessment materials and record-keeping forms, the teacher's written report constructs a profile or picture of the child in terminology that is meaningful and understandable to the parents (Horm-Wingerd, 1992; Krechevsky, 1991).

Current practices in how we should assess and report young children's progress favor the use of performance-based assessments. Authentic assessment methods combined with portfolios and written summary reports are proposed as models for assessment and reporting. Project Spectrum (Krechevsky, 1991), the Work Sampling System (Meisels, 1997), and the Child Observation Record (Schweinhart, 1993) all use a combination of authentic, performance-based assessment strategies, a record-keeping system, portfolio materials, and a written summary report. All three models have been carefully researched to ensure a quality assessment and reporting process that can be disseminated to early childhood educators.

PERSISTENT ISSUES IN THE ASSESSMENT AND REPORTING OF YOUNG CHILDREN'S PROGRESS

In spite of the positive steps being taken in developing appropriate assessments and reporting procedures, there are still concerns associated with their use. The time needed to initiate and maintain portfolios and compose written reports on children's progress is an issue for many teachers. When teachers first implement portfolio assessment, they feel that it is very time-consuming to make the many decisions about how to organize a portfolio and determine when and how to collect children's work. Later, when they are more experienced in the process, they are able to develop more time-efficient strategies.

Other issues focus on teacher accountability for portfolio assessment. Teachers are insecure about the validity and reliability of the assessment and reporting method. They are concerned about whether they are measuring accurately (validity) and whether the measurement is dependable (reliability). They are uncertain about whether they are grading the child's work appropriately. In some schools teachers are encouraged to use portfolios for assessment but are required to give letter grades. They find this a source of conflict and confusion (Goodwin & Goodwin, 1993; Guskey, 1994; Shepard, 1995). Guidelines for quality in portfolio assessment have been developed to assist teachers and include the following:

1. How representative is the work included in the portfolio of what students can really do?
2. Do the portfolio pieces represent coached work? Independent work? Are they identified as to the amount of support students received?
3. Do the evaluation criteria for each piece and the portfolio as a whole represent the most relevant or useful dimensions of student work?
4. How well do portfolio pieces match important instructional targets or authentic tasks?
5. Do tasks or some parts of them require extraneous abilities?
6. Is there a method for ensuring that portfolios are reviewed consistently and criteria applied accurately? (Arter & Spandel, as cited by Herman et al., 1992)

There are also concerns about the quality of performance assessments. Authentic assessment can also be time-consuming and can be more complex than more traditional types of assessment. Because assessment is integrated into instruction, teachers must clearly understand what they are looking for in assessment. A related issue is in scoring performance assessments. A common concern is who will determine the quality of performance assessments when they are used for grading (Bergen, 1994; Givens, 1997).

There are strategies now available to help teachers assess student progress or score student work when using performance assessments. Rubrics are one tool that can be used for qualitative evaluation of student performance. Wiggins (1996) defines a rubric as follows:

A rubric is a printed set of guidelines that distinguishes performances or products of different quality. . . . A rubric has descriptors that define what to look for at each level of performance. . . . Rubrics also often have indicators providing specific examples or tell-tale signs of things to look for in work. (p. VI-5: 1)

Rubrics provide guidelines to distinguish performance from one level to another. Indicators of performance can also be called the criteria for scoring. That is, they set the criteria for the score at each level of quality. Indicators can also describe dimensions of performance—different categories of indicators leading to the desired score. Rubrics can be used with interviews, games, work samples, projects, and other assessments that are considered to measure performance.

Rubrics can be central to developing quality performance assessments. In addition, other suggestions can help in the development of quality performance assessments:

- Base assessments on instructional goals.
- Use fully developed task descriptions for performance assessments.
- Review assessment criteria against instructional goals.
- Score systematically and recheck scoring strategies periodically.
- Compare rubric and other performance scoring with other informal assessments when appropriate.
- Use more than one assessment in making important decisions.
- Conduct assessments that are consistent for all students to eliminate bias. (Herman et al., 1992)

In these beginning years of the 21st century, teachers have an accumulation of instruments and strategies at hand. Some measures are required; others are choices that teachers may make for assessment. This chapter has explored both appropriate and inappropriate practices and measures. A major focus has been to describe some alternative methods for conducting assessment that permit children to demonstrate how they understand and use what they have learned. Although the progress of developing quality assessments is dynamic and needs constant refinement, teachers now have the opportunity to use a variety of assessment approaches and strategies that will provide maximum benefit for the child.

REFERENCES

Allington, R. L., & McGill-Franzen, A. (1995). Flunking: Throwing good money after bad. In R. L. Allington & S. A. Walmsley (Eds.), *No quick fix* (pp. 45–60). New York: Teachers College Press.

Barbour, A., & Desjean-Perrotta, B. (1998). The basics of portfolio assessment. In S. C. Wortham, A. Barbour, & B. Desjean-Perrotta, *Portfolio assessment: A handbook for preschool and elementary educators* (pp. 15–30). Olney, MD: Association for Childhood Education International.

Barrera, I. (1996). Thoughts on the asessment of young children whose sociocultural background is unfamiliar to the assessor. In S. J. Meisels & E. Fenichel (Eds.), *New visions for the developmental assessment of infants and young children* (pp. 69–84). Washington, DC: ZERO TO THREE: National Center for Infants, Toddlers, and Families.

Bergen, D. (1994). Authentic performance assessments. *Childhood Education, 70*, 99–102.

Bergen, D. (1997). Using observational techniques for evaluating young children's learning. In O. N. Saracho & B. Spodek (Eds.), *Issues in early childhood educational assessment and evaluation* (pp. 108–128). New York: Teachers College Press.

Engel, B. (1990). An approach to assessment in early literacy. In C. Kamii (Ed.), *Achievement testing in the early grades: The games grown-ups play* (pp. 119–134). Washington, DC: National Association for the Education of Young Children.

Farr, R. C. (1993). *Portfolio assessment teacher's guide grades K–8*. Orlando, FL: Harcourt Brace Jovanovich.

Fewell, R. R., & Glick, M. (1998). The role of play in assessment. In D. P. Fromberg & D. Bergen (Eds.), *Play from birth to twelve and beyond* (pp. 201–207). New York: Garland.

Fewell, R. R., & Rich, J. (1987). Play assessment as a procedure for examining cognitive, communication and social skills in multihandicapped children. *Journal of Psychoeducational Assessment, 2*, 107–118.

Foster, J. E. (1993). Retaining children in grade. *Childhood Education, 63*, 38–42.

Givens, K. (1997). Performance assessment tests: A problematic panacea. *Contemporary Education, 69*, 27–29.

Glazer, S. M. (1993, January). Assessment in the classroom: Where are we, where we're going. *Teaching K–8*, pp. 68–71.

Goodwin, W. L., & Goodwin, L. D. (1993). Young children and measurement: Standardized and nonstandardized instruments in early childhood education. In B. Spodek (Ed.), *Handbook of research on the education of young children* (pp. 441–465). New York: Macmillan.

Goodwin, W. L., & Goodwin, L. D. (1997). Using standardized measures for evaluating young children's learning. In B. Spodek & O. N. Saracho (Eds.), *Issues in early childhood educational assessment and evaluation* (pp. 92–107). New York: Teachers College Press.

Grace, C., & Shores, E. F. (1992). *The portfolio and its use: Developmentally appropriate assessment of young children*. Little Rock, AK: Southern Early Childhood Association.

Greenspan, S. I., Meisels, S. J., & the ZERO TO THREE Work Group on Developmental Assessment. (1996). Toward a new vision for the developmental assessment of infants and young children. In S. J. Meisels & E. Fenichel (Eds.),

New visions for the developmental assessment of infants and young children (pp. 11–26). Washington, DC: ZERO TO THREE: National Center for Infants, Toddlers, and Families.

Guskey, T. R. (1994). What you assess may not be what you get. *Educational Leadership, 51,* 51–54.

Herman, J. L., Aschbacher, P. R., & Winters, L. (1992). *A practical guide to alternative assessment.* Alexandria, VA: Association for Supervision and Curriculum Development.

Horm-Wingerd, D. M. (1992). Reporting children's development: The narrative report. *Dimensions of Early Childhood, 21,* 11–15.

Kamii, C., & Rosenblum, V. (1990). An approach to assessment in mathematics. In C. Kamii (Ed.), *Achievement testing in the early grades: The games grown-ups play* (pp. 146–162). Washington, DC: National Association for the Education of Young Children.

Katz, L. (1985). Dispositions in early childhood education. *ERIC/EECE Bulletin, 18,* 1, 3.

Kohn, A. (2001). Fighting the tests: Turning frustration into action. *Young Children, 56,* 16–18.

Krechevsky, M. (1991). Project Spectrum: An innovative assessment alternative. *Educational Leadership, 48,* 43–48.

Meisels, S. J. (1993). Remaking classroom assessments with the Work Sampling System. *Young Children, 48,* 34–40.

Meisels, S. J. (1997). *Work sampling in the classroom: A teacher's manual.* Ann Arbor, MI: Rebus.

Meisels, S. J. (2000). On the side of the child: Personal reflections on testing, teaching, and early childhood education. *Young Children, 55,* 16–19.

Meisels, S. J., Steele, M., & Quinn-Leering, K. (1993). Testing, tracking, and retaining young children: An analysis of research and social policy. In B. Spodek (Ed.), *Handbook of research on the education of young children* (pp. 279–292). New York: Macmillan.

National Association of Early Childhood Specialists in State Departments of Education (NAECS/SDE). (2000). *Still! Unacceptable trends in kindergarten entry and placement.* Washington, DC: Author.

National Association for the Education of Young Children (NAEYC) & National Association of Early Childhood Specialists in State Departments of Education (NAECS/SDE). (1992). Guidelines for appropriate curriculum content and assessment in programs serving children ages 3 through 8. In S. Bredekamp & T. Rosegrant (Eds.), *Reaching potentials: Appropriate curriculum and assessment for young children* (pp. 9–27). Washington, DC: National Association for the Education of Young Children.

National Education Goals Panel. (1998). *Principles and recommendations for early childhood assessments.* Washington, DC: Author.

Neill, M. (1997). Transforming student assessment. *Phi Delta Kappan, 79,* 34–40.

Perrone, V. (1990). How did we get here? In C. Kamii (Ed.), *Achievement testing in the early grades: The games grown-ups play* (pp. 1–13). Washington, DC: National Association for the Education of Young Children.

Perrone, V. (1991). On standardized testing. *Childhood Education, 68*, 132–142.

Pierson, C. A., & Beck, S. S. (1993). Performance assessment: The realities that will influence the rewards. *Childhood Education, 70*, 29–32.

Pierson, L. H., & Connell, J. P. (1992). Effect of grade retention on self-system processes, school engagement, and academic performance. *Journal of Educational Psychology, 84*, 300–307.

Ratcliff, N. J. (2001/2002). Using authentic assessment to document the emerging literacy skills of young children. *Childhood Education, 78*, 66–69.

Schweinhart, L. J. (1993). Observing young children in action: The key to early childhood assessment. *Young Children, 48*, 29–33.

Seefeldt, C. (1993). *Social studies for the preschool/primary child* (4th ed.). New York: Merrill/Macmillan.

Segal, M., & Webber, N. T. (1996). Nonstructured play observations: Guidelines, benefits, and caveats. In S. J. Meisels & E Fenichel (Eds.), *New visions for the developmental assessment of infants and young children* (pp. 207–230). Washington, DC: ZERO TO THREE: National Center for Infants, Toddlers, and Families.

Shepard, L. A. (1994). The challenges of assessing young children appropriately. *Phi Delta Kappan, 76*, 206–213.

Shepard, L. A. (1995). Using assessment to improve learning. *Educational Leadership, 52*, 38–45.

Shepard, L. A. (2000). The role of assessment in a learning culture. *Educational Researcher, 29*, 4–14.

Shepard L. A., & Graue, M. E. (1993). The morass of school readiness screening: Research on test use and validity. In B. Spodek (Ed.), *Handbook of research on the education of young children* (pp. 293–305). New York: Macmillan.

Smith, S. S. (1999). Reforming the kindergarten round-up. *Educational Leadership, 56*, 39–44.

Wesson, K. A. (2001). "The Volvo effect"—Questioning standardized tests. *Young Children, 56*, 16–18.

Wiggins, G. P. (1993). *Assessing student performance*. San Francisco: Jossey-Bass.

Wiggins, G. P. (1996). What is a rubric? A dialogue on design and use. In R. E. Blum & J. A. Arter (Eds.), *Student performance assessment in an era of restructuring* (pp. VI-5:1–VI-5:13). Alexandria, VA: Association for Supervision and Curriculum Development.

Wiggins, G. P. (1998). *Educative assessment*. San Francisco: Jossey-Bass.

Wortham, S. C. (1998). Introduction. In S. C. Wortham, A. Barbour, & B. Desjean-Perrotta. *Portfolio assessment: A handbook for preschool and elementary educators* (pp. 7–14). Olney, MD: Association for Childhood Education International.

Wortham, S. C. (2001). *Assessment in early childhood education* (3rd ed.). Englewood Cliffs, NJ: Prentice Hall.

Chapter 7

Shaking the Very Foundations of Emergent Literacy: Book Reading Versus Phonemic Awareness

LEA M. McGEE

Three teachers shift nervously in their seats in a large conference room prior to the beginning of an important meeting in their school district. They talk together quietly as they prepare to present a preliminary report on early literacy curriculum and instruction to the larger committee that will meet this morning. The purpose of the committee is to establish policies for prekindergarten programs in their system. The teachers are anxious about their presentation because as they were preparing their report, they discovered research about early literacy instruction that was contradictory to their current beliefs about early childhood education. They worked hard to prepare a report that they felt adequately represented the research on early literacy development, including research that was contradictory to their beliefs, and also represented their beliefs about the importance of child-centered early childhood education. This had taken many hours of reading, talking, and debate. Now the teachers were eager to share their thoughts with their colleagues.

The purpose of this chapter is to explore two areas of research that address the tension between two approaches to literacy instruction for 4- and 5-year-olds in preschool and kindergarten: reading aloud to children, on the one hand, and direct instruction in phonemics, on the other.

Major Trends and Issues in Early Childhood Education: Challenges, Controversies, and Insights, Second Edition. Copyright © 2003 by Teachers College, Columbia University. All rights reserved. ISBN 0-8077-4350-X (pbk), ISBN 0-8077-4351-8 (cloth). Prior to photocopying items for classroom use, please contact the Copyright Clearance Center, Customer Service, 222 Rosewood Dr., Danvers, MA 01923, USA, tel. (508) 750-8400.

Recent reviews of research have called into question a widespread and universally accepted practice associated with the emergent literacy perspective—the practice of reading aloud to children. At the same time, extensive research on children's development of phonemic awareness and its role in future reading achievement has prompted researchers to recommend that preschool and kindergarten programs include direct instruction in phonemic awareness, letter–sound associations, and word decoding. In this chapter I trace the historical tension between these two approaches to early literacy instruction. Discussed is research that downplays the role of reading aloud for children's literacy development as well as research that emphasizes the role of phonemic awareness. Finally, I examine recommendations from the National Research Council presented in *Preventing Reading Difficulties in Young Children* (Snow, Burns, & Griffin, 1998) for insights into resolving these tensions.

PRINT SKILLS VERSUS BOOKS: A HISTORICAL PERSPECTIVE

Early childhood programs have typically focused on activities that support growth in the full range of children's abilities. Some literacy activities, such as reading books to children and reciting nursery rhymes, were included in preschool programs; however, the purpose of these activities was to develop language rather than literacy abilities. Literacy received more emphasis in kindergarten programs, but from the readiness perspective (Morphett & Washburne, 1931). From this perspective children were not thought to be ready to read until reaching a particular level of mental maturity. Reading readiness tests assessed children's knowledge of prerequisite reading skills such as recognizing alphabet letters and associating sounds with letters. Children were taught the prerequisite skills in a sequence of direct-instruction lessons.

Since the late 1970s and early 1980s, research on children's early literacy learning in highly literate homes and preschools spurred a different perspective on literacy instruction in both preschool and kindergarten (Teale & Sulzby, 1986). This perspective—the emergent literacy perspective—stressed meaningful interactions during read-alouds and shared reading and writing activities, such as shared journal writing, and literacy-enriched play with the guidance and modeling of teachers. Instruction followed from children's responses rather than from a sequenced curriculum.

Despite emergent literacy's strong, current research base and overwhelming support from literacy professionals since its inception, programs in kindergarten, in particular, have continued to be influenced by both the emergent literacy and reading readiness perspectives (McMahon, Richmond, & Reeves-Kazelskis, 1998). Even side by side in the same school, teachers shaped their kindergarten programs more toward one perspective or the other (Nielsen & Monson, 1996).

These two perspectives on literacy instruction—reading readiness and emergent literacy—could be considered to share some common ground. Both programs may include reading books aloud to children, although the emergent literacy perspective places overwhelmingly more emphasis on the importance of this activity than the reading readiness perspective. Both programs address children's need to learn alphabet letters and acquire the alphabetic principle. The reading readiness approach to these print learning goals involves direct instruction in letter recognition and letter–sound relationships outside the context of actual reading and writing. In contrast, the emergent literacy approach to print learning emphasizes embedded activities within shared reading and writing.

Despite the fact that common ground might be expected in the two perspectives on kindergarten literacy instruction, children experience very different curricula in these classrooms (McMahon, et al., 1998). According to recent research (Nielsen & Monson, 1996), in reading readiness classrooms, 60.5% of instruction involved completing paperwork or procedural activities, mainly oriented toward print concepts, and only 4.5% involved reading aloud. In contrast, in emergent literacy classrooms, 19.6% of instruction was devoted to writing and 16.7% to reading aloud. Print-related instruction was embedded within writing activities and reading aloud. Differences in the amount of instructional time teachers allocated to various activities were related to differences in activities children selected for independent exploration. Children in reading readiness classrooms selected activities with print-related props, which consisted of teacher-made or commercial materials pertaining to concepts such as matching upper- and lowercase letters and identifying letter sounds. In contrast, children in emergent literacy classrooms more frequently elected to use books, engage in writing, or interact with familiar print in the classroom, such as charts of poems or songs. As I show later in this chapter, neither an exclusive focus on writing and sharing books nor an exclusive focus on learning letter–sound relationships seems to provide the range of literacy experiences that children need in order to become powerful early readers and writers.

THE ERODING BASE FOR READING BOOKS ALOUD

While not the only component of instruction in emergent literacy classrooms, reading books aloud is certainly considered an important, if not essential, component of the emergent literacy program (Ballenger, 1999; Cochran-Smith, 1984). Numerous literacy professionals assert that reading aloud to young children is one of the most important activities for literacy development. For example, an influential review of reading development and instruction argued that "the single most important activity for building the knowledge required for eventual success in reading is reading aloud to children. This is especially true during the preschool years" (Anderson, Hiebert, Scott, & Wilkinson, 1985, p. 23).

In general, research has demonstrated that reading aloud allows children to develop vocabulary (Robbins & Ehri, 1994; Senechal, Thomas, & Monker, 1995; Whitehurst et al., 1994a, 1999), acquire syntax and literary vocabulary associated with written versus spoken texts (Purcell-Gates, McIntyre, & Freppon, 1995), recall stories better (Morrow & Smith, 1990), and develop concepts about the organizational structures of narrative and informational text (Duke & Kays, 1998; Morrow & Smith, 1990). That is, numerous research studies have revealed a relationship between reading aloud to children and their development of various reading-related abilities such as language development, emergent literacy concepts, and story retellings. However, when researchers examined the relationship between reading aloud and conventional measures of reading acquisition, studies showed only modest relationships between frequency and quality of parent–child read-alouds during preschool and later conventional reading achievement in first grade and beyond (Scarborough & Dobrich, 1994).

Research on teachers' reading aloud in preschool and kindergarten also provides a mixed picture. One study revealed that the amount of analytic talk used by children during read-alouds in preschool was related to level of growth in vocabulary and story understanding in kindergarten (Dickinson & Smith, 1994). Several read-aloud studies have shown gains in preschool children's expressive language development and vocabulary acquisition, especially of vocabulary from the books included in the program, even when the duration of the programs was as short as only 4 weeks (Whitehurst et al., 1994a, 1994b, 1999). However, other research has questioned the importance of reading aloud in kindergarten. In one study, the amount of time that kindergarten teachers devoted to various instructional activities, including reading aloud and providing instruction in phonics, was calculated (Meyer, Wardrop, Stahl, & Linn, 1994). A negative relationship was found between the amount of time teachers spent reading aloud and children's knowledge of letters, sounds, and decoding. In contrast, a strong positive relationship was found between the amount of time spent in phonics activities and several reading achievement measures. The researchers argued that the amount of time teachers spent reading aloud displaced other activities, such as learning letter names and letter–sound relationships, that have a more direct relationship with reading achievement.

To interpret the results of the study conducted by Meyer and colleagues (1994), the amount of time kindergarten teachers devoted to reading aloud versus phonics activities needs to be examined. Teachers in one of the three districts included in the study devoted 40 minutes to literacy instruction, with 30 minutes spent in phonics activities, 5 minutes in reading aloud, and 5 minutes in other literacy activities. In contrast, teachers in a second district allocated 15 minutes to literacy instruction, with 5 minutes devoted to phonics, 5 minutes to reading aloud, and 5 minutes to other literacy activities. Teachers in the third district allocated 30 minutes to literacy instruction, with 5 minutes spent on phonics and 25 minutes spent in reading aloud. Therefore, children in one district were exposed to a great deal of phonics instruction but had limited book experiences. In a second district, children received little literacy instruction in either phonics or books. In the third district, children had extensive opportunities to share books with their teacher but limited instruction in phonics.

It is not surprising that children made better gains in literacy acquisition in classrooms where they received phonics instruction. Most literacy assessments at the kindergarten level focus on letter recognition, letter–sound associations, and word decoding. However, the notion that reading aloud—which at most received 25 minutes of instructional time—could *displace* time needed for more critical activities seems a misinterpretation of the data. Within the kindergarten day (even in a half-day program), teachers could find adequate time to read aloud *and* provide instruction in print-related concepts.

PHONEMIC AWARENESS: MOVING TO CENTER STAGE
IN EARLY LITERACY INSTRUCTION

It is not possible here to review all the research focusing on the development of phonemic awareness—the ability to blend and segment all speech sounds, or phonemes, in a spoken word. Numerous studies have examined not only correlations between preschool and kindergarten phonological skills and later reading skills acquisition, but also the effects of instructing young children in various phonological skills (for a review, see Snow et al., 1998; Whitehurst & Lonigan, 1998). These studies have informed the field regarding early literacy development; however, much about this research does not fit within the emergent literacy perspective (McGee & Purcell-Gates, 1997). Instruction follows a prescribed sequence regardless of children's responses. Children are often instructed without regard for their prior knowledge about phonemic awareness, letter recognition, or concepts about written language. Even when children are pretested on phonemic awareness and selected for training programs based on these pretests, conclusions imply that training with direct, explicit, systematic instruction should apply to, if not all young children, then children like those included in the study.

These issues are illustrated in two recent studies by Lonigan, Burgess, Anthony, and Baker (1998) and by Torgeson and colleagues (1999). Lonigan and colleagues (1998) assessed the phonological sensitivity of 2- through 5-year-old children. They found that some children as young as 2 and 3 years old exhibit early levels of phonological sensitivity. Sensitivity increased with age, and higher-SES children exhibited higher levels and more consolidated knowledge of phonological sensitivity at earlier ages than lower-SES children. These researchers concluded that it was possible to assess phonological sensitivity at very early ages and that these assessments could be used to guide instruction for very young children. This begs the question of whether there is a need to know the level of phonological awareness of 2- and 3-year-olds.

Torgeson and colleagues (1999) assessed a large group (N = 1,436) of kindergartners on a variety of literacy measures, including phonological sensitivity, to identify children most in need of intervention instruction. Of the total sample, 180 children (12%) with the lowest letter-naming and phonemic awareness scores were randomly assigned to three treatment groups and a control group. The first treatment group received intensive and explicit instruction in phonemic awareness and phonics; the second treatment group received balanced instruction in phonemic awareness and phonics; and the third treatment group received instruction that was coordinated with classroom reading instruction. All three treatment groups received one-on-one tutoring four times a week for 20 minutes a day from the second semester of kindergarten through second grade. The treatment group in which children received intensive and explicit instruction in phonemic awareness and phonics (including instruction in reading decodable books) outperformed the other treatment groups in word reading assessments and scored highest of all groups on the Woodcock Reading Mastery Test (Woodcock, 1987) on word reading level, with scores on grade level and within the average range. There were no significant differences among the three treatment groups in comprehension scores; however, when the test scores were converted to age-based standard scores, the explicit-instruction group again scored highest.

Torgeson and colleagues (1999) concluded that the explicit-treatment condition lacked sufficient depth in instruction on constructing meaning and the other treatments lacked sufficient depth of instruction in alphabetic reading skills. They also stated that "what may be required for many children like those included in this study is *much more than 20 minutes a day of systematic, explicit instruction in phonemic decoding skills* along with high-quality comprehension-oriented instruction and experiences" (p. 592; emphasis added). It is important to keep in mind that the children included in the study were only 12% of the total sample of all kindergarten children, the ones with the lowest beginning knowledge of letter names and phonological awareness.

PREVENTING READING DIFFICULTIES IN YOUNG CHILDREN: RECOMMENDATIONS FOR PRESCHOOL AND KINDERGARTEN PROGRAMS

How do teachers resolve the apparent contradictions in the current research on best practices in early literacy instruction? Teachers may be tempted ignore the research that suggests reading aloud to young children is only minimally related to later reading achievement. From a commonsense perspective, time spent enjoying a good book in the company of a sensitive teacher and inquisitive peers ought to be related to reading success. It is difficult to imagine how children will figure out what reading is for if adults do not read aloud to them. However, it could be that merely sharing books together is not powerful enough to boost children's literacy and language concepts and strategies. Certainly, research has demonstrated that when teachers increased the amount of children's verbal and nonverbal contributions during book sharing, especially at levels of higher cognitive demand, their learning was enhanced (Dickinson & Smith, 1994; Whitehurst et al., 1994a, 1994b). Further, when teachers extended children's experiences with books by having them retell (Morrow & Smith, 1990) or dramatize (Pellegrini & Galda, 1982) stories, their understandings increased.

On the other hand, it seems impossible to ignore the research on the importance of phonemic awareness and early instruction that is foundational to discovering the alphabetic principle. Overwhelmingly, research supports the value of such knowledge in reading development. Embedded within this research is a powerful nod toward using commercial programs to structure direct, systematic instruction with the argument that these programs are more explicit.

A recent national report written by the Committee on the Prevention of Reading Difficulties ought to be one professional resource to which teachers could turn in making decisions about early literacy programs and resolving conflicts regarding contradictory research results. It is interesting to note that the committee's report, *Preventing Reading Difficulties in Young Children* (Snow et al., 1998), did ignore the research that downplays the role of reading aloud in young children's literacy development. In the chapter on preventing reading difficulties before kindergarten, the editors briefly acknowledged the findings of Scarborough and Dobrich (1994) that reading aloud had little effect on reading achievement. However, the committee concluded that parents should read aloud with their young children. Further, it recommended that preschool and day-care teachers allow children access to books and read aloud to them.

In contrast, the role of phonemic awareness and instruction focusing on the alphabetic principle received considerable attention. In a large section of the chapter on preschool literacy programs, the editors reviewed several studies that examined the effects of phonemic awareness instruction with 4- and 5-year olds. It is interesting that one study explained in detail used commercially available phonemic awareness training materials also used in Torgeson and colleagues' (1999) study (described earlier in this chapter). Snow and colleagues (1998) concluded:

> Instruction [in preschool] in phonological awareness ought to be accompanied by *training in letters and letter–sound associations* also. Children who *enter school* with these competencies will be better prepared to benefit from formal reading instruction. (pp. 154–155; emphasis added).

The current federal mandate to organize reading programs, even preschool programs, around instructional techniques that have been proven effective by scientifically based research makes it is even more crucial to read research with a critical eye. It is noteworthy that even the National Research Council downplayed the implications of some research, while emphasizing the results of other research.

WHAT WE DO AND DO NOT KNOW: MAKING DECISIONS ABOUT EARLY LITERACY PROGRAMS

One solution to the tension between programs that emphasize reading aloud, shared reading, and emergent writing compared to programs emphasizing direct instruction in phonemic awareness and letter–sound relationships is to include instruction that addresses the underlying concepts in both programs. Currently research suggests that young children have access either to much instruction related to the alphabetic principle or to rich interactions around books. Whitehurst and Lonigan (1998) argued that what young children need are programs that provide access to both. According to their framework, early literacy encompasses two separate domains of knowledge. One domain includes language and concept development and the other, phonological awareness, letter knowledge, and the ability to use letter–sound associations to decode words. These two domains of knowledge are not the product of the same instructional experiences, nor do they influence reading achievement in the same way. Reading aloud to children may facilitate the development of one domain of early literacy knowledge, while instruction related to the alphabetic principle may facilitate the development of the other domain.

Despite our considerable knowledge from research about the two domains of early literacy and especially regarding reading aloud to young children and phonemic awareness training, we have relatively little research that provides insights into the levels of competencies we might expect for preschoolers and kindergarteners as outcomes for these activities. For example, what level of phonemic awareness should be expected before children enter kindergarten? *Preventing Reading Difficulties in Young Children* (Snow et al., 1998) suggested that the level is fairly high, but we do not have research indicating which levels of phonemic awareness are essential at various age and grade levels.

We also have research that validates the effectiveness of direct and systematic instruction in phonemic awareness. But does this instruction need to be direct, systematic, and based on a highly sequenced commercial program? At least one study suggested that phonemic awareness instruction can be embedded within book reading and does not need to be as systematic as suggested (Ukrainetz, Cooney, Dyer, Kysar, & Harris, 2000). In this study children read books that included rhyming words or alliteration. Three or four times during the book reading, teachers demonstrated segmenting words into phonemes. They helped children count phonemes in short and long words and segment words into onsets, rimes, and phonemes. No particular sequence in teaching phonemes was followed, and the groups included children with both high levels and low levels of phonological awareness. All children made significant gains in phonological awareness compared to children who merely listened to and talked about stories. This research suggests that literacy instruction for 4- and 5-year-olds does not necessarily have to be direct or systematic, but it must be intentional. While the teachers in this program were guided by children's interest in particular words in the story text, they also intentionally selected words from the story that would provide rich opportunities for phonemic exploration.

CONCLUSION

As the three teachers finish their presentation, their colleagues begin a discussion of issues highlighted in the report. As the morning comes to a close, the committee votes to set policy for literacy curriculum in prekindergarten literacy programs that will include instruction in two domains of early literacy development. One domain will focus on concept and language development, and the other will focus on developing foundations for children's acquisition of the alphabetic principle. The committee makes a recommendation that instruction in prekindergarten programs should be intensive and intentional.

Reading aloud to children will call upon children's use of analytical thinking and literary vocabulary. Phonological awareness instruction will ensure that children discover and manipulate phonemes as well as learn to associate letters with phonemes. Both should occur in the context of meaningful literacy activities that connect with the child's world.

REFERENCES

Anderson, R. C., Hiebert, E. H., Scott, J. A., & Wilkinson, I. A. (1985). *Becoming a nation of readers: The report of the commission on reading.* Washington, DC: National Institute of Education.

Ballenger, C. (1999). *Teaching other people's children: Literacy and learning in a bilingual classroom.* New York: Teachers College Press.

Cochran-Smith, M. (1984). *The making of a reader.* Norwood, NJ: Ablex.

Dickinson, D. K., & Smith, M. W. (1994). Long-term effects of preschool teachers' book readings on low-income children's vocabulary and story comprehension. *Reading Research Quarterly, 29,* 104–122.

Duke, N. K., & Kays, J. (1998). "Can I say 'once upon a time'?": Kindergarten children developing knowledge of information book language. *Early Childhood Research Quarterly, 13,* 295–318.

Lonigan, C. J., Burgess, S. R., Anthony, J. L. & Baker, T. A. (1998). Development of phonological sensitivity in 2- to 5-year-old children. *Journal of Educational Psychology, 90,* 294–311.

McGee, L. M., & Purcell-Gates, V. (1997). "So what's going on in research on emergent literacy?" *Reading Research Quarterly, 32,* 310–318.

McMahon, R., Richmond, M. G., & Reeves-Kazelskis, C. (1998). Relationships between kindergarten teachers' perception of literacy acquisition and children's literacy involvement with classroom materials. *Journal of Educational Research, 91,* 173–182.

Meyer, L. A., Wardrop, J. S., Stahl, S. A., & Linn, R. L. (1994). Effects of reading storybooks aloud to children. *Journal of Educational Research, 88*, 69–85.

Morphett, M. V., & Washburne, C. (1931). When should children begin to read? *Elementary School Journal, 31*, 496–508.

Morrow, L. M., & Smith, J. K. (1990). The effects of group setting on interactive storybook reading. *Reading Research Quarterly, 25*, 211–231.

Nielsen, D. C., & Monson, D. L. (1996). Effects of literacy environment on literacy development of kindergarten children. *Journal of Educational Research, 89*, 259–271.

Pellegrini, A. D., & Galda, L. (1982). The effects of thematic-fantasy play training on the development of children's story comprehension. *American Educational Research Journal, 19*, 443–452.

Purcell-Gates, V., McIntyre, E., & Freppon, P. A. (1995). Learning written storybook language in school: A comparison of low-SES children in skills-based and whole language classrooms. *American Educational Research Journal, 32*, 659–685.

Robbins, C., & Ehri, L. C. (1994). Reading storybooks to kindergartners helps them learn new vocabulary words. *Journal of Educational Psychology, 86*, 54–64.

Scarborough, H. S., & Dobrich, W., (1994). On the efficacy of reading to preschoolers. *Developmental Review, 14*, 245–302.

Senechal, M., Thomas, E., & Monker, J. (1995). Individual differences in 4-year-old children's acquisition of vocabulary during storybook reading. *Journal of Educational Psychology, 87*, 218–229.

Snow, C. E., Burns, M. S., & Griffin, P. (Eds.). (1998). *Preventing reading difficulties in young children.* Washington, DC: National Academy Press.

Teale, W. H., & Sulzby, E. (1986). Emergent literacy as a perspective for examining how young children become writers and readers. In W. H. Teale & E. Sulzby (Eds.), *Emergent literacy: Writing and reading* (pp. vii–xxv). Norwood, NJ: Ablex.

Torgesen, J. K., Wagner, R. K., Rashotte, C. A., Rose, E., Lindamood, P., Conway, T., & Garvan, C. (1999). Preventing reading failure in young children with phonological processing disabilities: Group and individual responses to instruction. *Journal of Educational Psychology, 91*, 579–593.

Ukrainetz, T. A., Cooney, M. H., Dyer, S. K., Kysar, A. J., & Harris, T. J. (2000). An investigation into teaching phonemic awareness through shared reading and writing. *Early Childhood Research Quarterly, 15*, 331–355.

Whitehurst, G. J., Arnold, D. S., Epstein, J. N., Angell, A. L., Smith, M., & Fischel, J. E. (1994a). A picture book reading intervention for children from low-income families. *Developmental Psychology, 30*, 679–689.

Whitehurst, G. J., Epstein, J. N., Angell, A. L. Payne, A. C., Crosne, D. A., & Fischel, J. E. (1994b). Outcomes of emergent literacy intervention in Head Start. *Journal of Educational Psychology, 86*, 542–555.

Whitehurst, G. J., & Lonigan, C. J. (1998). Child development and emergent literacy. *Child Development, 69*, 848–872.

Whitehurst, G. J., Zevenbergen, A. A., Crone, D. A., Schultz, M. D., Velting, O. N., & Fischel, J. E. (1999). Outcomes of an emergent literacy intervention from Head Start through second grade. *Journal of Educational Psychology, 91*, 261–272.

Woodcock, R. W. (1987). *Woodcock Reading Mastery Tests—Revised.* Circle Pines, MN: American Guidance Service.

Chapter 8

Sensitivity to the Social and Cultural Contexts of the Play of Young Children

FERGUS HUGHES

Play is not a one-dimensional construct but one that takes many forms and serves many purposes depending on the sociocultural conditions in which it occurs. The need for sensitivity to cultural context was highlighted recently by a haunting image from the war in Afghanistan. On the wall of a half-destroyed building, children had drawn a variety of images of battle. There were planes dropping bombs and anti-aircraft weapons shooting at the planes. There were depictions of bodies, many missing arms or legs. The drawings indicated who the children are and how they view the world. The same drawings might not have been found in other countries or in other times. They were unique to a particular time and place. Another lesson from the battered wall is that, even when discouraged from doing so, children find ways to play. The most adverse of circumstances and the most oppressive social conditions cannot keep them from their play.

Twenty-five years of teaching an undergraduate course on play could lead one to become a "true believer," seeing play as beneficial for all children under all circumstances. There is a danger, however, in true belief. Play could easily be romanticized, assigned greater significance in children's lives than it deserves, or valued over other childhood activities such as learning, exploration, and work. Even greater is the danger of ethnocentrism, in the form of failure to appreciate the cultural context of play.

Students have a talent for challenging the assumptions of their professors, particularly by the questions they raise. As an example, a student recently asked: If free play is beneficial for preschool children, and if

Korean American teachers are less likely than Anglo Americans to incorporate play into their classrooms, should Korean American teachers be encouraged to change their teaching approaches? Another student, after learning of the correlation between block play and spatial reasoning ability, asked if teachers should actually *require* that preschool girls spend greater amounts of time in the block corner.

Such questions may arise for the following reason: On the one hand, play is seen as facilitating cognitive, social, and emotional development and, as such, is strongly endorsed for its developmental benefits by the National Association for the Education of Young Children (Bredekamp & Copple, 1997). Thus, one could conclude that play, particularly imaginative play, should be encouraged. On the other hand, play is reflective of the social and cultural contexts in which children live. If educators are respectful of those contexts, they should also respect variations in play and pay heed to the possibility that if they change play behaviors, they are changing an aspect of culture. Should child development professionals recommend that play be encouraged if it does not occur normally in the environment? If all children are encouraged to play, and in ways that the experts believe are most beneficial, could this reflect an insensitivity to individual, cultural, and gender differences? It is questions of this type that are addressed in this chapter.

EVIDENCE OF CONTEXTUAL INFLUENCES ON PLAY

Variations in attitudes toward and opportunities for play are found across families, schools, communities, and entire societies. What do the variations mean, and should there be a uniform standard applied to children's opportunities to play?

Individual Caregiver Variations

Even in the second year of life, when children acquire the capacity for symbolic play and caregivers often assume the roles of play partners, there is compelling evidence of contextual variation in play. Within our own culture, it has been observed that sensitive play partners, whose children are most likely to play in a developmentally appropriate manner, tend to be successful at getting their toddlers to participate in social games that involve taking turns. The most effective adult play partners avoid being overly directive and refrain from constantly asking questions, giving commands, or offering hints as to how a child should play a game (Glick, Wheeden, & Spiker, 1997).

Individual differences in the parent's tendency to assume a structuring role in play have often been described in terms of the presence or absence of parenting skills. For example, the variable of maternal responsiveness has been invoked as an explanation for differences: A highly responsive mother is sensitive to the social signals emitted by her child and responds promptly and consistently to even subtle behaviors. Conversely, an unresponsive mother is more focused on her own interests and moods than on those of her baby and interacts with the child primarily because the interaction meets her own needs.

An assumption underlying much of the research on variation in play partner style is that unwillingness to play is an indication of inability to play or even of a basic insensitivity to children's needs. There are alternative explanations, however. Some adults may simply choose not to play with young children or may live in a cultural milieu in which play with a young child is seen as inappropriate behavior for an adult. Perhaps educators and psychologists need to look beyond an examination of whether play does or does not occur. Instead of comparing the overall amount of play observed in various cultures, they should be asking how children—and adults—*use* play differently in the different environments in which they live (Roopnarine, Shin, Donovan, & Suppal, 2000).

Cross-Cultural Variation

There is considerable variation across cultures in the overall amount of adult–toddler play and also in the purposes that play serves. As an illustration, Tamis-LeMonda, Bornstein, Cyphers, Toda, and Ogino (1992) studied the behavior of American and Japanese toddlers and their mothers at free play and found that, while Japanese mothers encouraged their children to engage in interactive, other-directed kinds of pretense, Americans emphasized the functional uses of toys and spoke more about the characteristics of the toys themselves. Japanese mothers used play to teach communication skills, while Americans used play to teach their children about the world and to encourage them to explore it on their own.

Cross-cultural variations reveal more that just a difference in the perceived purposes of play. In many societies, play between an adult and a young child is seen as inappropriate; a parent's role is not to play but to provide the basic necessities of life. Indonesian mothers, for example, tend to be reserved and unplayful; they view play primarily as an opportunity to develop children's minds and bodies and to help them learn to cooperate (Farver & Wimbarti, 1995). In many East African cultures, the mother's role is to protect and teach the child and to intervene in the child's play only if intervention is necessary (Edwards & Whiting, 1993).

Variations Within a Culture

Even within the United States, cultural groups vary considerably in their appreciation of symbolic play, as illustrated in studies of the social pretend play of Korean American preschool children (Farver, Kim, & Lee, 1995; Farver & Shin, 1997). Social pretend play occurs less often in all-Korean preschools than in schools attended primarily by Anglo American children. Even though the teachers in the Korean schools were Korean Americans educated in American universities, they still emphasized traditional Korean values. They saw the purpose of nursery school as teaching academic skills and encouraging task perseverance and passive involvement in learning. The schoolday was highly structured, creative play materials were not available, and play of any sort was rarely seen. By contrast, teachers in the Anglo American schools typically encouraged independent thinking and problem solving, engaged the children actively in learning, and provided numerous opportunities for social interaction and for play.

Is one approach better than the other in an absolute sense, or would the preferred approach to using play in the preschool depend on the perceived purposes of education and on the larger values of the community? In fact, the Korean American teachers' attitudes toward play did reflect the values of the larger Korean American community, and those values in turn appeared to depend on the degree to which community members had become "Americanized." When Farver & Lee-Shin (2000) examined the extent to which Korean-immigrant mothers living in the United States had been assimilated into American culture, they found that those mothers who were "separated" or "marginal" in their acculturation styles were less accepting and encouraging of their children's play, and less likely to play with their children, than were those characterized as more assimilated.

Sociocultural variations in play depend not only on the attitudes of parents, teachers, and society in general but even on such variables as the amount of play space and time that is available to children (Roopnarine, Lasker, Sacks, & Stores, 1998). The context of play has not been well understood. Child development experts have amassed a considerable amount of information about the role of play in development but have been far less successful in understanding the contexts within which play occurs (Roopnarine et al., 2000).

GENDER AS A CONTEXT FOR PLAY

A major element of the context of children's play is the cultural variable of gender. For reasons not completely understood, boys and girls play differently, and a significant question for educators is how these differences should be addressed. Should gender differences simply be appreciated as elements of the sociocultural context in which children develop, or should efforts be made to minimize the differences as much as possible?

Very young children typically display an awareness of gender differences and a preference for gender-typed toys at some time between the ages of 2 and 3, and in some studies children show preferences for gender-appropriate toys as early as 18 to 24 months of age (Caldera, Huston, & O'Brien, 1989; Serbin, Poulin-Dubois, Colburne, Sen, & Eichstedt, 2001). These preferences are usually attributed to cultural factors, in particular to the socializing influences of adults, peers, and the mass media. Adults are likely, for example, to offer gender-appropriate toys to very young children and to reinforce children for playing with gender-appropriate toys (Caldera et al., 1989; Will, Self, & Datan, 1976). Peers reinforce play with toys seen as gender-appropriate, and gender-typed toy preferences are more likely to be observed when such preferences conform to the social expectations of people in children's immediate physical environments (Caldera et al., 1989; Raag, 1999; Raag & Rackliff, 1998).

In fantasy play, girls are more likely to choose domestic and family roles, such as mother and baby, while boys prefer roles that are more adventurous, action-oriented, fictitious, and far removed from the domestic environment. Danger and high adventure characterize the make-believe play themes of boys, with vehicles and assorted weapons likely to be incorporated into the action. Girls tend to enact scenes pertaining to family relationships, use dolls as characters in their play, and rely more on verbal interaction and less on physical activity than boys do (Connolly, Doyle, & Ceschin, 1983).

Males engage in more play fighting than females do (Pellegrini, 1985), a difference that is particularly evident among children of elementary school age (Humphreys & Smith, 1984) and has been observed in a variety of cultures (Whiting & Edwards, 1973). Finally, traditional girls' games have been described as less complex in their rule structure than boys' games (Parker, 1984) and are less likely to have teams with specialized roles, umpires, or referees. Boys' games tend to be played in larger groups (Waldrop & Halverson, 1975), are more competitive and longer-lasting, and require a greater amount of physical skill than do girls' games (Lever, 1976).

Gender differences in play are of significance to early childhood educators because of their correlations with other variables during childhood or even later in life. For example, school-aged boys who indicate the strongest preference for "boy" toys demonstrate superior spatial skills and score higher on mathematics and science achievement tests; girls who are the most likely to play with feminine-stereotyped toys are the most likely to display superior verbal skills (Serbin & Connor, 1979; Tracy, 1987). This pattern seems to continue into adulthood, since adults who show a preference for spatially oriented toys perform better on standard spatial tasks than do adults who do not show such a preference (Voyer, Nolan, & Voyer, 2000). Gender-typed play is also related to children's involvement in sports, with female athletes being more likely than nonathletes to have played with traditionally masculine toys (e.g., guns, sports equipment) and in traditionally masculine ways (e.g., rough-and-tumble) and less likely to have engaged in traditionally feminine play activities (e.g., playing with dolls or jump ropes) (Greendorfer, 1993).

In general, it appears that gender differences in children's play are correlated with, and may actually contribute to, the development of different skills, abilities, and preferences (Giuliano, Popp, & Knight, 2000). With this in mind, should a parent or educator attempt to change the culture of gender by actively promoting cross-gender forms of play and the use of cross-gender play materials? Is there a problem to be addressed, or should child development professionals simply accept gender differences as a healthy sign of diversity?

RESOLVING THE DILEMMA

What should an early childhood educator do to communicate both an appreciation of the multiple values of play *and* a sensitivity to individual and cultural variation in an increasingly multicultural society? As a long-time believer in the immeasurable benefits of play, I would still suggest that a delicate balance is required, a balance between work and play in a child's life as well as a balance between encouraging children to play and providing the opportunity for them to do so.

Balancing Work and Play

Play differs from work in that, even when enjoyable, work is extrinsically motivated, while the motivation for play is the sheer joy of the activity. Play is freely chosen, while work is not usually optional, and play is always pleasurable, while work is often not.

An interesting model for striking an appropriate balance between work and play in early childhood classrooms was suggested by Goodman (1994), who rejected the idea that play and work are direct opposites. There are purely work-related activities, as when a child struggles with an unpleasant assignment, and there is pure play, as when a child cavorts in waves at the beach. Somewhere between the two is a type of activity that

Goodman called play/work because it contains elements of both. For example, a child might struggle with a frustrating and difficult project but at the same time be completely absorbed and self-motivated. It is here, at the midpoint between play and work, that the best teaching is thought to occur (Goodman, 1994).

Balancing Encouragement and Opportunity

Children do not need to be encouraged to play. They need to be allowed to do so. Even though parents and teachers of young children differ considerably in their understanding of, appreciation of, and ability to play, children will find the means to play if the environment at least affords an opportunity to do so.

A child's desire to play can be fulfilled in many ways. As was discussed earlier, parents in some cultures rarely play with young children, but in some of those same cultures, the infant's or toddler's need to play is met by older siblings. As an example, in terms of making suggestions to younger siblings, commenting on their play, and actually joining in play with them, Mexican siblings closely resemble American mothers (Farver, 1993). A similar pattern is found in Indonesia, where parents are not particularly playful but close and harmonious sibling relationships are highly valued. Older brothers and sisters in Indonesia are sophisticated play partners, assuming many of the structuring roles that American mothers do (Farver & Wimbarti, 1995).

Creating a Climate of Acceptance

The climate for play must include acceptance of children's play choices as well as acceptance of the cultural context out of which children's identities are formed. Nevertheless, an educator should always be ready to make new play options available. For example, children may display gender segregation in their preference for playmates (Hoffman & Powlishta, 2001), but educators can certainly allow and indicate that they approve of play with opposite-sex peers. Male children may gravitate toward the block corner, while females may seek out the housekeeping area. However, an educator could send a message of permission by simply removing the physical barriers between these areas and making sure that all children have access to a variety of play materials.

Such an approach was taken by Theokas, Ramsey, and Sweeney (1993), who modified a kindergarten classroom by combining the housekeeping and block areas into an "outer-space" environment, with androgynous space clothing, "space food," and a space capsule constructed in the block area. The outer-space environment appeared to alter the children's gender-typed play behavior. Before the intervention, boys spent 25% of their free play time in the block area and only 2% in the housekeeping corner; girls were in the housekeeping area 10% of the time but spent only 2% of their play time with the blocks. During the intervention, however, girls spent 19% of their time in the block area, while the time boys spent in the housekeeping section increased from 2% to 10%! It is clear that behavioral change can occur when children are simply given permission to change.

The creation by teachers of a climate of acceptance might provide the framework for addressing student questions of the sort mentioned at the beginning of this chapter. Should teachers pressure little girls into playing with blocks or encourage little boys to venture into the housekeeping corner? It seems unreasonable and unnecessary to attempt to force children to play with materials that they wouldn't ordinarily select. It is instructive that in the study by Theokas and colleagues (1993), children were simply given opportunities to play in nontraditional ways but were not required to do so. Should teachers in cultures in which preschool play is not highly valued be encouraged to change their teaching approaches? To do so would reflect a marked insensitivity to the cultural context in which children are educated and would probably be ineffective in any case. On the other hand, there is always value in informing those who work with children of the multiple benefits that play can have for young children.

It is necessary to remember that play is an important, and perhaps an essential, ingredient in children's lives. Nevertheless, it should not be romanticized. It should not be seen as the primary, or even the most valuable, activity of the preschool years, or as the only way in which young children learn. Most important, it should be respected and accepted in its many variations rather than prescribed. If it is truly play, it is free and it is individual. It is an aspect of a child's identity, formed in a particular social, cultural, and physical environment.

REFERENCES

Bredekamp, S., & Copple, C. (Eds.). (1997). *Developmentally appropriate practice in early childhood programs serving children from birth through age 8* (rev. ed.). Washington, DC: National Association for the Education of Young Children.

Caldera, Y. M., Huston, A. C., & O'Brien, M. (1989). Social interactions and play patterns of parents and toddlers with feminine, masculine, and neutral toys. *Child Development, 60,* 70–76.

Connolly, J., Doyle, A., & Ceschin, F. (1983). Forms and functions of social fantasy play in preschoolers. In M. B. Liss (Ed.), *Social and cognitive skills: Sex roles and children's play* (pp. 71–92). New York: Academic Press.

Edwards, C. P., & Whiting, B. B. (1993). "Mother, older sibling, and me": The overlapping roles of caregivers and companions in the social world of two- to three-year-olds in Ngeca, Kenya. In K. MacDonald (Ed.), *Parent–child play: Descriptions and implications* (pp. 305–329). Albany: State University of New York Press.

Farver, J. M. (1993). Cultural differences in scaffolding pretend play: A comparison of American and Mexican mother–child and sibling–child pairs. In K. MacDonald (Ed.), *Parent–child play: Descriptions and implications* (pp. 349–366). Albany: State University of New York Press.

Farver, J. A., Kim, Y. K., & Lee, Y. (1995). Cultural differences in Korean- and Anglo-American preschoolers' social interaction and play behaviors. *Child Development, 66,* 1088–1099.

Farver, J. A., & Lee-Shin, Y. (2000). Acculturation and Korean-American children's social and play behavior. *Social Development, 9,* 316–336.

Farver, J. A., & Shin, Y. L. (1997). Social pretend play in Korean- and Anglo-American preschoolers. *Child Development, 68,* 544–556.

Farver, J. A., & Wimbarti, S. (1995). Indonesian children's play with their mothers and older siblings. *Child Development, 66,* 1493–1503.

Giuliano, T. A., Popp, K. E., & Knight, J. L. (2000). Footballs versus Barbies: Childhood play activities as predictors of sport participation by women. *Sex Roles, 42,* 159–181.

Glick, M. P., Wheeden, A., & Spiker, D. K. (1997, April). *Predicting play and language skills of low birthweight toddlers: The influence of maternal directiveness and turntaking.* Poster presented at the biennial meeting of the Society for Research in Child Development, Washington, DC.

Goodman, J. F. (1994). "Work versus play" and early childhood care. *Child and Youth Care Forum, 23,* 177–196.

Greendorfer, S. L. (1993). Gender role stereotypes and early childhood socialization. *Psychology of Women Quarterly, 18,* 85–104.

Hoffman, M. L., & Powlishta, K. K. (2001). Gender segregation in childhood: A test of the interaction style theory. *Journal of Genetic Psychology, 162,* 298–313.

Humphreys, A. P., & Smith, P. K. (1984). Rough-and-tumble in preschool and playground. In P. K. Smith (Ed.), *Play in animals and humans* (pp. 241–270). London: Blackwell.

Lever, J. (1976). Sex differences in the games children play. *Social Problems, 23,* 478–487.

Parker, S. T. (1984). Playing for keeps: An evolutionary perspective on human games. In P. K. Smith (Ed.), *Play in animals and humans* (pp. 271–294). London: Blackwell.

Pellegrini, A. D. (1985). Social-cognitive aspects of children's play: The effects of age, gender, and activity centers. *Journal of Applied Developmental Psychology, 6,* 129–140.

Raag, T. (1999). Influences of social expectations of gender, gender stereotypes, and situational constraints on children's toy choices. *Sex Roles, 41*, 809–831.

Raag, T., & Rackliff, C. L. (1998). Preschoolers' awareness of social expectations of gender: Relationships to toy choices. *Sex Roles, 38*, 685–700.

Roopnarine, J. L., Lasker, J., Sacks, M., & Stores, M. (1998). The cultural context of children's play. In O. N. Saracho & B. Spodek (Eds.), *Multiple perspectives on play in early childhood education* (pp. 194–219). Albany: State University of New York Press.

Roopnarine, J. L., Shin, M., Donovan, B., & Suppal, P. (2000). Sociocultural contexts of dramatic play: Implications for early education. In K. A. Roskos & J. F. Christie (Eds.), *Play and literacy in early childhood* (pp. 205–230). Mahwah, NJ: Erlbaum.

Serbin, L. A., & Conner, J. A. (1979). Sex-typing, children's play preferences, and patterns of cognitive performance. *The Journal of Genetic Psychology, 134*, 315–316.

Serbin, L. A., Poulin-Dubois, D., Colburne, K. A., Sen, M. G., & Eichstedt, J. A. (2001). Gender stereotyping in infancy: Visual preferences for and knowledge of gender-stereotyped toys in the second year. *International Journal of Behavioral Development, 25*, 7–15.

Tamis-LeMonda, C. S., Bornstein, M. H., Cyphers, L., Toda, S., & Ogino, M. (1992). Language and play at one year: A comparison of toddlers and mothers in the United States and Japan. *International Journal of Behavioral Development, 15*, 19–42.

Theokas, C., Ramsey, P. G., & Sweeney, B. (1993, March). *The effects of classroom interventions on young children's cross-sex contacts and perceptions.* Paper presented at the biennial conference of the Society for Research in Child Development, New Orleans.

Tracy, D. M. (1987). Toys, spatial ability, and science and mathematics achievement: Are they related? *Sex Roles, 17*, 115–138.

Voyer, D., Nolan, C., & Voyer, S. (2000). The relation between experience and spatial performance in men and women. *Sex Roles, 43*, 891–915.

Waldrop, M. L., & Halverson, C. L. (1975). Intensive and extensive peer behavior: Longitudinal and cross-sectional analyses. *Child Development, 46*, 19–26.

Whiting, B., & Edwards, C. P. (1973). A cross-cultural analysis of sex differences in the behavior of children aged three through eleven. *Journal of Social Psychology, 91*, 171–188.

Will, J. A., Self, P. A., & Datan, N. (1976). Maternal behavior and perceived sex of infant. *American Journal of Orthopsychiatry, 46*, 135–139.

Chapter 9

Educational Technology in the Early and Primary Years

SUDHA SWAMINATHAN
JUNE L. WRIGHT

Visualize an inclusive preschool classroom set up in centers, including two recently acquired computers. The two teachers are taking a quick break to share their technology concerns with their faculty trainer. "What do I do when the sound is gone? How do I weave technology into my theme-based curriculum? What are they learning from computers? Won't it isolate them?" Suddenly, everyone's attention is drawn to 4-year-old Sarah, who is listening enraptured to the computer's lyrical narration of a popular book. After a while she walks over to the book center, extracts the same book, comes back to the computer, and starts reading the book. Her eyes are still on the book as two children join her, and Sarah directs them to the screen and the book. All three remain absorbed in the book and the computer for almost 15 minutes. As the adults watch the scene silently, one of the teachers comments, "You know Sarah has multiple neurological disabilities. She rarely interacts with anyone."

Instances like these happen in many early childhood classrooms. Teachers do begin their venture into educational technology with trepidation and caution but gradually become more comfortable and willing as they see children react like Sarah did. Historically, the advent of any new technology into the classroom has been accompanied by cries of caution as well as promises of great benefits for the young child (Wartella & Nancy, 2000). Advocates highlight their arguments with vignettes of children making powerful discoveries while using educational technology. Protestors caution that these stories are neither generalizable nor prevalent across all classrooms. In the following sections, we address several issues, controversial or otherwise, that educational technology has faced. For each, we discuss the nature of the controversy and share potential new teaching and learning options.

APPROPRIATENESS OF COMPUTERS FOR YOUNG CHILDREN

In the early 1980s, numerous studies were launched in response to the fear that computers in the classroom would draw children away from traditional concrete activities, such as manipulative play and art, and adversely affect peer social interactions. All of the results demonstrated that following a novelty effect lasting 1 to 2 weeks, the children returned to their typical play patterns and the computer corner became one of many learning centers.

Revisiting the same argument some 20 years later, we hear similar concerns that children need active learning experiences involving real objects that they can manipulate (Armstrong & Casement, 2000; Cordes & Miller, 2000; Healy, 1998). Can technology adequately meet that need? Is it developmentally appropriate for young children to engage in a medium that is two-dimensional, abstract, and potentially debilitating? This continues to be the single most critical technology dilemma in the field.

However, children as young as 3 years of age have been observed to engage in meaningful interactions with the computer. Appropriate computer software can be particularly useful for facilitating the social and cognitive growth of young children. It has facilitated preschoolers to work competently beyond their normal capabilities and to engage in advanced problem-solving processes. The software can actually scaffold children's journey toward more symbolic thinking. As such, children's computer usage calls for a reevaluation of what traditionally has been considered "concrete." Does concrete allude simply to what is physical and tangible, or can it also include ideas and actions that are meaningful to and manipulable by the young child? Clearly, dismissing the computer as an abstract medium inappropriate for young children fails to acknowledge its tremendous metacognitive potential. (For more on these ideas, see Clements, 1999.)

SMART TOYS—HOW SMART ARE THEY?

Perhaps some of the early suspicions of technology have been revived and escalated by the new wave of toys and software (lapware) targeted for toddlers and infants. The position statement on technology from the National Association for the Education of Young Children calls for well-designed and well-planned technology for use by young children starting at age 3 (NAEYC, 1996). The kaleidoscopic special effects of color, music, and actions of many high-tech toys, intended for toddlers, require only a random reaction. When toddlers spend an overabundance of time with these playthings, the development of the child's brain may be impeded (Healy, 1998). Therefore, younger children do need more exposure to toys that encourage imagination and exploration as they learn to play (Barnette, 2001).

Novelty effect holds for toddlers, too. Having explored the antics of moving animals or dollhouses with sound effects, 2- to 4-year-olds often return to the stuffed hand puppet or blockhouse to play out their story scripts. Others who are more inventive incorporate the special features of these toys into their play scenarios. For example, a 1-year-old boy modified a toy that rotates disks and flowers to the same repetitive music by tossing balls or duplos on the disks. He would observe their twirling motions, remove a few pieces and add others. Or he would hold one disk steady and watch the others move.

Children who have not developed such imaginative play ability may be cognitively limited by the "smart toys." Adults should monitor children's use of these toys to evaluate their effects, to help children maintain control of the play scenario, and to scaffold their play (Oravec, 2000/2001). On the other hand, early research suggests that computerized toys may increase the active engagement of children with disabilities (Wilds, 2001). Certainly there is a need for further research that focuses on the effects of such toys on children's learning and behavior.

Interactive toys, such as the robots that elementary school children learn to build and program (with adult scaffolding), are educationally sound. The programmable brick, a microprocessor capable of receiving sensor data and powering motors, enables elementary school children to build a Lego object, program the brick with the computer, embed it in the Lego object, and direct its function. Such intelligent tools motivate children to construct knowledge through meaningful projects. Perhaps educators can urge toy developers to design more smart toys that promote child actions rather than reactions.

EFFECTS OF EDUCATIONAL TECHNOLOGY

The advantages (or disadvantages) of educational technology use can be studied under the four domains of child development, namely physical, cognitive, emotional, and social.

Physical Development

A strong critic of computers, the Alliance for Childhood claims that computers put children at risk for repetitive stress injuries (RSIs), eyestrain, and obesity (Cordes & Miller, 2000). Many of these problems are more likely to occur during uninterrupted and prolonged use of computers, something that neither the technology standards nor classroom practitioners advocate. Another concern—that the ultraviolet radiation of the monitor might injure eyes—has been set aside by the American Optometric Association. The actual amount of radiation is too minimal to have any effect on the eyes beyond eyestrain—again, caused by continuous staring at the monitor. Possible injuries can be avoided by monitoring children's computer time, regulating the lighting, using appropriate furniture, and positioning the monitor properly (Swint, 2000).

Cognitive Development

Does educational technology enhance children's cognitive development? The Alliance for Childhood also has deep concerns about the technocrats' alleged push for faster learning and claims that computers have not been proven to enhance cognitive growth (Cordes & Miller, 2000). In truth, even staunch proponents of educational technology do not cite speed as its main attraction. Rather, it has been utilized for the unique opportunities it offers for creative problem solving, self-guided instruction, and reflective exploration.

Research on the cognitive impact of technology does offer some insights into the specific gains shown by young children (Haugland, 1999). Preschoolers who used computers with supporting activities showed significantly greater developmental gains than did those without computer experiences. These children showed gains in intelligence, structural knowledge, nonverbal and verbal skills, long-term memory, and problem solving. Kindergarten and primary school children showed gains in creativity, mathematical thinking, and motivation. In another study, preschoolers with disabilities who were taught with computer-assisted instruction (CAI) enhanced their abilities to match shape, color, numbers, and letters (Hitchcock & Noonan, 2000).

Emotional Development

Are children emotionally affected by the use of educational technology? Children interacting with appropriate software have been observed to exhibit active and positive facial expressions as well as more vocalizations than those watching television (Wartella & Nancy, 2000). Computers can also give a sense of control and self-worth to children hitherto lacking in self-esteem (Primavera, Wiederlight, & DiGiacomo, 2001). These particular children, hailing from low-income families, were more patient and exhibited greater impulse control and greater peer cooperation at the computers than elsewhere in the classroom. They also appeared more interested in learning in general when at the computers.

Social Development

Does using the computer isolate children from their classmates? Researchers report that the social effects of having computers in the classroom have been strongly positive (Bergin, Ford, & Hess, 1993). The computer learning center is a place where language development flourishes. Computers provide opportunities to build social skills, even facilitating social interaction for shy children and those who haven't found their niche. They allow children to create a shared problem space where experts may emerge to mediate with their peers, thus promoting cooperative learning (Freeman & Somerindyke, 2001).

INTEGRATION INTO THE CURRICULUM

For teachers, one of the most difficult pedagogical issues is learning to integrate educational technology into their curricula. While there are many ways to do so, the most effective approach is also the most complex. The dynamic interactivity offered by several of the technological tools necessitates innovative changes to current pedagogy but also demands revolutionizing the content of our children's learning.

The simplest integration is the tutor approach, whereby technology supplements an existing curriculum by providing additional practice sessions, usually at the end of a unit. Hardly anyone advocates following this method. It is recommended that teachers take the more difficult and yet more effective approach: use of technology as an integral tool (Gullo, 2000; Hutinger & Johanson, 2000; McNabb, 2001). Here, technology functions as one more useful tool in the classroom, along with the papers and pencils, the manipulatives, and the books. For instance, calculator explorations have led many elementary grade students to "discover" for themselves negative numbers and rational numbers (Reys & Arbaugh, 2001). Using digital cameras, second-graders were able to study the symmetry in human faces and to create symmetrical images (Johnson & Bomholt, 2000). Students participating in online science projects were able to compare their results of specific ecological experiments, thereby making cross-climactic study more meaningful. Thus, curricular integration of educational technology should enable children to use technology for its unique and most powerful capability: to inquire, to engage in problem solving, and to develop ideas (Clements & Sarama, 2002).

Beyond these transformations of the curricula, technology also challenges teachers to make a revolutionary change within the content matter. For example, how important is it for children to learn good penmanship and accurate spelling? In one study, researchers found that the writing of first-graders using word processors was significantly better in terms of content than that of the children who wrote by hand (Barrera, Rule, & Diemart, 2001). Therefore should 6-year-old children practice writing the spelling of multisyllable words for half an hour every day for five days, or should they spend four of those periods in accessing information, writing down their thoughts, and revising their writing? Some of these traditional skills are neither practically needed today nor do they serve as gateways to essential conceptual understanding (Papert, 1998; Tinker, 2001). Shouldn't our nation's teachers be focusing on fostering skills that children would actually use and need? For those of us who grew up with spelling tests, these are not easy conversions of the mind.

ARE OUR TEACHERS READY TO TEACH WITH TECHNOLOGY?

In 2000, the International Society for Technology in Education (ISTE) established six standards for technology proficiency of teachers. These standards ask teachers not only to be skillful operators of technology but also to be designers and users of learning environments and curricula that maximize the learning of diverse students. Do our nation's teachers meet these standards? Sadly, changes in teacher attitudes, training, and school policies have been much slower than the concomitant advances in technology (Cuban, 2001).

A 1998 survey revealed that teachers felt that they lacked the necessary expertise to use technology and that their classrooms were poorly equipped (Wood, Willoughby, & Specht, 1998). Even in 2001, with more early childhood teachers exuding greater comfort and frequency of use, effective use of technology by teachers continues to be a rarity (Cuban, 2001).

Discomfort with technical skills is becoming less prevalent, with more of the 1970s generation becoming teachers themselves. Nevertheless, technical skills continue to be an important concern, and it is recommended that teacher preparation programs address it in a separate introductory course rather than including technical skills within a curricular methods course (Beasley & Wang, 2001). Many teachers are as yet unaware that input devices such as the mouse and the keyboard can be customized to match the technical ability of their children.

Personal commitment to or belief in technology is heavily emphasized as a critical factor in teachers' use of technology (Bielefeldt, 2001). While it is difficult to affect innate belief systems, research has proven that most teachers who support technology enthusiastically are also those who are fairly computer-literate and those who are able to take ownership of the new tool (Wetzel, 2001/2002). These are important considerations for teacher educators.

Integrating technology effectively into the curriculum needs practice and support and often calls for a radical shift in one's teaching strategies. Research shows that significant change was observed in teachers' use of technology only in the second year of training (Dwyer, Ringstaff, & Sandholtz, 1991). In the second year, the teachers reported personal mastery of the technology. An important change was their increasing tendency to reflect on their own teaching, to question old patterns, and to speculate about the causes behind the changes. Therefore, for our preservice teachers to conceptualize, internalize, and implement an integrated approach to technology, they need in-depth training and practice.

Many grant efforts are currently underway to train preservice and inservice teachers. The next step in these efforts would be to create field experiences where preservice teachers are mentored and supported (Thompson, 2001). Within teacher education, a growing trend is online learning. Online education does offer greater variety in courses and flexibility in course timings, but it comes with many pitfalls. Problems with Internet access, lack of face-to-face communication, difficulty assessing learning, and the quality of the courses are some issues that need to be addressed before online learning can become a viable professional development option.

THE CHALLENGE OF SELECTING QUALITY SOFTWARE

Ideally, the types of software that teachers choose are directly related to their theoretical orientation and educational goals, just as literature and manipulatives match teachers' philosophy of how children learn. The depth and complexity of the software chosen increases as teachers gain technical mastery and are able to focus on children's responses and the thinking processes promoted by the software.

The nature of the experience that the software offers the child is the key variable in deciding its worth. The most frequently stated criterion for quality is that the program be interactive and the child be in control. This interactivity has been used to defend the time spent at computers as compared to the passivity found when watching TV. However, Bennett (1998) points out that "interactivity" is a slippery concept and a great marketing buzzword. The real question is whether that control is meaningful and leads to active learning.

Bowman (1998) describes software as points on a continuum ranging from open and active to closed and passive. The most open-ended software reflects the thinking of the user and allows the child to play with ideas (word processor, graphics programs, LOGO). Closely related are simulations that provide a structure for children to discover new ideas. Next come computer applications that provide information asked for by the user (encyclopedias, the Internet). The most closed-ended software packages set problems and determine the correct answers (CAI). Educators who wish to evaluate software independently may want to use scales such as the Haugland Developmental Software Scale (Haugland & Wright, 1997).

THE EDUCATOR'S ROLE IN SOFTWARE DEVELOPMENT

Some of the finest software developed over the past 15 years has been discontinued. Small innovative companies are not able to sustain themselves and are either taken over by a larger company or disappear. With increasing awareness of exciting innovations and better communication via Web sites such as http://techandyoungchildren.org and listservs such as ECETECH-L@listserv.uiuc.edu, educators can now bring such products to the attention of their peers.

Our first challenge is to preview programs and return those that do not meet our standards, with an explanation to the publishers of how to make them appropriate. Only if we respond to the developers and advocate for the standards we believe in can we expect their products to improve. When reading reviews on www.childrensoftware.com, readers could utilize the embedded feature to send feedback to the publishers and to other readers.

Perhaps one of the most encouraging developments in software production is the emergence of products created in relation to specific curriculum models. Researchers and educators are creating teams to develop programs that are based on theories such as constructivism (Ferguson, 2001) and Vygotsky's zone of proximal development (ZPD) (Luckin, 2001). In such cases, the theory provides the framework for the software design. One such effort, sponsored by the National Science Foundation, is a DLM (developmental learning materials) math software for preschoolers (Clements & Sarama, 2003) that embeds the software in a curriculum. A second example, sponsored by the U.S. Department of Education, was developed at the Erikson Institute and reflects the Reggio Emilia philosophy ("Ani's Rocket Ride," 2001).

UNIVERSAL ACCESS TO EDUCATIONAL TECHNOLOGY

If as educators we believe that children gain enhanced self-esteem, communication skills, new ideas, and new ways of thinking when interacting with technology, then it follows that all children should have this advantage. A number of projects have been initiated to assure equity of exposure to technological advances. Family resource centers and libraries have offered opportunities for both parents and children to explore the potential of the computer as a learning tool. As early as 1984, the National Head Start Association lifted its ban on computers in the classroom. Teachers and researchers discovered that low-income children who were typically considered candidates for "remedial," or drill-and-practice, activities responded to open-ended programs with excitement and a capacity for higher-order thinking and creativity (Mobius, 1990). A second outcome of these projects was that parents became involved in the computer activity center and requested further training so that they could enter the job market with advanced skills.

Surveys conducted in 1983 and again in 1998 (Becker, 2000) revealed that although access to computers was becoming more equitable, use of open-ended programs was still not prevalent. Bowman (1998) explains the necessity for providing all children opportunities to represent their thinking using open-ended software tools. Failing to provide such tools to low-income and minority children only accentuates their separation from the mainstream.

ENCOURAGING FAMILY INVOLVEMENT

Today most parents believe that their children will be better able to cope with the demands of the 21st century if they are technologically competent. However, many do not know how to select activities or when to scaffold their children. Workshops at schools, libraries, and community centers open the door to adults eager to learn. Introducing a variety of activities—from surfing the Web and scanning photographs to word processing and playing adventure games—allows parents to interact with their children using a mode that appeals to both of them.

Reports of family-centered decision making are frequent in relation to special education technology (Lindstrand, 2001; Parrette, VanBiervliet, & Hourcade, 2000). Parents' awareness of children's abilities included observations of increased concentration, quality social interaction (particularly by children with autism), and creative word processing by children with physical and learning disabilities.

While it is beyond the scope of this chapter to report the many benefits technology provides for those with special needs, the high level of parental involvement in accessing and facilitating assistive technology is a model worth emulating.

Research projects facilitated by placing laptops or reconditioned computers into the homes of low-income families have shown the power of increased communication between teachers and parents through e-mail and personal Web pages. In spite of the ongoing debate over the appropriateness of using technology with young children, careful reading of the reports from parents and teachers tells us that a unique component has been added to our learning environment.

A new international online course for teachers—Documentation in the Digital World by George Forman—has just begun. Utilizing an interactive listserv and a CD with video files of children's interactions, the group will investigate such topics as the forms of documentation, using technology to enhance documentation, using technology with children to make their thinking visible, and creating better parent relations using technology. The fact that more than 100 individuals have signed up for such a course through the NAEYC Technology and Young Children Interest Forum Listserv (ECETECH-L@listserv.uiuc.edu) tells us that educators are serious about finding powerful ways to support children, parents, and teachers in their development.

CONCLUDING THOUGHTS

Bringing this chapter to a close, we offer a few provocative, instructional, and pedagogical questions to consider:

- Do educators use the following criteria to evaluate technology use: Who is in control—the child or the computer? Who does the thinking? Can the same activity be done as well without the technology? (If the last question receives an affirmative answer, we recommend a serious instructional revision or not using technology for that activity.)
- Has technology offered us a new window into the child's mind that leads us to rethink our teaching strategies?
- How can teachers influence the design and the marketing of educational technology? Rather than being passive recipients of commercial products, let us be at the forefront advocating for technological advances that we know are best.
- Should we teach our current curricula with newer tools, or should we reevaluate what children need to learn and develop an integrated curriculum for the 21st century?
- How can we advocate for equal access to the full potential of technology for all children and families?

REFERENCES

Ani's rocket ride [Computer software]. (2001). Evanston, IL: Apte.

Armstrong, A., & Casement, C. (2000). *The child and the machine*. Beltsville, MD: Robins Lane Press.

Barnette, M. (2001). Tech toys: How are they really affecting your child? [On-line]. Available: www.child.com/your_child/media_and_technology/techtoys.jsp

Barrera, M. T., Rule, A. C., & Diemart, A. (2001). The effect of writing with computer versus handwriting on the writing achievement of first-graders. In D. D. Shade (Ed.), *Information technology in childhood education annual* (pp. 215–228). Charlottesville, VA: Association for the Advancement of Computing in Education.

Beasley, W., & Wang, L.-C. C. (2001). Implementing ISTE/NCATE technology standards in teacher preparation: One college's experience. In D. D. Shade (Ed.), *Information technology in childhood education annual* (pp. 33–44). Charlottesville, VA: Association for the Advancement of Computing in Education.

Becker, H. J. (2000). Who's wired and who's not: Children's access to and use of computer technology. *Children and Computer Technology* [On-line], *10*(2), 44–75. Available: www.futureofchildren.org

Bennett, S. (1998). *The plugged-in parent: What you should know about kids and computers.* New York: Random House.

Bergin, D. A., Ford, M. E., & Hess, R. D. (1993). Patterns of motivation and social behavior associated with microcomputer use of young children. *Journal of Educational Psychology, 83*(3), 437–445.

Bielefeldt, T. (2001). Technology in teacher education: A closer look. *Journal of Computing in Teacher Education, 17*(4), 4–15.

Bowman, B. (1998, October/November). *Equity and young children as learners.* Paper presented at the Families, Technology, and Education Conference, Chicago. Available on-line: ericeece.org/pubs/books/fte/general/bowman.pdf

Clements, D. H. (1999). "Concrete" manipulatives, concrete ideas. *Contemporary Issues in Early Childhood* [On-line], *1*(1), 45–60. Available: www.triangle .co.uk/ciec

Clements, D. H., & Sarama, J. (2002). The role of technology in early childhood learning. *Teaching Children Mathematics, 8*(6), 340–343.

Clements, D. H., & Sarama, J. (2003). DLM math software. Columbus, OH: SRA/McGraw-Hill.

Cordes, C., & Miller, E. (2000). *Fool's gold: A critical look at computers in childhood* [On-line]. Available: www.allianceforchildhood.net/projects/computers/computers_reports.htm

Cuban, L. (2001). *Oversold and underused: Computers in the classroom.* Cambridge, MA: Harvard University Press.

Dwyer, D. C., Ringstaff, C., & Sandholtz, J. H. (1991). Changes in teachers' beliefs and practices in technology-rich classrooms. *Educational Leadership, 48*, 45–52.

Ferguson, D. (2001). Technology in a constructivist classroom. In D. D. Shade (Ed.), *Information technology in childhood education annual* (pp. 45–56). Charlottesville, VA: Association for the Advancement of Computing in Education.

Freeman, N. K., & Somerindyke, J. (2001). Social play at the computer: Preschoolers scaffold and support peers' computer competence. In D. D. Shade (Ed.), *Information technology in childhood education annual* (pp. 203–213). Charlottesville, VA: Association for the Advancement of Computing in Education.

Gullo, D. F. (2000). Integrating computer technology into the early childhood curriculum: A constructivist approach. *Journal of Early Education & Family Review, 7*(5), 7–15.

Haugland, S. W. (1999). What role should technology play in young children's learning? *Young Children, 54*(6), 26–31.

Haugland, S. W., & Wright, J. L. (1997). *Young children and technology: A world of discovery.* Boston: Allyn & Bacon.

Healy, J. F. (1998). *Failure to connect: How computers affect children's minds—for better and worse.* New York: Simon & Schuster.

Hitchcock, C., H., & Noonan, M. J. (2000). Computer-assisted instruction of early academic skills. *Topics in Early Childhood Special Education, 20*(3), 145–158.

Hutinger, P. L., & Johanson, J. (2000). Implementing and maintaining an effective early childhood comprehensive technology system. *Topics in Early Childhood Special Education, 20*(3), 159–173.

Johnson, I. D., & Bomholt, S. K. (2000). Picture this: Second graders "see" symmetry and reflection. *Teaching Children Mathematics, 7*(4), 208–209.

Lindstrand, P. (2001). *Parents of children with disabilities evaluate the importance of the computer in child development* [On-line]. Available: www.unlv.edu/Colleges/Education/ERC/JSET

Luckin, R. (2001). Designing children's software to ensure productive interactivity through collaboration in the zone of proximal development. In D. D. Shade (Ed.), *Information technology in childhood education annual* (pp. 57–85). Charlottesville, VA: Association for the Advancement of Computing in Education.

McNabb, M. L. (2001). In search of appropriate usage guidelines. *Learning & Leading with Technology, 29*(2), 50–54.

Mobius Corporation. (1990). *Computers in Head Start classrooms: Recommendations for the Head Start/IBM partnership project.* Alexandria, VA: Author.

National Association for the Education of Young Children (NAEYC). (1996). Position statement on technology and young children—Ages three through eight. *Young Children, 51*(6), 11–16.

Oravec, J. A. (2000/2001, Winter). Interactive toys and children's education: Strategies for educators and parents. *Childhood Education, 77*(2), 81–85.

Papert, S. (1998). *Technology in schools: To support the system or render it obsolete* [On-line]. Available: www.mff.org/edtech/article.taf?_function=detail& Content_uid=106

Parrette, P., VanBiervliet, A., & Hourcade, J. J. (2000). Family-centered decision making in assistive technology. *Journal of Special Education Technology* [On-line], *15*(1), 1–7. Available: www.unlv.edu/Colleges/Education/ERC/JSET

Primavera, J., Wiederlight, P., & DiGiacomo, T. M. (2001, August). *Technology access for low-income preschoolers: Bridging the digital divide.* Paper presented at the American Psychological Association, San Francisco.

Reys, B. J., & Arbaugh, F. (2001). Clearing up the confusion over calculator use in grades K–5. *Teaching Children Mathematics, 8*(2), 90–94.

Swint, S. (2000). *Computer-related problems: When the eyes have had it* [On-line]. Available: http://my.webmd.com/content/article/1728.58531

Thompson, A. (2001). New directions: Focus on preservice K–12 field experiences that integrate technology. *Journal of Computing in Teacher Education, 18*(1), 2, 4.

Tinker, R. (2001). Future technologies for special learners. *Journal of Special Education Technology* [On-line], *16*(4), 1–9. Available: www.unlv.edu/ Colleges/Education/ERC/JSET

Wartella, E. A., & Nancy, J. (2000). Children and computers: New technology— old concerns. *Children and Computer Technology* [On-line], *10*(2), 31–43. Available: www.futureofchildren.org

Wetzel, D. R. (2001/2002). A model for pedagogical and curricular transformation with technology. *Journal of Computing in Teacher Education, 18*(2), 43–49.

Wilds, M. (2001). It's about time! Computers as assistive technology for infants and toddlers with disabilities. *Zero to Three, 22*(2), 37–41.

Wood, E., Willoughby, T., & Specht, J. (1998). What's happening with computer technology in early childhood education setting? *Journal of Educational Computing Research, 18*(3), 237–243.

PART III

Policy and Professional Development Issues

When we asked a group of early childhood majors to select a metaphor, a symbol that might characterize their professional role, these were some of their responses:

- A student teacher said: "I picture myself as a bird in a cage. I can't escape, yet everyone else can casually walk by and see what I do and how I am struggling."
- A rather traditional kindergarten teacher remarked: "It's like building with blocks—first you make the base, then you stack them, one at a time, on top of one another."
- An experienced Montessori teacher said: "I chose the metaphor of a swimmer. You can dive in or wade in. You might find yourself in deep water or in freezing cold water or even turning to the lifeguard (support services) for help. When you swim, you can rely on a floatation device for a while, but eventually you select and develop your own style. Above all, if you are a swimmer, you swim."

As this sampling of metaphors suggests, teachers view their professional roles very differently. Often, it is the larger context—the backdrop, if you will, against which the role of the teacher is performed—that influences early childhood educators' perspectives. The three chapters in Part III focus on broad social policy issues, global education, and the status of the early childhood profession.

Frances O'Connell Rust examines public policy affecting children and families and the consequences of such policies, both intended and unintended, in Chapter 10. She discusses five critical policy issues in the field of early childhood education and offers recommendations for the future.

In Chapter 11, Louise Boyle Swiniarski examines early childhood education from a global perspective. She begins by presenting the twelve key attributes of global education and argues for broadening our perspectives to encompass a world view, a perspective that holds the greatest promise for educating citizens of the world.

Doris Pronin Fromberg, in Chapter 12, takes a fresh look at the social, political, and educational factors that have contributed to the low status of the early childhood profession. She presents a working definition of professionalism followed by a perspective on historical and philosophical traditions of the field, an interpretation of its knowledge base, and other pertinent trends. The chapter concludes with a discussion of the consequences of professionalization and reflections on the broader implications of elevating the social status of those who dedicate their lives to the care and education of the very young.

Together, these three chapters address teacher professional development issues and raise the question that provides a framework for Part III: *How does the larger social context influence public policy affecting children and families and the early childhood professional's role?*

Chapter 10

Counting the Cost of Caring: Intended and Unintended Consequences of Early Childhood Policies

Frances O'Connell Rust

SCENARIO ONE

Ted and Joan are a young couple in Big City. They are in search of child care for their 4-month-old son. Ted is a full-time doctoral candidate earning $20,000. Joan is an elementary school teacher in the city. Her salary is $45,000 and she has a generous health benefit package that covers the entire family. They live in subsidized housing provided by Ted's university and pay $1,200 a month for a two-bedroom apartment. Over the past 6 months, they have made inquiries about day-care facilities that will take infants. They have identified 12 that they think they can afford and that meet their criteria for quality care. Only one will have room for their son. The cost is $250 a week. Luckily, it is within an easy drive from Joan's school, so she can drop their son off in the morning and pick him up at the end of her workday.

SCENARIO TWO

Steve and Irene are a young couple also living in Big City. They, too, are in search of child care for their 4-month-old son. Steve has two part-time jobs: He works as a cashier 20 hours a week at a local supermarket, where he earns $9 an hour, and he works another 20 hours a week at a fast food restaurant, where he earns $8.25 an hour. Irene is a clerk in a government office. She earns $11 an hour, or about $22,000 a year, and she has health benefits for basic care for herself and her family. Together, Steve and Irene make too much money to qualify for a city-funded day-care program or for Head Start when their child is older. Their rent is $800 a month. Their public transportation expenses run about $140 a month. They figure the most they can afford to spend for child care is $200 a week. Their choices are very limited. They identify five centers that they can afford. Only one has room for their child. It will cost $195 a week. Steve and Irene discuss Steve's giving up one of his jobs to stay home with the baby, but the hours of his work cannot be adjusted to fit Irene's schedule unless he decides to work at the supermarket at night.

SCENARIO THREE

Miguel and Maria are a young couple also living in Big City. They, too, are in search of childcare for their 4-month-old son. Though neither speaks English well, both are working: Miguel as a day laborer at $6.25 an hour; Maria at a local hotel chain at $5.75 an hour. In a good week, Miguel will bring home $250 and, with tips, Maria will, too. In a good year, their combined salaries come to about $21,000. Though above the poverty line ($14,650 for a family of three), they are within the range that makes them eligible for Medicaid and for federally funded day care. The problem is that they have not been able to find a program that can take their baby. On the days when Miguel has work, they have resorted to leaving the child with an unlicensed neighbor who takes in children. They pay her $4 an hour. They leave their child with her approximately 30 hours each week. They hope that they will be able to use the local Head Start center when their son is older.

POLICY AND EARLY CHILDHOOD

Policy emerges from need. It is a response to a problem. The value and appropriateness of a policy depend on the underlying assumptions and intent of those who frame it and the extent to which the policy defines the problem correctly. In the area of early childhood, defining the problem is a critical issue. Head Start is an example of early childhood policy that is both consistent with need and an appropriate to a problem; welfare-to-work programs that reduce families' incomes, such as those in Riverside, California, and Grand Rapids, Michigan, are examples of policy mandates that are harmful to children (Children's Defense Fund [CDF], 2001).

In the United States, policies focused on young children are fragmented, reflecting an internal struggle between the role of the federal government and the roles of state and local governments. For the most part, our early childhood policies are directed toward the poor and their education. These policies tend to focus on education as distinct from the family and the social, cultural, and economic surroundings in which the child matures, thus skewing policy away from some of the fundamental needs of young children and their families.

According to Goffin, Wilson, Hill, and McAnich (1997), there are two dominant perspectives that shape policy discourse in early childhood. In one view, the child is "at risk" and therefore in need of saving so that the society as a whole will be able to sustain itself economically and socially; in the other view, the child is a resource whose rightful support and education will shape the society of the future.

The first view has largely shaped policies directed toward children of poverty and can be discerned in such federal mandates such as Head Start and Aid for Families with Dependent Children. From this perspective, poverty is the critical issue, and the government steps in because the family cannot provide (Goffin, 1988; Gordon, 1994; Wrigley, 1991).

Policies emanating from the second perspective tend to be subtler, directed at education, and ingrained in the national consciousness. One of the most obvious ramifications of this perspective is compulsory education: While government steps into family life in hugely intrusive ways requiring everything from vaccinations to testing, we, without protest, accommodate our schedules and shape our family lives to the requirement that every child between the ages of 7 (5 in some states) and 18 will be in school.

Neither the perspective of the "child-to-be-saved" nor the perspective of the "child-as-savior" encompasses the larger social network of the family and community in which the child resides. As Goffin and colleagues (1997) write, "Romanticizing the child as an innocent and worthy recipient of public funds justifies investment in programs created for the child, rather than in larger social and economic dimensions affecting childhood" (p. 17).

Both perspectives posit children as human capital, that is, a resource with good possibility for future yield; both perspectives posit childhood as what Goffin and colleagues (1997) describe as "a unique moment for intervention" (p. 15). Both are premised on understandings of early childhood and of the relationship of government to children and their families that emerge from an idealized notion of the family as the proper and rightful locus of support and guidance for children. This line of thinking does not situate the family as an integral unit in the general society; instead, each family is viewed as separate and unique. Following this line of thinking dictates that if government does interfere, it should do so only in situations in which the family is failing—often because of struggling with the stresses of poverty.

Unfortunately, both perspectives seem not to recognize the already powerful presence that government has in the lives of young children and their families. Both are premised on an erroneous view that education that happens outside of the public school setting cannot be affected by public policy. Both work against efforts to develop coherent structures that could address the needs of and provide support for all of our children and their families.

DEFINING THE ISSUES

To name the problem correctly requires that we push the focus of policy making for early childhood beyond the parameters defined by these two prevailing perspectives. The critical issues here transcend the boundaries of race, culture, and class that currently define much of this country's early childhood policy. The issues are largely economic, and they have everything to do with the way we value children and families, that is, where we choose to place our resources. We have to look at the entire surroundings of all young children, not just the children of poverty. To name the problem correctly, we must ask probing questions about who cares for children and what young children need in order to live healthy lives and to grow into educated citizens in a democracy.

Availability of Child Care

Finding adequate and appropriate child care has become one of the major economic issues of our time. As of the fall of 1994, 20.2 million children (53%) under the age of 12 were in child care (Fields, Smith, Bass, & Lugaila, 2001). The numbers have undoubtedly increased since then. Close to 67% of married women in the United States are in the labor force (Bureau of Labor Statistics, 1999), but, unlike many other democracies around the world (Kammerman, 2000), we have no national child-care policy. Instead, we have what Olson (2002) describes as a "'nonsystem,' in which most of the onus falls on families to find, pay for, and monitor the quality of the early learning their children receive" (pp. 10–11).

"In most other industrialized nations," writes Olson (2002), "ensuring the safety and care of young children is viewed as a shared responsibility between parents and the public" (p. 16). In Sweden, Germany, Finland, Austria, Spain, Italy, and Canada, according to Kammerman (2000), "women and children have full health care or health insurance that covers pre-natal care, pregnancy-related care, hospitalization, and post-natal pregnancy care—in addition to job protection, benefit, and seniority protection" (p. 10). The policies that these countries have enacted are premised on the belief that the care and education of young children is critical to a strong economy, and this premise has been borne out in these settings over the past 20 years.

The United States, Australia, and New Zealand are the only countries in the Organization for Economic Cooperation and Development (which includes the countries of the European Union as well as the major industrialized nations) that do not have a policy of paid family leave. Although the United States passed the Family and Medical Leave Act (FMLA) in 1993, it is, as Kammerman (2000) writes, "a modest policy, far less generous in every way than the prevailing policies in other countries" (p. 12). Only 55% of our work force is covered by FMLA, in contrast to coverage for almost all working parents in other countries.[1]

Doherty (2002) describes the child-care arrangements in this country as a "mismatch" in which only 12% of the 15 million children eligible for federal child-care subsidies actually receive assistance. "No state," writes Olson (2002), "has a comprehensive system of early care and education that makes high-quality services available to all families of young children who want help" (p. 14). And the quality child care that is available is often out of reach for low- and moderate-income families. In New York City, for example, Child Care, Inc. (2000) found that "a two parent family with one preschool child and earning $21,000 would spend 62% of their gross income to secure quality center-based care at the current state market rate" (p. i).

Research tells us that the quality and reliability of child care shapes parents' attitudes toward their employment (Kagan & Cohen, 1997; Kammerman & Kahn, 1981). This relates to the impact that child-care policy has across a society: Parents who are satisfied with their child-care arrangements are more productive at work and less anxious about their children than are parents who have not found adequate arrangements (CDF, 2001; Kammerman & Kahn, 1981). With 67% of all married women in the work force, policy makers in this country can ill afford to ignore the issue of child care or to think that its only impact is on the children of poverty. We have the resources; we can do better.

Quality in the Child-Care Field

Among the biggest obstacles to developing quality child care are low salaries and levels of education for early childhood educators. Whether they are medical, legal, or education professionals, those who work with young children and their families are perceived to have low status relative to their peers. In part, this has to do with the fact that the care and education of young children have traditionally been thought of as women's work. In part, it has to do with the fact that young children do not vote. Whatever the reason, those who work with young children and their families, irrespective of their professional field, tend to be paid less than their peers. This is nowhere more obvious than in salaries for education-related work in early childhood.

The average annual salary of a child-care worker in 2000 was $15,430. With annual salaries of $19,610—less than half of what the average elementary school teacher earns—preschool teachers, who typically work with 3- to 5-year-olds, don't fare much better (CDF, 2001; Doherty, 2002; Olson, 2002). "As a nation," writes Olson (2002), "the United States pays about as much to parking lot attendants and dry-cleaning workers as it does to early childhood educators" (p. 21).

Often, preparation for the field is also minimal. Currently, "no state has included content requirements for child care as part of its licensing system for child care providers" (Doherty, 2002, p. 56). According to Olson (2002),

> In many states, individuals who work with young children are not required to hold any certificate or degree, and ongoing training requirements are minimal. Every state, for example, requires kindergarten teachers to have at least a bachelor's degree and a certificate in elementary or early childhood education. But only 20 states and the District of Columbia require teachers in state-financed pre-kindergartens or preschool programs to meet similar requirements. (p. 13)

This situation prevails despite research that makes a strong connection between teacher quality and student achievement (National Institute of Child Health and Human Development Early Child Care Research Network, 2000; Sanders & Rivers, 1996). It is especially startling in early childhood, where the quality of child care has been directly linked with the preparation and compensation of early childhood educators (Kagan & Cohen, 1997; National Institutes of Health, 2001; Peisner-Feinberg et al., 2000).

Better pay and conditions for children and adults can go a long way toward decreasing turnover in the field, enhancing the status of early childhood and family-related services and ensuring that all our children arrive into public school ready to learn to read and write.

Health Care Coverage

Health care is another critical issue facing young children and their families. Seven percent of all children in the United States die before age 1, and 10.8 million children under the age of 18 lack health insurance (Bureau of the Census, 2001). While parental employment is clearly a factor in our current system, nearly 90% of uninsured children have at least one working parent and 66% have a parent who works full time and year round (CDF, 2001, p. 26).

The problem of coverage is exacerbated by a lack of coordination between social service programs and health care agencies as well as by a cumbersome bureaucracy. There is a vast difference between what middle-class families encounter as they negotiate the health care system and the obstacles that poor families must overcome (CDF, 2001). The Kaiser Family Foundation reports that nearly 60% of parents with Medicaid-eligible children failed to enroll because of difficulties encountered in the process (Kaiser Commission on Medicaid and the Uninsured, 2000).

In the long run, the failure to provide a uniform health care policy affects the society as a whole as resources are drawn away from life-enhancing areas into crisis management of the sort described in a July 1997 report from the National Center for Health Statistics (CDF, 1998), which shows "that uninsured children are six times as likely as privately insured children to go without needed medical care, five times as likely to use the hospital emergency room as a regular source of health care, and four times as likely to have necessary health care delayed"(p. 25).

One of the most promising policy initiatives for children came in 1997 when Congress enacted the State Children's Health Insurance Program (CHIP) as part of the Balanced Budget Act signed by President Clinton. CHIP is designed primarily to help children in working families with incomes too high to qualify for Medicaid but too low to afford private family coverage. All states and the District of Columbia offer health coverage through CHIP and Medicaid. The Children's Defense Fund (2002) reports that "more than 3.3 million children were enrolled in the Children's Health Insurance Program (CHIP) in fiscal year 2000, an increase of almost 1.4 million from the previous year. However, 5.8 million children remain eligible for, but not enrolled in, either CHIP or Medicaid" (p. 23), in large part because of bureaucratic obstacles and lack of publicity regarding the program. Despite the clear improvement in children's health coverage that can be attributed to CHIP, the fact remains that a significant number of our children are uninsured and that the very poor are twice as likely to be uninsured as children with higher family incomes (Bureau of the Census, 2001; CDF, 2002; Newacheck, Hughes, Hung, Wong, & Stoddard, 2000).

A National Safety Net for Poor Working Families

In 1999, the poverty line for a family of three was an income of less than $13,290. The number of families with children who lived in extreme poverty—that is, with cash income below $6,645—yet received no welfare or similar means-tested cash benefits increased 16% between 1995 and 2000 (from 1.0 million to nearly 1.2 million). Whereas a majority of extremely poor families received welfare or similar means-tested cash assistance prior to the signing of national welfare legislation in 1996, only one in three got such help in 2000 (CDF, 2001). Of children living in poverty who are uninsured, 40.8% are White, 31.7% are Hispanic, 19.8% are Black, 5.1% are Asian or Pacific Islander, and 2.6% are American Indian or Alaskan Native (CDF, 2001, p. 26); 30% live in cities, 23% live in rural areas, and 32% live in the suburbs, with residency data not available for the remaining 15% (Bureau of the Census, 2001). Despite this diversity, no national safety net exists for families.

In the year 2000, the number of American children living below the poverty line fell to 11.6 million, or 16.2%, the lowest poverty rate in 20 years, according to data released by the U.S. Census Bureau (2001). This decrease in the proportion of children in poverty—to one in six—resulted from the enactment of the national welfare legislation of 1996 combined with the unprecedented period of economic prosperity that lifted income and rolled back poverty for most Americans in the 1990s. The poverty rate among adults age 18 to 64 also reached its lowest point in two decades.

However, child poverty rose in full-time working families according to Census Bureau (2001) figures. The number of poor children who live in families with a full-time year-round worker rose to 4.1 million (37% of poor children) in 2000, up from 3.8 million in 1999—an increase of 326,000 children—according to an analysis by the Children's Defense Fund (2001). The problem for these families is that even if both parents are working at minimum wage, the minimum wage is too low to lift a family of three out of poverty and its obvious consequences.

The growing number of children living in poverty despite their parents' best efforts suggests a significant breach in the nation's social contract that places young children and their families in jeopardy. What is needed are policies that acknowledge the needs of all children and their families, that recognize that most young families will be at the low end of the wage scale since most are just entering the work force, and that are consistent with our fundamental democratic ideals.

Ideology and Policy

Shannon (1998) suggests that our differing views of the causes and cures for poverty in America have profound consequences for the social policies that we enact. He identifies ideological perspectives on poverty ranging from conservative to radical Democrat. Conservatives, he argues, "blame government policies for the social problems that surround poverty. They argue that social-support policies create a 'blight of dependency' and, in fact, have taught the poor to rely on others rather than themselves" (p. 60). Radical Democrats, he writes, "do not accept the absolute definition of poverty. Rather, they suggest that the poverty line is set too low for a family to support itself" (p. 69) and "seek to transform the structures of the economic and political systems to achieve greater cultural and economic justice" (p. 72). In between are those who essentially believe either that willpower is enough or that with effort and a little help anyone can achieve a reasonable standard of living.

Shannon's (1998) argument effectively removes both the child and the family from the spotlight and places political ideology at the center of deliberations surrounding economic and social policies that affect young children and their families. He pushes us as citizens toward an examination of current early childhood policies with an eye toward underlying assumptions of need, with questions about what stops our investing in the future, and with concerns about who benefits by our not choosing to do so.

LOOKING AHEAD

As a nation, we clearly face problems that we do not know how to solve. However, the problems of early childhood care and education are not among them. The needs are clear: Universal child care and health care cannot be ignored, and we must develop a national safety net for families to make both possible.

It is shortsighted to think about making schools better and improving student achievement, as the Leave No Child Behind Act of 2002 dictates, without simultaneously thinking about and planning carefully for the early care and education of our children. It is foolish not to see that the education of children is more than what takes place in public schools and that education for children begins far earlier than their first public school experiences.

We need to reenvision the education of all our children, to understand it as a continuum that begins at birth and extends both inside and outside of schools. This means ensuring a context for optimal learning experiences and recognizing that healthy and well-cared-for children will achieve. This means policies that focus on early childhood have to ensure that educational institutions bring thoughtful, knowledgeable, and highly skilled people into early childhood education and ensure that they have a high level of preparation. It means supporting quality child care for all.

We cannot separate care, health, and education for children, especially young children. We must begin to think of other people's children as the children of us all and understand that if we as citizens and educators are to transform our educational systems and provide a stable future, meeting these needs is the least we can do for *our* children.

NOTE

1. "The act requires employers with 50 or more employees to provide up to 12 weeks unpaid, job-protected leave each year to eligible employees to care for a newborn, newly adopted or foster child, a child, a spouse, or parent with a serious health condition, or for a serious health condition of the employee, including maternity-related disability. Workers in the private sector are eligible to take leave if they have worked for a covered employer for least one year and for at least 1,250 hours during that year, and if there are at least 50 employees working for their employer within a 75-mile radius of their worksite" (Kammerman, 2000, p.12).

REFERENCES

Bureau of the Census, U.S. Department of Commerce. (March 2001). *Current Population Survey*. Washington, DC: Author.

Bureau of Labor Statistics, U. S. Department of Labor. (1999). *Occupational Employment and Wage Estimates*. Washington, DC: Author.

Child Care, Inc. (2000). *A child care primer. Key facts about child care and early education services in New York City*. New York: Author.

Children's Defense Fund (CDF). (1998). *The state of America's children. Yearbook 1998: Leave no child behind*. Washington, DC: Author.

Children's Defense Fund (CDF). (2001). *The state of America's children. Yearbook 2001: Leave no child behind*. Washington, DC: Author.

Children's Defense Fund (CDF). (2002). *General health facts* [On-line]. Available: www.children'sdefensefund.org

Doherty, K. M. (2002). Early learning. *Education Week, 21*(17), 54–56.

Fields, J., Smith, K., Bass, L. E., & Lugaila, T. (2001). *A child's day: Home, school, and play. (Selected indicators of child well-being). 1994*. Washington, DC:

U.S. Department of Commerce, Economics and Statistics Administration, U.S. Census Bureau.

Goffin, S. (1988). Putting our advocacy efforts in a new context. *Young Children, 43*(3), 52–56.

Goffin, S., Wilson, C., Hill, J., & McAnich, S. (1997). Policies of the early childhood field and its public: Seeking to support young children and their families. In J. P. Isenberg & M. R. Jalongo (Eds.), *Major trends and issues in early childhood education. Challenges, controversies, and insights* (pp. 13–28). New York: Teachers College Press.

Gordon, L. (1994). *Pitied but not entitled: Single mothers and the history of welfare, 1890–1935.* New York: Free Press.

Kagan, S. L., & Cohen, N. E. (Eds.). (1997). *Not by chance: Creating an early care and education system for America's children.* New Haven, CT: Bush Center in Child Development and Social Policy, Yale University.

Kaiser Commission on Medicaid and the Uninsured. (2000). *Medicaid and children overcoming barriers in enrollment. Findings from a national survey.* Washington, DC: Author.

Kammerman, S. B. (2000). Parental leave policies: An essential ingredient in early childhood education and care policies. *Social Policy Report. Giving Child and Youth Development Knowledge Away, 14*(2), 3–15.

Kammerman, S. B., & Kahn, A. J. (1981). *Childcare, family benefits, and working parents.* New York: Columbia University Press.

National Institute of Child Health and Human Development Early Child Care Research Network. (2000). Relation of child care to cognitive and language development. *Child Development, 71*(4), 960–980.

National Institutes of Health—National Institute of Child Health and Human Development. (April 2001). *NIH Backgrounder: Preschoolers who experienced higher quality care have better intellectual and language skills.* Press release.

Newacheck, P. W., Hughes, D. C., Hung, Y. Y., Wong, S., & Stoddard, J. J. (2000). The unmet health needs of America's children. *Pediatrics, 105*(4), 989–997.

Olson, L. (2002). Starting early. *Education Week, 21*(17), 10–14, 16–21.

Peisner-Feinberg, E. S., Burchinal, M. R., Clifford, R. M., Culkin, M. L., Howes, C., Kagan, S. L., Yazejian, N., Byler, P., Rustici, J., & Zelazo, J. (2000). *The children of cost, quality, and outcomes study go to school.* Technical report. Chapel Hill: Frank Porter Graham Child Development Center, University of North Carolina.

Sanders, W. L., & Rivers, J. C. (1996). *Cumulative and residual effects of teachers on future student academic achievement.* Knoxville: University of Tennessee Value-Added Research and Assessment.

Shannon, P. (1998). *Reading poverty.* Portsmouth, NH: Heinemann.

Wrigley, J. (1991). Different care for different kids: Social class and child care policy. In L. Weiss, P. G. Altbach, G. P. Kelly, & H. Petrie (Eds.), *Critical perspectives on early childhood education* (pp. 189–209). Albany: State University of New York Press.

Chapter 11

Global Education: Why and When to Teach It?

LOUISE BOYLE SWINIARSKI

"What do you teach?" asks one colleague at a conference on higher education policy.

"I'm a professor in our education department. I teach several courses, but my specialties are early childhood and global education." I reply.

"Oh, Yes . . . well I know what early childhood education is, but whatever is global education?" the colleague continues.

"Isn't it when you teach children about Africa and other countries [*sic*]. You know, my children have a wonderful food fair at their school for their global awareness day," offers another conference colleague.

"That's nice, but isn't it enough for youngsters just to read and to count in these early years," adds another member of our group.

"Oh, no!" I groan.

Many conversations I have with personal friends or professional colleagues often sound like the above dialogue. Many people have no idea about the meaning of global education. Here lies the first issue in the field—the definition of *global education*. To further complicate this issue, those who profess to know think of global education in terms of the worst stereotypes and inaccuracies. There are two ways to respond to the question "What is global education?—a short response or a lengthy explanation. This chapter explores a succinct but balanced in-depth definition of global education along with the issues involved in teaching it to young children.

This chapter begins by considering what global education is and what is it not. It also examines the rationale for global education as an important curriculum area for early childhood education programs. Global education addresses many controversies. Among them is the debate of when to begin the teaching of worldwide issues. Traditionally, such issues are delayed until the upper middle school years and relegated to the social studies curriculum. Further, this chapter challenges families and educators of young children to infuse a global perspective in all that they teach in the child-care center, preschool, or primary grade settings and at home. Finally, the chapter discusses current models of *best practices* in teaching global education to young children, implications of trends and movements in the field of global education, and directions for the implementation of global education in the early years of childhood.

WHAT IS GLOBAL EDUCATION?

Global education has many interpretations, but common to all are several themes and principles. First, global education promotes a perception of the world in terms of "unity within diversity" (Swiniarski, Breitborde, & Murphy, 1999, p. 4). That is to say, global education develops in children a point of view in which they "are a part of a world community and able to accept the differences among cultures" (p. 4). Kenneth Tye (1990) defines global education as "seeing things through the eyes and minds of others—and it means the realization that while individuals and groups may view life differently, they also have common needs and wants" (p. 5). Other definitions of global education include the concepts of teaching world cultures, world issues, and world systems as interconnected and interdependent (Swiniarski et al., 1999).

Twelve principles explain the scope of the concept and enable educators or family members to implement a comprehensive view of global education (Swiniarski & Breitborde, 2003). These principles include guidelines that serve as a theoretical framework for both formal and informal educational opportunities for young children:

1. *Global education is basic.* Global education is a part of the basic curriculum. It involves all the academic areas such as language arts, mathematics, the sciences, the social studies, and the arts, while it promotes the affective skills of social development, critical thinking in decision making, and creative expression in artistic endeavors. Rather than added to an ever-growing laundry list of curriculum requirements, global education can be infused throughout the cur-

riculum as an interdisciplinary topic or as a lens through which to view a global perspective of a particular subject area. For example, story time can be enhanced by presenting a familiar story in two languages, possibly English and Spanish.

2. *Global education is lifelong learning.* Traditionally, the teaching of global educational issues emerges in the upper elementary grades, but research has shown that attitudes and cultural identity are formed in infancy and that the socialization process continues throughout life (Swiniarski et al., 1999). Learning about your own culture while respecting others is a lifelong pursuit and needs to begin in the child's early years to avoid the onset of bias and prejudices. Bring children to their local library, bookshop, or museum to find materials that teach about the world and illustrate how people share common experiences in diverse cultural expressions. Enjoy the excursions together.

3. *Global education is cooperative learning.* Living together in the world requires cooperation. Cooperative learning experiences enhance the skills necessary for collaboration and communication. Working together is essential for the projects of the globally aware classroom. For example, design "group chores" in which each child shares designated responsibilities for the care and decoration of the classroom environment.

4. *Global education is inclusive.* Bringing all the diverse segments of society together is an aim of global education. To reach that end, global education endorses the United Nations Convention for the Rights of the Child. This convention supports children and families who are challenged by special needs, social and political conditions, economic hardships, and discrimination.

5. *Global education is education for social action.* Global education teaches about world issues to encourage solutions to problems and responsible behavior. Knowing and doing need to go hand in hand. Teachers who advocate for causes such as support of a clean environment can have their classes make and display posters on pollution control to model effective activist roles and involve their students as well. Such proactive behavior demonstrates how personal initiative seeks to improve the well-being of all.

6. *Global education is economic education.* The themes of interdependence and interconnection are evident in the world's economy. Businesses are global and seek an educated work force. Concerns for safe and equitable working conditions worldwide are promoted in the global education curriculum. Understanding economic concepts is important for children who are consumers in today's marketplace. Children can learn to make wise choices. Necessary math skills and

economic concepts can be taught in learning centers around topics such as the farm, the store, the bank, or the travel agency.

7. *Global education involves technology.* Technology connects the world. Its use in education is open-ended. Distance learning, researching on the computer, conferencing on the Internet, and mapping the world with remote sensing are a few global technologies suitable for early childhood education. Equal access to technology needs to be provided in early childhood programs so that all children develop sufficient computer literacy skills to navigate around their world through technology.

8. *Global education requires critical and creative thinking.* Global education encourages children to discover new ideas, to compare and contrast, to analyze and synthesize, to evaluate and formulate, to create, and to believe in themselves and their own endeavors. Inquiry-based projects promote these ideals.

9. *Global education is multicultural.* Global education broadens the scope of multicultural education. Global education helps children locate their place in the world, while multicultural education encourages children to identify the world in their community. Global education presents a mosaic of the multicultural world, as multicultural education depicts a global village in a local neighborhood or municipality. Both global education and multicultural education encourage young children to accept and appreciate likeness and difference among people.

10. *Global education is moral education.* Global education seeks the moral imperatives and revisits character education. Notions of justice, wisdom, courage, temperance, and tolerance are universal virtues that can be examined at circle time in an early childhood class. Children need time to engage in reflection to develop personal codes of behavior that define just and fair treatment of all in a caring classroom climate.

11. *Global education supports a sustainable environment.* Global education endorses the protection of the planet. Understanding that events in one part of the globe affect another part of the world is a key tenet of global education. Global education requires the reciprocal responsibility of young children as world citizens to preserve and nurture the planet in their daily experiences.

12. *Global education enhances the spirit of teaching and learning.* The spirit of teaching and learning invites children to take an educative journey into the world of ideas, to develop a sense of wonder about their world, and to live harmoniously together. Global education permits children to engage in introspection to learn about themselves, to be comfortable with themselves and responsive to each other so

as to encourage empathy for other people and an openness to other cultures and new ideas.

In summary, these 12 principles elaborate and clarify the definition of global education and guide families and educators to infuse a worldview into the education of their children. The principles are open to interpretation and revision because they recognize the importance of home/school relationships in teaching young children about their family cultures as the foundation for learning about others. They also constitute a theoretical framework that helps children learn about and appreciate their families, their communities, and their world. The principles were designed to avoid perceptions of what global education is not.

WHAT IS NOT GLOBAL EDUCATION?

Global education is not a one-day event, be it in school, at home, or in the community. While Earth Day, Children's Day, and the annual international food fair are worthwhile endeavors in themselves, they do not constitute a global education curriculum. Global education needs to be an ongoing, integral part of the whole curriculum and the child's daily life. It is not an occasional happening, nor is it a seasonal look at another's holidays.

Special events need to connect to the lives of young children, be related to their daily experiences, and evolve meaning from an in-depth study. Values and attitudes develop from social interactions. Situations that promote taking a worldview, allow for study of how the world works, and treat children as citizens of the world need to be continuous occurrences that emerge from the children's backgrounds.

Teaching global education requires approaches that are relevant to the child's immediate world. Children learn about others by knowing about themselves, their families, and their own culture. To reach beyond borders, it is important to begin with the familiar and then search for common bonds to appreciate differences. Any special event can be part of a thematic unit or the child's daily routines.

Louise Derman-Sparks's *Anti-Bias Curriculum* (1989) clearly addresses the need for global as well as multicultural experiences that avoid stereotyping other cultures with simplistic interpretations or portraying other peoples as foreign exotics (Seefeldt, 1993). Derman-Sparks defines the superficial celebration of holidays and customs around the world as the "tourist curriculum" (Seefeldt, 1993, p. 122). Similarly, British educators label such unconnected activities as *The Cook's Tour* of global studies. To avoid these traps, Carol Seefeldt (1993) recommends connecting holidays and celebrations to children's experiences, in which "the routines of the regular school day are preserved, . . . parents or other members of the community are involved to ensure sensitivity to the culture of the children, [and] . . . few key concepts are selected for development" (p. 123). Other educators concur with Seefeldt's recommendations when school policies attempt to balance holiday offerings in kindergarten with respect to the ideals of separation of church and state, their students' family traditions, and the traditions of others around the world (Myers & Myers, 2001/2002).

Subtle messages in the classroom speak volumes. To provide a balanced view of other cultures, teachers should display appropriate images and use sensitive language to explain common life experiences. For example, note that cars in England are driven on the *left* side of the road, not the *wrong* side; likewise, Indian girls do not wear *costumes*, they wear *saris*!

WHY TEACH GLOBAL EDUCATION?

The rationale for global education typically emanates from the literature on themes of the *shrinking world*, caused by such influences as the impact of technology, the global economy, political/social movements, and massive immigration. Certainly, through the advancements of the Internet, the development of e-mail, and the World Wide Web, children are connected to a broader community. It behooves schools to prepare children for a smaller, more interactive world with knowledge about that world, understandings of how its people and institutions function, and skills for living together peacefully.

Multinational corporations have called for school and curriculum reform to meet the challenges of a global economy. Schools worldwide are charged to educate a diverse, highly literate and skilled work force along with informed consumers. Children can readily recognize the world economy's impact on their lives by simply noting where their clothes, toys, and household items are made or identifying the origins of the foods they eat. Children, consumers in today's global marketplace, are producers of its future. Learning how to negotiate and manage the global economy is critical for effective citizenship for children of all nations.

Many countries are adopting and adapting a standards-based approach in their educational reforms that includes global issues in the curriculum. In the United States, national and individual state reform measures concur with the international trend for a standards-based global perspective in mandated curriculum frameworks. To cite an example, the National Council for the Social Studies (NCSS) requires "analyzing patterns and relationships within and among world cultures such as economic competition and interdependence" in the ninth thematic strand, Global Connections, of its Curriculum Standards for the Social Studies (NCSS, 1996, p. C1).

Another justification for global education is evident in world events. Everywhere, children witness war, disaster, famine, and floods, as well as political, social, and economic upheaval. The assault on America of September 11, 2001, exemplifies the reality that no nation is exempt from terrorism or destruction. All children feel vulnerable to catastrophe. Global education's overarching goal—to provide a safe and accepting school environment in which every child can learn—mirrors Nel Noddings's (1992) premise that primary in all education is a caring relationship. Establishing a school climate that is protective of all children, appreciative of the worth of the individual as well as each person's connection to the community's heritage, is the challenge of this global education mandate. Jane Roland Martin (1992) proposes such a school climate, rooted in the work of John Dewey and Maria Montessori, when she exchanges the idea of the "schoolhouse" for the "schoolhome" with an emphasis on care, concern, and connection.

At an early age, children recognize differences in the appearances, languages, and habits of others (Seefeldt, 1993). Young children need guidance in appreciating diversity to avoid predisposed notions of superiority and prejudices. Children attend classes with political refugees seeking asylum or recent immigrants hoping for a better life. Conversation, cooperation, and collaboration set the tone in many classrooms, where teachers have begun to facilitate understanding, to dispel dissension and mistrust, and to provide basic rights for all. One such approach focused on "human needs across cultures" in which children in primary grades used novels and stories as a "springboard for discussion of basic needs" (NCSS, 1996, p.C6).

To offset differences and disparities that exist in nations, communities, and families, many curriculum resources have been developed for bringing children together. Such offerings promote consensus among diverse populations through recognition of the common bonds and rights people share. Organizations such as Educators for Social Responsibility, UNICEF, or the Teaching Tolerance Project develop policy and produce materials and curricula in support of human rights and the rights of the child. One recommendation is the UNICEF publication, *For Every Child*, a beautifully illustrated book that interprets the principles of the UN Convention on the Rights of the Child (Castle, 2000). A unique program guide for teaching "tolerance, justice and peace" to young children is the Teaching Tolerance Project's (1997) *Starting Small*.

Outreach programs endorse the tenets of global education. School- and community-based programs ensure the protection of common rights when they address "the vast differences in the quality of schooling" offered to children across race, class, and community (Breitborde & Swiniarski, 2001). The full-service school, a recent trend in the United States that is like the Nordic nations' community center educational models, opens its doors to the whole community and extends the schoolday to meet family needs with services from an array of social, medical, and educational providers. The Partnership for the Educational Village at the Ford School in Lynn, Massachusetts, is an exemplary model of a full-service school in an urban northeast community that attempts to bring a diverse population of peoples together. Its after-school care, tutoring sessions, evening parent classes, English as a second language community programs, and on-site medical and social counseling provide equity and equal opportunity for the most recently immigrated family or the five-generations American family (Breitborde & Swiniarski, 2001). Likewise, distance learning programs, funded by the U.S. Department of Education Star School Grant, have been produced as outreach to a national audience for forging home–school–community partnerships. Two television series, *Taking the First Steps: Parents as Teachers* (Swiniarski, 1999b) and *Building Bridges for Excellence in the Early Grades* (Swiniarski, 1999a)—now available as in videos for preschool and primary school children—focus on the importance of family culture and heritage in all teaching and learning situations. Both series present a multicultural and international population of children and their families engaged in activities and reflections that link unity and diversity, the familiar and the unfamiliar, and local with global concerns.

Lastly, environmental agencies, scientists, and advocates value the goals and mission of global education. The concern for protection of the planet, the need to preserve the world's natural resources, and the international movement for clean air and water resonate with both concerned scientists and educators globally. Their campaigns, research projects, and writings can be woven into early childhood curricula. These efforts are in concert with the goals of global education because they illustrate how global events and needs are interdependent and interconnected and why they require systematic study.

WHEN CAN GLOBAL EDUCATION BEGIN?

The dilemma of teaching global education often centers on the question of when to begin. With so many abstract concepts, distant places, and complicated details at the heart of global issues, how can young children—

who are concrete, immediate, and direct—deal with ambiguous concerns? Traditionally, early educators follow the dictum offered by Lucy Sprague Mitchell in 1921. She contended that young children learn best about the "here and now" rather than the vague, the fanciful, or the unfamiliar. Indeed, the familiar is interesting to children and not until a "transitional period of . . . about seven years of age" does the child become "poignantly aware of the world outside his own immediate experience—of an order, physical or social, which he does not determine" (Mitchell, 1921, p. 15). Yet many educators note that children younger than 7 can transcend beyond their immediate environment to bond with others (Teaching Tolerance Project, 1997). The teacher who knows how to present the unfamiliar and the unknown in context with the child's personal world experiences can lead the child to discover new pathways for learning and living beyond a parochial milieu. Beginning in the preschool years, children can start with themselves to learn and care about other people and places.

Universals of childhood help teachers move children beyond their egocentric worldview. Toys and play, family and community culture, and daily life experiences that connect people across borders address the "here and now" and act as conduits for exploring the distant and unknown. Toys, in particular, are of interest to children everywhere and have been used to teach global education concepts (Swiniarski, 1991). There are more commonalities than differences among toys of various nations. Some common toys are dolls, animals, musical instruments, games, puzzles, and movement toys such as cars, trucks, trains, planes or wagons. The national distinctions in toys are usually in the decoration or presentation.

Whether the toy is handmade or produced by an international toy manufacturer, the opportunity to learn about the world is always present in its message to the child. Board games such as Monopoly are reproduced in at least 32 versions around the globe. By comparing sample editions, children can easily see how countries are represented differently in place names, language, and money; yet the game is the same in concept, design, and rules of play. Collecting toys from other parts of the world can enhance geographic awareness. Valuing toys made by children from areas where ownership of toys is considered a privilege promotes sensitivity to other lifestyles and economies.

One controversial global education issue concerns the teaching of the United Nations Convention of the Rights of the Child to children themselves. To date, all UN member nations, except the United States and Somalia, have signed the convention, a contract that binds member nations of the United Nations to the provision, protection, and participation of all children in their inalienable rights (Castle, 2000; Le Blanc, 1995).

While most nations agree with the spirit of the convention, many nations internally debate sovereignty issues, the children's right to know their rights, and the conflict between children and their families for autonomy to participate in their rights. In Great Britain, some parents feel that involving children in their rights means giving over control (Marshall, 1997). Canadian educators recommend grade 6 or age 11 as the developmentally appropriate time for introduction to the rights (Covell & Howe, 2000). In contrast, Anne Smith of New Zealand defends teaching the rights to young children, whose views she contends have been readily dismissed and underestimated. She applauds efforts that encourage young children to participate in defining and protecting their rights because they respect and honor young children's points of view (Smith, 2000). In the United States, successful models for teaching the Convention of the Rights of the Child are evident in many preschool, kindergarten, and primary classrooms. In such settings, children post their rights on school bulletin boards or interpret in readers' theater the messages of picture books published by the United Nations to explain the principles of the convention (Swiniarski et al., 1999). The question from the child's point of view seems not to be "Should I know about my rights?" but rather "When am I too young to know?" The answer begs a collaborative solution rather than a disputed discourse.

IMPLICATIONS FOR THE FUTURE:
GLOBALLY LITERATE EDUCATORS

Global education as basic and inclusive of all children should begin in the early childhood years. It is important to teach global concepts, in terms of the children's experiences, about a world that feels familiar and in the context of an accepting and caring school climate. Central to the success of global education is the teacher—one who is literate about the world, involved in social and political happenings, and responsible in addressing challenges. A globally literate teacher advocates for international policies that improve the lives of children, creates alliances that share *best practices*, and advocates for necessary changes that protect and provide for the rights of children. Being sensitive to the cultural aspects of the unity within diversity theme, this teacher helps children find their place in the world and accept the world that inhabits their homes, neighborhoods, school, and community.

Historically, early childhood educators have been internationalists. The kindergarten movement has its antecedents in Froebel's German disciples who planted the seeds of early education globally throughout the

19th century. Elizabeth Peabody, a kindergarten pioneer, projected visions of early education as a global endeavor with the formation of the International Kindergarten Union. Today, international organizations and governmental agencies such as the Association for Childhood Education International (ACEI), the World Organization for Early Childhood Education (Organization Mondiale pour L'Education Préscolaire, or OMEP), and the United Nations Children's Fund (UNICEF) speak to common concerns and issues. ACEI and OMEP jointly fund symposia to create and debate international guidelines for 21st-century early childhood education or to critique the guidelines (Moss, 1999). The United Nations convenes special sessions for a General Assembly on Children to define *A World Fit for Children* (UN Bureau of the Preparatory Committee for the Special Session of the General Assembly on Children, 2001). The Organization for Economic Co-operation and Development (OECD) continually reviews and compares its member nations' early childhood programs to seek out efficacious models. In recent studies, the OECD (1996) identified lifelong learning projects that begin with the earliest years and extend through senior citizenship as being critical to a healthy world economy. The organization has continued its research of early education by comparing educational provisions and care of children prior to compulsory school entrance (Lubeck, 2001). Findings show that although the Nordic nations lead in advocating for families and children, all early educators have much to learn from each other to ensure and promote democratic ideals (Lubeck, 2001).

Like young children, the world is small and, at times, fragile. Its future is in the hands of its youngest children. The teachers of these children can't be the folks in the introductory dialogue. They need to be professionals committed to individual enlightenment and global citizenship as well as innovators who encourage divergent thinking (Breitborde & Swiniarski, 1999). Their task is not merely to transmit information to their students but to join with them to build and transform a global society.

REFERENCES

Breitborde, M., & Swiniarski, L. (1999). Constructivism and reconstructionism: Educating teachers for world citizenship. *Australian Journal of Teacher Education, 24*(1), 1–15.

Breitborde, M., & Swiniarski, L. (2001, September). *Family education and community power: New structures for new visions in the educational village.* Paper presented at the Oxford Conference on Education and Development, United Kingdom.

Castle, C. (2000). *For every child: The UN convention on the rights of the child in words and pictures.* New York: Phyllis Fogelman Books/UNICEF.

Covell, K., & Howe, R. (2000). Children's rights education: Implementing Article 42. In A. Smith, M. Gollop, K. Marshall, & K. Nairn (Eds.), *Advocating for children: International perspectives on children's rights* (pp. 42–50). Otago, New Zealand: University of Otago Press.

Derman-Sparks, L. (1989). *Anti-bias curriculum: Tools for empowering children*. Washington, DC: National Association for the Education of Young Children.

Le Blanc, L. (1995). *The convention on the rights of the child: United Nations lawmaking on human rights*. Lincoln: University of Nebraska Press.

Lubeck, S. (2001, November). Early childhood education and care in cross-national perspective. *Phi Delta Kappan, 83*(10), 213–215.

Marshall, K. (1997). *Children's rights in the balance: The participation-protection debate*. Edinburgh, UK: Her Majesty's Stationery Office.

Martin, J. R. (1992). *The schoolhome*. Cambridge, MA: Harvard University Press.

Mitchell, L. S. (1921). *Here and now story book*. New York: Dutton.

Moss, Peter. (1999, July). International standards or one of many possibilities. In World Organization for Early Childhood Education & the Association for Childhood Education International, *Early childhood education and care in the 21st century: Global guidelines and papers from an international symposium* (pp. 19–29). Olney, MD: Association for Childhood Education International.

Myers, M., & Myers, B. (2001/2002, Winter). Holidays in the public school kindergarten: An avenue for emerging religious and spiritual literacy. *Childhood Education, 78*(2), 79–83.

National Council for the Social Studies (NCSS). (1996, October). Classroom focus: Global education. *Social Education, 60*(7), C1–C8.

Noddings, N. (1992). The challenge to care in schools. In R. Reed & T. Johnson (Eds.), *Philosophical documents in education* (2nd ed.). (pp. 243–258). New York: Longman.

Organization for Economic Cooperation and Development (OECD). (1996). *Lifelong learning for all*. Paris, France: Author.

Seefeldt, C. (1993). *Social studies for the preschool-primary child* (4th ed.). New York: Merrill.

Smith, A. (2000). Children's rights and early childhood education: The rights of babies and young children. In A. Smith, M. Gollop, K. Marshall, & K. Nairn (Eds.), *Advocating for children: International perspective on children's rights* (pp. 191–205). Otego, New Zealand: University of Otego Press.

Swiniarski, L. (1991). Toys: Universals for teaching global education. *Childhood Education, 68*(3), 161–163.

Swiniarski, L. (1999a). *Building bridges for excellence in the early grades: A home-school partnership* [TV/videotape series]. Cambridge, MA: Massachusetts Corporation for Educational Telecommunications.

Swiniarski, L. (1999b). *Taking the first steps: Parents as teachers* [TV/videotape series]. Cambridge, MA: Massachusetts Corporation for Educational Telecommunications.

Swiniarski, L., & Breitborde, M. (2003). *Educating the global village: Including the child in the world* (2nd ed.). Upper Saddle River, NJ: Merrill/Prentice Hall.

Swiniarski, L., Breitborde, M., & Murphy, J. (1999). *Educating the global village: Including the young child in the world.* Upper Saddle River, NJ: Merrill Prentice Hall.

Teaching Tolerance Project. (1997). *Starting small: Teaching tolerance in preschool and the early grades.* Montgomery, AL: Southern Poverty Law Center.

Tye, K. (Ed.). (1990). *Global education: From thought to action. 1991 yearbook of the Association for Supervision and Curriculum Development.* Alexandria, VA: Association for Supervision and Curriculum Development.

UN Bureau of the Preparatory Committee for the Special Session of the General Assembly on Children. (2001, March). *A world fit for children* (Revised draft outcome document). New York: Author.

Chapter 12

The Professional and Social Status of the Early Childhood Educator

DORIS PRONIN FROMBERG

My first teaching position was in a New York City public school kindergarten in Bedford-Stuyvesant after completing a bachelor of arts degree with a dual major in early childhood education and psychology. My mother-in-law wondered whether I would qualify for teaching in a high school after I had gained additional experience. Her view may be close to the way many laypeople view early childhood education. Growing out of the transparent work of women and motherhood as taken-for-granted, unpaid labor, the group care of other peoples' children in exchange for fees is a relatively recent phenomenon. Laypeople often find it difficult to locate the specialized mastery of a body of knowledge and skills in the external practice of early childhood education (1) because the most exemplary practice needs to look playful and (2) because most early childhood workers are not required to have specialized professional preparation. Early childhood education is, therefore, a public relations nightmare.

During the time that I received my preparation to teach, New York State offered a self-standing teaching certificate, nursery through third grade. The N–3 teacher certification was consistent with the abundant evidence that specially prepared early childhood personnel have a positive educational impact on the experience of young children in group settings (Bowman, Donovan, & Burns, 2001; Bredekamp, 1995; National Association of Early Childhood Teacher Educators & National Association of Early Childhood Specialists in State Education Departments, 1993/2001). However, that certification was discontinued more than three decades ago, and not until 2004 will New York State begin to offer a self-standing early childhood teaching certificate (birth–grade 2). In the past few years, an "annotation in early childhood" has been passed, an add-on to the preK–6 teacher certification. This means that when initially certified teachers begin their employment with young children, they usually have had no preparation to work with this age group because most of their field experiences and courses focused on grades 1–6.

It is paradoxical, therefore, that there is often unnecessary regulation of what should be reasonable professional behavior alongside a lack of support for professional standards that can assure a better quality of educational services for young children. Current federal and state policies narrowly prescribe minimalist phonics, mathematical computation, and occasionally science information examinations. High-stakes examinations and policy prescriptions have influenced the narrowing of early curriculum practices toward passing the examinations (American Educational Research Association, 2000; Cochran-Smith, 2000; Kohn, 2000a; Shepard, 2000; Wasserman, 2001). Higher-quality teaching and "high-stakes services for our children" (Hilliard, 2000, p. 293) have not typically accompanied the testing programs. "Those groups already marginalized may be further punished and potentially cut off disproportionately from further academic opportunities and employment" (Brennan, Kim, Wenz-Gross, & Siperstein, 2001, p. 210). The problem inherent in this paradox lies in the absence of a profession of early childhood that regulates itself, like law and accounting.

This chapter considers the paradox of professionalism and supplies a working definition of professionalism. It also takes a look at the historical perspectives and philosophical traditions of early childhood education, provides an interpretation of its knowledge base and other ongoing contemporary issues and trends, and concludes with implications and challenges for the future of early childhood teacher education.

THE PARADOX OF PROFESSIONALISM

A professional status for the field of early childhood education does not now exist. The field reflects an outgrowth of "commonsense" approaches that more nearly comprise an occupation rather than a profession. In addition, a practical distinction exists between professionals who serve individuals, such as physicians, and those who engage in a "public service profession," such as teachers and social workers (Howe, 1980). This distinction has its roots in historical events, public ideologies and perceptions, and sociopolitical and economic considerations.

In a sense, professionalism that is defined by high standards is not a democratic concept because it limits entry into its ranks. As an exclusive expertise, professional practice separates the professional from ordinary life and action. The dual systems of public school (requiring teachers to hold B.A. degrees) and nonpublic school (with a variety of standards) forms of early childhood services further compound the dilemma of early childhood education and professionalism. Early childhood teaching and status, therefore, are in a state of amateurism when compared with the composite definition of professionalism discussed below.

A WORKING DEFINITION OF PROFESSIONALISM

This chapter takes the position that the difference between a professional person and a technician resides in the confluence of the six factors discussed below. The professional is an expert who can assess, plan, adapt, and act with flexibility, based upon access to a broad field of alternatives (Gibboney, 1998). The early childhood professional has a high tolerance for ambiguity. It is the scope and depth of understanding as well as the capacity to see patterns and flexibly juggle alternatives, however, that differentiate the functionary from the professional.

Professional practice involves six distinct characteristics: (1) ethical performance that is fair; (2) a high level of "essential" expertise and skill (Katz, 1987, p. 3) combined with "sensitivity" to meaningful patterns and the capacity to use "varying levels of flexibility in their approach to new situations" (Bransford, Brown, & Cocking, 1999, p. 19); (3) a body of deep knowledge and skills that laypeople do not possess (Wise & Liebbrand, 1993); (4) considerable autonomy in practice and control of entry into the profession; (5) commensurate compensation; and (6) a professional organization. Each of these characteristics will be discussed in detail.

Ethical Performance

Early childhood education needs to be a distinctly ethical profession because the clientele are vulnerable and relatively powerless. Young children tend to want to please adults. That they can please adults by conforming to adults' wishes does not mean that they should be expected to conform to those expectations that are not in the best interests of the children or of society. Much of existing early childhood education is organized in ways that require children to adapt rather than ways that adapt to young children. For example, toddlers patiently watch as their teachers shamelessly worship the calendar each day or 5-year-olds engage in a letter-of-the-week ritual or sit for long periods of time to be tested in work-books. Equally stultifying for both children and teachers is the practice of teachers' reading children a literally "scripted" activity with directions, questions, and single, expected answers found in many published teachers' guides (Pogrow, 2000; Starnes, 2000). Too many teachers' manuals are based on static and fragmented bits of trivial information. Such technical, unre-flective practices by adults abuse young children's willingness to please.

Ethical considerations, therefore, need to enter into the development of standards for personnel preparation, ongoing practice, and professional development. The profession needs to specify the knowledge base—belief systems and philosophical premises—on which teacher preparation is based and how that study relates specifically to the involvement of young children in the process of meaningful learning. The "inclusionary" model, when using the behaviorist orientation of some special educators, for example, creates a conflict within the practice of a nonbehaviorist early childhood program orientation.

The *Code of Ethical Conduct and Statement of Commitment* (Feeney & Kipnis, 1990) of the National Association for the Education of Young Children (NAEYC) addresses the ways in which personnel interact with their clients, client families, and one another. An ethical field also has to focus on the part of the code that says that no harm will be done to chil-dren. Diminished self-esteem is harmful; learning to deny one's feelings is harmful; and wasting time with trivial pursuits is harmful. Ethical prac-tice, for example, assures that each child will feel competent and engage in significant, culturally relevant, and meaningful learning.

High Level of Expertise and Skill

A professional is capable of expert practice if it is based on rigorous and protracted preparation. Representing the National Council for the Accredi-tation of Teacher Education (NCATE), Arthur Wise (1989) contends that professional teacher education should occur in accredited college-level educational programs that include initiation and apprenticeship, leading in turn to licensing and to advanced accreditation.

Some states have increased the regulations and duration of preservice teacher programs, while others, like Texas, have limited baccalaureate preparation outside the liberal arts to as little as 18 semester hours. A full-time student may become cataclysmically transformed from a citizen into a teacher, sometimes within a year. This person typically may not have any postgraduate contact with university personnel. This is distinctly dif-ferent from other professions. Medical preparation, for example, requires internships and residencies after 4 years of graduate education; legal preparation entails 3 years of graduate work; and both require ongoing professional development.

Early childhood teachers with bachelor's degrees, whether in the public or the private sector, often find that their principal or director has less background in early childhood than they. Although some states require a master's degree for permanent teacher certification, it need not be in the field of early childhood education. State certification standards for school administrators do not require preparation in early childhood education, despite a supportive publication of the National Association of Elementary School Principals (1990). It would be difficult to warrant, therefore, that ongoing induction into the field of early childhood was taking place on the job.

Within the early childhood field, when "professionalism" defines longer periods of costly preparation, it may disadvantage the already-employed, low-income, often minority-group child-care personnel, most of whom are women. An industry of community-based organizations has grown up to serve this population with isolated workshops and conferences that fulfill fragmented social service or health agency regulations for clock-hour staff development contacts. Within their separate tracks, Head Start and the Child Development Associate (CDA) also offer staff development, some of which is coordinated. Very few of these alternative staff development activities translate into college-level credits leading to state teacher certification. If Head Start funds during the past 30 years had been translated into college teacher education scholarships, instead of infused into personnel development workshops, the benefit might have been returned to Head Start children in the form of a reduced attrition rate for increasingly credentialed personnel (Waxler, 1993). It is only recently that funds have become available to support some Head Start personnel, 50% of whom will be expected to hold a 2-year degree in higher education by 2003 (Organization for Economic Co-operation and Development [OECD], 2000). There is a need to ask "Who is served?" Our best answers need to focus on ethical services for young children and their families.

Mastery of Specialized Knowledge and Skills

A specialized, professional-level body of knowledge, skills, and attitudes is based on a coherent theory that accounts for the need of professionals to know what to do, how to do it, and why they have selected particular strategies and tactics from among the available range of alternatives. Thus, professional practice moves beyond simply replicating personal experience and opinions. Beyond knowledge, the professional uses wisdom (Whitehead, 1929), the capacity to *consciously* use knowledge.

The various national proposals and standards for preparing entry-level early childhood personnel devote an enormous percentage of attention to safety and health and focus far less on wisdom—decision making and issues of meaningful curriculum, assessment, and environmental design in the service of significant meanings (Council for Early Childhood, 1993; NAEYC, 1994). The contrast is apparent in the following anecdote:

A young child has taken a chair to the window and is standing on it.

NOVICE ADULT (an assistant, rushes over): Get down. You could hurt yourself. [This adult assesses the physically obvious.]

EDUCATIONALLY ORIENTED ADULT (moves quickly beside the child): What are you seeing outside? (personal communication, B. Nilsen, 1994). [The educationally oriented adult assesses the child's focus, values the child's curiosity and independence, encourages descriptive language and imagery-building, while remaining close enough to provide safety from falling. In effect, the context (background) provides a basis for new text (meanings), rather than becoming the focus and closure.]

This anecdote demonstrates the difference between aides or beginning student teachers, who focus first on how effective they will be in practice by asking "What can I do?" (with a focus on technical skills), and educated and experienced student teachers, who focus on "What can the child do? What will be the child's experience/learning?" (focused on integrating meanings and new connections).

Autonomy in Practice

A professional engages in autonomous practices within a profession that maintains the autonomy to set standards for, control entry into, and monitor retention within the field. The medical profession offers an autonomous model of a profession that regulates itself through credentials, examinations and other standards, and membership in professional organizations.

There has not been a single professional voice in early childhood education that has loudly countered the acceptance of regulations that are noxious to the learning and development of young children. Disregard for the qualifications of a mainly female work force in early childhood may influence the use of high-stakes standardized tests that assume a percentage of failure—and policy makers focus on the failure. Alfie Kohn (2000b) reminds us that if everyone passed the tests, then the public would assume that the tests are too easy.

Commensurate Compensation

Early childhood educators are underpaid, particularly those employed outside the public schools. Public school early childhood teachers tend to be compensated at the same rate as other teachers with credentials that include at least a bachelor's degree. In nonpublic settings, however, early childhood program directors, with or without a bachelor's degree, often earn less than the base salary of a new public school teacher. It is not uncommon to find early childhood personnel, often with a high school diploma and sometimes with a 2- or 4-year college degree, employed at or close to the national minimum wage level. These people have been compensated at so low a rate that a personnel turnover rate between 26% and 41% (compared with a 5.6% public school turnover rate) is typical (Whitebook, Phillips, & Howes, 1993). There is evidence

> that lack of preparation actually contributes to high [teacher] attrition rates and thereby becomes a disincentive to long-term teaching commitments and to the creation of a stable, high-ability teaching force. Lack of preparation also contributes to lower levels of learning, especially for those students who most need skillful teaching in order to succeed. (Darling-Hammond, 2001, p. 61)

Much of the tension involved in the transformation of early childhood education from a cottage industry to a profession centers on economics. Parents' and policy makers' concern for quality confronts the economic problem of scarce resources in families and the competition for budgetary resources in government. Quality, affordability, and professional compensation are often antagonistic rather than integrated elements. In a climate of competing resources, early childhood education has historically been cut or merely been maintained. The exploitation of uncertified personnel who are low-income, often minority-group, women has, in effect, been subsidizing child-care services.

Professional Organization

A strong professional organization has the potential to influence autonomous practice. Admission to professional organizations, such as the American Association of University Professors or the United Federation of Teachers, is open to those who have the required credentials. The democratic scope of the NAEYC, which includes anyone who works within (or takes an interest in) the broadly defined field of young children, whether professionally prepared or not, stands in contrast to this practice. The National Association of Early Childhood Teacher Educators (NAECTE) exists to further early childhood teacher education and admits to membership all those who are concerned with early childhood teacher education. Current practices, therefore, highlight the fragmented status of advocacy forums.

However, several initiatives have begun to point the field in the direction of professionalism. The leadership of NAEYC has attempted to develop a career ladder as well as to work with NCATE as a specialty professional association in teacher preparation program accreditation of universities. NAEYC has become involved with the National Board for Professional Teaching Standards (NBPTS), an organization that will assess teachers' actual performance as well as their conceptual and technical knowledge. NAEYC and NAECTE have developed position papers advocating for the development in each state of a self-standing early childhood teacher certification that includes a minimum of a baccalaureate degree. NAECTE, together with the National Association of Early Childhood Specialists in State Education Departments, advocate that all school building administrators need specialized preparation in early childhood curriculum and related supervision. National movements, however, have not yet affected the variability of teacher certification present across different states (McCarthy, Cruz, & Ratcliff, 1999).

HISTORICAL AND PHILOSOPHICAL TRADITIONS OF THE FIELD

When Shirley Morgenthaler's mother finished her first year of college in 1935 and returned to her farm community in the Midwest, she was asked to teach because she was the most educated person in her community (S. Morgenthaler, personal communication, 1993). Let us consider what it means to be the most educated person today.

The United States has moved from a primarily agrarian to an industrial and then an informational/communications/services kind of society. The idea of the community offering schooling to its children was rooted in the 17th-century goal that children learn enough to read the Bible. Schools today continue to remain centered mainly on the isolated, technical teaching of the "basic" 3Rs. Motives for changing from this narrow definition of schooling to the development of critical thinkers, connection makers, and responsible employees have grown more recently out of the business community. Nevertheless, the high-stakes tests engendered by concern for standardization and easily identified minimalist skills contradict the demands of a global economy.

In some communities, various forms of literacy qualify one to teach. Historically, and in agricultural societies even today, an apprenticeship system qualified one to teach. Usually, the apprentice would not be expected to learn more than the master but to conserve and replicate practices. It was a finite, skills-based approach to education.

There has been a historical trend, however, for elementary school teachers to function with increasingly more education than one year beyond their students. The requirements developed from completion of a program in a "normal" school/technical teachers' college (still prevalent in England, Australia, and New Zealand), to undergraduate degrees, and finally today to undergraduate degrees plus master's degrees. The following information (Wise, 1989) suggests this trend in the United States:

1935	10% of elementary teachers held a B.A.
1946	15 states required teachers to complete a B.A.
1956	35 states required teachers to complete a B.A.
1955	70% of all elementary teachers had a B.A.; 97% of all high school teachers had a B.A.

All states now require public school teachers to hold a baccalaureate, although "emergency" and "alternate" entries exist for those who have fewer qualifications, often in urban settings. The periodic infusion of uncertified personnel into the public schools further confounds the public image of professionalism and fuels the debate about lower standards for teachers and privatizing education for children (Berliner, 2000; Darling-Hammond, Berry, & Thoreson, 2001; Walsh, 2001). Other professions typically do not accept emergency licenses.

In general, the historical increase of qualifications for public school teachers has had little impact on nonpublic early childhood personnel. Another consideration is that the historical association of child care with social services to young children and to low-income families compounds the image that "professionals tend to take on the status of their clients" (Howe, 1980, p. 180). Along with the elderly, the very young and low-income populations are often tacitly devalued as inept.

THE ISSUE OF DEFINING KNOWLEDGE BASES

Knowledge in early childhood education and early childhood teacher education is continuously changing. The research database in early childhood teacher education is smaller than in the field of teacher education in general, but there are related and parallel findings to consider.

Awareness of the knowledge base answers the question: What are the assumptions about the image of an effective professional teacher—held in common within an institution—that guide preservice work, preparation and placement in student teaching, and initial supervision and mentoring, as well as the transformation of teaching practice? Shared knowledge bases can serve to provide continuity between preservice and inservice teacher professional education. An additional challenge is the current emphasis on accountability in the form of performance assessment (Hyson, 2000). Early childhood teachers who work ethically in a nonlinear, interdisciplinary mode need to make explicit the ways in which they assess learning and "will need help in learning to use assessment in new ways" (Shepard, 2000, p. 36).

A "core" body of informational modules, in contrast, relates mainly to linear, technical activity. The isolated, eclectic study of individual children's predetermined development and the behaviorist use of stars and other extrinsic rewards also exist as technical activities. Within today's diverse society, however, attention to children's sociocultural contexts and family cultures requires an interdisciplinary, holistic preparation that provides a stronger platform on which teachers might build curricula with children. Thoughtful issues about equitable curricula need to be the center of professional education.

Teachers today should expect to deal with the realities of predictable unpredictability, which describe the nature of each early childhood group setting that takes an ethical stance in relation to children. Professional teachers, of course, prepare ideas and materials for flexible use with the children based on their assessment/professional judgment of what will have meaning to the children. To work from this perspective, teachers need preparation and encouragement in risk taking, being comfortable with ambiguity, and connection making.

It makes sense to support highly skilled and caring early childhood teachers who can provide children with multiple forms of representation, long blocks of time, and a reasonable variety of choices. The scarcity of a sufficient number of such professionally prepared early childhood teachers suggests that a massive effort of staff development is needed. At the same time, the preparation of master teachers who can work with preservice teachers is a next step in professionalization. Institutions of higher education, within the context of the professional development school model, have the potential to create growth for cooperating teachers as well as college teachers. This view is consistent with the notion that inservice professional transformation can take place when there is a focus on capacity building (Fullan, 1999). A next step in advocacy needs to be the preparation of school administrators who understand early childhood curricula and how to provide support for professional teaching practice.

IMPLICATIONS FOR PROFESSIONALIZING EARLY CHILDHOOD TEACHER EDUCATION

Unique forms of early childhood teacher education would be reflected in the implementation of four interconnecting dimensions of work:

1. *Linking/bridging—emphasizing what to teach.* The early childhood teacher needs to actively integrate a rich background of knowledge and diverse cultural experiences in order to be able to appreciate and adapt to young children's ways of learning. This dimension is consistent with Dewey's (1916) notion that the teacher's role is to help children move toward humanity's fund of knowledge in ways that help learners make connections. A contemporary egalitarian definition of "humanity's fund" would include consideration of varied perspectives such as culture, gender, race, variously abled persons, and other orientations. The ways in which prospective teachers have been taught and the ways in which they have learned also form part of the "fund" that they acquire. There has been attention to a paradigm shift (Fromberg, 2002) and the essential importance of "interdisciplinary preparation for diverse early childhood settings" (National Institute on Early Childhood Development and Education, 2000, p. 7).

2. *Alternatives—emphasizing how to teach.* The early childhood educator needs to acquire a repertoire of alternative strategies and tactics, paying particular attention to the inclusion of play in the educational program. Additional interconnected conditions for learning include inductive experiences, cognitive dissonance, social interaction, physical experiences, revisiting, and a sense of competence (Fromberg, 1995). Environmental design is yet another distinctive feature of early childhood teacher education because, for young children, a decentralized physical setting can help to support the conditions for learning. The capacity to thoughtfully employ a variety of "pedagogical orientations" (Delpit, 1995, p. 24) is particularly relevant in working with diverse students.

   The preservice teacher should be given practice, with a gradual increase of responsibility. In order to develop the power to select from among alternatives, it is useful for preservice teachers to take responsibility for independent planning and working with children, while receiving coaching support; they would engage in a series of experiences with the same small group over time and then with groups of increasing size. Coherent programs of preservice teacher education need to include field placements that are consistent with the college's conceptual framework. Field placements, therefore, need to be collaboratively developed between the college and the school district rather than dictated as "rewards" to inservice teachers or "help" for inept teachers.

3. *Reflecting—emphasizing why to teach*. Reflecting on work with young children by using audio-/videotape and transcripts provides an opportunity for teachers to increase their self-awareness and to rehearse alternative ideas as each one replays events. Such critical self-study makes it possible to focus practice in each subsequent encounter with children, thereby building spontaneity and flexibility along with additional insights for future plans. The teacher who works in these ways engages in a form of participatory curriculum research that blends practice, theory, and research in a recursive process. Evidences of reflectivity represent authentic forms of assessing teaching competence. The NBPTS process of advanced certification includes such assessment.

4. *Community and family involvement—emphasizing who teaches*. Early childhood education has a distinct, caring commitment to working closely with families and communities. Teachers need to learn how to welcome family and community involvement through a variety of forms. The kinds of activities in which teachers can engage to promote community acceptance include the following: articulating the purposes and practices of early childhood education in order to attempt to guarantee acceptance of ethical practices; sharing information concerning local and state early childhood education initiatives, writing to legislators, and explaining program purposes to family and community members as well as other school people; and attending teacher conferences, school board meetings, and professional meetings, along with interviewing community members concerning educational and cultural issues.

ADDITIONAL ISSUES AND TRENDS

Economic and political as well as sociocultural forces interact to create the issues of compensation, staff composition, development, and regulation that affect early childhood education as a profession in the United States. The following challenges to professional status continue:

1. Low compensation influences the choice of teaching as a career (Bracey, 2001; Su, 1996). A single professional organization has the potential to address this issue.
2. Although there is a growing population of young children from minority groups, children of color, and children who are English-language learners in the United States, there are fewer minority

teachers and teachers of color (less than 10%) among baccalaureate graduates (Haberman, 1989). Because research shows that
qualified minority teachers can improve the quality of education
for minority children through modeling and sensitivity to cultural
nuances and learning needs (King, 1993), it makes sense to recruit
minority teachers from among the larger pool (50%) of 2-year colleges graduates (Haberman, 1999). Moreover, recruitment of a
diverse teacher corps from community-based organizations needs
to be accompanied by "sufficient social-service supports such as
child care, transportation, family support, and financial aid" (Adair,
2001, p. 233). Job sharing, scholarships, and colleges that accommodate schedules to the longer day of child-care personnel are
other necessary forms of support.

3. The diffusion of responsibility for early childhood education within
state and federal agencies often results in parallel, nonintegrated
regulations concerning standards for early childhood personnel.
A profession would be better served by a single agency for early
education within each state that deals respectfully with a single
association that represents the profession. Such a meaningful collaboration has the potential to improve the coherence of quality
teacher education programs and services to children.

If. This chapter began by considering the paradox of professionalism
in early childhood education, and it closes with concern that this paradox continues. The state of the field would be very much improved if each
state had a self-standing early childhood teacher certificate for initial entry
into the field; if each college of education were to qualify for NCATE
accreditation; and if each state were in a full partnership arrangement with
NCATE. If each policy maker were to imagine the need for each teacher
to be good enough for his or her children, grandchildren/future grandchil-
dren, nieces, nephews, and neighbors, perhaps there might be some movement toward a professional ideal.

But. In reality, it is likely that early childhood educators will need to
engage in significant advocacy initiatives in order to move toward such
an ideal. The reality of affordability may mean that early childhood personnel will need to negotiate differentiated staffing formats that include
coherent opportunities for a career ladder. Another reality is that the
issues of autonomy versus external regulation of a public service profession, opportunities to ensure a high quality of distinct and expert preparation versus a history of voluntarism and commonsense perspectives, and
ethical fairness versus commensurate compensation will need to be re-
solved over time, in a way that leads to an evolving awareness of what sort

of self-organizing system we might expect for early childhood education as a profession. On the way, influenced by sensitive dependence on initial conditions, there will be plenty of phase transitions, bifurcations, and very strange attractors in the form of political waves.

REFERENCES

Adair, V. C. (2001). Poverty and the (broken) promise of higher education. *Harvard Educational Review, 71*(2), 217–239.

American Educational Research Association. (2000). Position statement of the American Educational Research Association concerning high-stakes testing in preK–12 education. *Educational Researcher, 29*(8), 24–25.

Berliner, D. C. (2000). A personal response to those who bash teacher education. *Journal of Teacher Education, 51*(5), 358–371.

Bowman, B. T., Donovan, S., & Burns, M. S. (Eds.). (2001). *Eager to learn: Educating our preschoolers.* Washington, DC: National Academy Press.

Bracey, G. W. (2001). Why so few Asian American teachers? *Phi Delta Kappan, 83*(1), 14–15.

Bransford, J. D., Brown, A. L., & Cocking, R. R. (Eds.). (1999). *How people learn: Brain, mind, experience, and school.* Washington, DC: National Academy Press.

Bredekamp, S. (1995). Early childhood education. In J. Sikula, T. J. Buttery, & E. Guyton (Eds.), *Handbook of research on teacher education* (pp. 323–347). New York: Macmillan/Association of Teacher Educators.

Brennan, R. T., Kim, J., Wenz-Gross, M., & Siperstein, N. (2001). The relative equitability of high-stakes testing versus teacher-assigned grades: An analysis of the Massachusetts Comprehensive Assessment System. *Harvard Educational Review, 71*(2), 173–216.

Cochran-Smith, M. (2000, April). *The outcomes question in teacher education.* Paper presented at the AERA annual meeting, New Orleans.

Council for Early Childhood. (1993). *Child Development Associate credential.* Washington, DC: Author.

Darling-Hammond, L. (2001). *The research rhetoric on teacher certification: A response to "Teacher certification reconsidered."* Palo Alto, CA: Stanford University National Commission on Teaching and America's Future.

Darling-Hammond, L., Berry, B., & Thoreson, A. (2001). Does teacher certification matter? Evaluating the evidence. *Educational Evaluation and Policy Analysis, 23*(1), 57–77.

Delpit, L. (1995). *Other people's children: Cultural conflict in the classroom.* New York: New Press.

Dewey, J. (1916). *Democracy and education.* New York: Macmillan.

Feeney, S., & Kipnis, K. (1990). *Code of ethical conduct and statement of commitment.* Washington, DC: NAEYC.

Fromberg, D. P. (1995). *The full-day kindergarten: Planning and practicing a dynamic themes curriculum* (2nd ed.). New York: Teachers College Press.

Fromberg, D. P. (2002). *Play and meaning in early childhood education.* Boston: Allyn & Bacon.

Fullan, M. (1999). *Change forces: The sequel.* Philadelphia, PA: Falmer.

Gibboney, R. A., with Webb, C. D. (1998). *What every great teacher knows.* Brandon, VT: Holistic Education Press.

Haberman, M. (1989). More minority teachers. *Phi Delta Kappan, 70*(10), 771–776.

Haberman, M. (1999). Increasing the number of high-quality African American teachers in urban schools. *Journal of Instructional Psychology, 26*(4), 208–212.

Hilliard, A.G., III. (2000). Excellence in education versus high-stakes standardized testing. *Journal of Teacher Education, 51*(4), 283–304.

Howe, E. (1980). Public professions and the private model of professional professionalism. *Social Work, 25*(3), 179–191.

Hyson, M. (2000). Growing teachers for a growing profession: NAEYC revises guidelines for early childhood professional preparation. *Young Children, 55*(3), 60–61.

Katz, L. G. (1987). The nature of professions: Where is early childhood education? In L. G. Katz & K. Steiner (Eds.), *Current topics in early childhood education* (Vol. 7; pp. 1–16). Norwood, NJ: Ablex.

King, S. H. (1993). The limited presence of African-American teachers. *Review of Educational Research, 63*(2), 115–149.

Kohn, A. (2000a). Burnt at the high stakes. *Journal of Teacher Education, 51*(4), 315–327.

Kohn, A. (2000b). Education in a dark time. *Education Update, 43*(1), 1, 4.

McCarthy, J., Cruz, J., Jr., & Ratcliff, N. (1999). *Early childhood teacher education licensure patterns: A state by state analysis.* Washington, DC: NAEYC.

National Association of Early Childhood Teacher Educators & National Association of Early Childhood Specialists in State Education Departments (2001). *Early childhood teacher certification: Executive summary.* New York: Authors. (Original work published 1993)

National Association for the Education of Young Children (NAEYC). (1994). NAEYC position statement: A conceptual framework for early childhood professional development. *Young Children, 49*(3), 68–77.

National Association of Elementary School Principals. (1990). *Early childhood education and the elementary school principal.* Alexandria, VA: Author.

National Institute on Early Childhood Development and Education. 2000). *New teachers for a new century: The future of early childhood professional preparation.* Washington, DC: U.S. Department of Education.

Organization for Economic Co-operation and Development (OECD). (2000). *Early childhood education and care policy in the United States of America.* Paris: Author. Available on-line: www.oecd.org/

Pogrow, S. (2000). Success for all does not produce success for students. *Phi Delta Kappan, 82*(1), 67–80.

Shepard, L. A. (2000). *The role of classroom assessment in teaching and learning*. Washington, DC: Center for Research on Education, Diversity and Excellence.

Starnes, B. A. (2000). On dark times, parallel universes, and déjà vu. *Phi Delta Kappan, 82*(2), 108–114.

Su, Z. (1996). Why teach: Profiles and entry perspectives of minority students as becoming teachers. *Journal of Research and Development in Education, 29*, 117–133.

Walsh, K. (2001). *Teacher certification reconsidered: Stumbling for quality*. Baltimore: Abell Foundation.

Wasserman, S. (2001). Quantum theory, the uncertainty principle, and the alchemy of standardized testing. *Phi Delta Kappan, 83*(1), 28–40.

Waxler, T. (1993, June). Head Start staff development. Paper presented at the NAEYC National Professional Development Institute, Minneapolis.

Whitebook, M., Phillips, D., & Howes, C. (1993). *Four years in the life of center-based childcare in America*. Report of the National Child Care Staffing Study Revisited. Oakland, CA: Child Care Employee Project.

Whitehead, A. N. (1929). *The aims of education*. New York: Mentor.

Wise, A. (1989). Graduate teacher education and teacher professionalism. In A. E. Woolfolk (Ed.), *Research perspectives on the graduate preparation of teachers* (pp.169–178). Englewood Cliffs, NJ: Prentice Hall.

Wise, A., & Liebbrand, J. (1993, October). Accreditation and the creation of a profession of teaching. *Phi Delta Kappan, 75*(2), 133–136, 154–157.

Epilogue

In the film *Listening to Children* (Squires, 1995), psychiatrist and author Robert Coles describes how a chance occurrence in 1960 inaugurated more than 30 years of research. While on his way to a professional conference in New Orleans, Coles came upon an angry mob that was protesting the desegregation of public schools in Louisiana. The first African American child to set foot in an all-White school was a diminutive 6-year-old named Ruby Bridges. She emerged from a car, accompanied by two burly marshals, and walked to the school, a scene that has been commemorated in a Norman Rockwell painting of a Black girl in a white dress walking past a tomato-stained wall. Coles was inspired to complete a case study of Ruby Bridges, and in the film he remarks that Ruby has been one of his greatest teachers. He also comments that "in a better America" everyone would know the Ruby Bridges story and honor her.

It is fitting to end this book about early childhood with this story of a young child, partly so that more educators will take this story to heart and partly as a reminder that not only do adults exert a powerful influence on children, but children also have a profound effect on adults. It is also fitting to conclude this book with the Ruby Bridges story because trends, issues, challenges, controversies, and insights are encapsulated in this single, symbolic event that shaped the future of American public education. Interestingly, since the publication of the first edition of this book, Ruby Bridge's courage has been celebrated through a children's book with a text by Robert Coles (1995), an autobiographical book (Bridges & Lundell, 1999) and a Disney book and movie about her life (Otto, 1997).

As set forth in the Introduction, our original goal in writing MAJOR TRENDS AND ISSUES IN EARLY CHILDHOOD EDUCATION: CHALLENGES, CONTROVERSIES, AND INSIGHTS was to give readers the advantage of multiple perspectives on where the early childhood field has been, where it appears to be headed, and why. Unlike many other areas in the educational field, early childhood educators have achieved a higher level of consensus about what young children need in order to thrive. The task before society is to move beyond the democratic ideal of optimizing every child's potential and make it a reality. Ongoing debate about how to attain this worthy goal stems not so much from discrepancies in early childhood educators' collective vision for children but rather from the moral, social, pedagogical, and political challenge of communicating those ideals to various publics, marshaling the necessary resources, and altering society so that children are truly put first.

Returning to the metaphor of the lens that has provided a framework for this book, we hope that the multiple perspectives represented here are comparable with yet another sort of lens. If you visit national parks around the United States you will often come upon a scenic overlook selected so that visitors can "take it all in." Frequently that site will be equipped with a set of powerful lenses mounted in large metal stand that pivots, swivels, and adjusts the focus to each person's vision, enabling the user to scan the landscape, detect what would be impossible to see with an unaided eye, and focus on significant details. When this looking is combined with what visitors knew or read recently about the site as well as information supplied by tour guides, on a recorded message, or from fellow travelers, the sightseers see more than scenery. They have, to borrow a phrase from Elliot Eisner (1991), an "enlightened eye," one that simultaneously sees things clearly and delves beneath the surface.

The editors and authors assembled to produce the second edition of MAJOR TRENDS AND ISSUES IN EARLY CHILDHOOD EDUCATION: CHALLENGES, CONTROVERSIES, AND INSIGHTS have worked to make the field of early childhood more accessible to our readers just as that special lens supports the goals of sightseers. Everyone who contributed to this volume fully appreciates that it will take an enlightened view of early childhood education to do the right things for young children. As professionals in a field dedicated to the care and education of the very young, we need to stand together, join with families, and collaborate with professionals in other fields to improve the quality of life for every young child.

REFERENCES

Bridges, R., & Lundell, M. (1999). *Through my eyes*. New York: Scholastic.
Coles, R. (1995). *Story of Ruby Bridges*. New York: Scholastic.
Eisner, E. W. (1991). *The enlightened eye*. New York: Macmillan.
Otto, C. (1997). *Wonderful world of Disney: The Ruby Bridges story*. Orlando, FL: Disney Press.
Squires, B. (Producer/Director). (1995). *Listening to children: A moral journey with Robert Coles* [Videotape]. Available from Customer Support Center/ PBS Video, 1320 Braddock Place, Alexandria, VA 22314-1698.

About the Editors and the Contributors

Joan Packer Isenberg is professor of education and director of the Advanced Studies in Teaching and Learning Program at George Mason University in Fairfax, Virginia, where she has twice received the distinguished faculty award for teaching excellence. She has taught young children and held administrative positions in both public and private school settings. Among her most recent publications are two co-authored books, *Creative Expression and Play in Early Childhood* (with Mary Renck Jalongo) and *Exploring Your Role: A Practitioner's Introduction to Early Childhood Education* (with Mary Renck Jalongo) (Merrill/Prentice-Hall). She has served on the NCATE Board of Examiners and as president of the National Association of Early Childhood Teacher Educators (NAECTE) and of the Metro Area Branch of the Association for Childhood Education International (ACEI). Her research interests are in early childhood curriculum and education and the advanced professional development of teachers. Dr. Isenberg received her Ed. D. in elementary education from Rutgers University. She is currently serving as the first visiting scholar for the National Board for Professional Teaching Standards (NBPTS) and is providing leadership with higher education initiatives and reform of advanced master's degrees for practicing teachers.

Mary Renck Jalongo is a teacher, writer, editor, and educational consultant. As a classroom teacher, she taught preschool, first grade, and second grade; worked with children and families of migrant farm workers; and taught in the laboratory preschool at the University of Toledo. Currently she is a professor at Indiana University of Pennsylvania, where she earned the university-wide award for outstanding teaching and is Coordinator of the Doctoral Program in Curriculum and Instruction. As a writer, she has published 20 books, many of them textbooks in the field of early childhood education, and has earned three national awards for excellence in writing. She is editor-in-chief of the international publication *Early Childhood Education Journal*. As an educational consultant, Mary Renck Jalongo has made presentations throughout the world.

Doris Bergen is a professor and former chair of the Department of Educational Psychology at Miami University in Oxford, Ohio. She has been an early childhood educator in inclusive classrooms at preschool, primary, and university levels. Her research has focused on the play, social, and humor development of young children, including the play development of children with disabilities. Her published work includes books on play development, infant/toddler transdisciplinary team assessment, and infant/toddler curriculum; her most recent book is on the implications of brain research for educators.

Doris Pronin Fromberg is professor and chairperson of the Department of Curriculum and Teaching at Hofstra University, where she also serves as director of early childhood teacher education. She is a past president of the National Association of Early Childhood Teacher Educators (NAECTE) and of the NAECTE Foundation, and has chaired the Special Interest Group on Early Education and Child Development of the American Educational Research Association as well as the Special Study Group on Elementary Education of the American Association of Colleges of Teacher Education. She was the recipient of the 1996 Early Childhood Teacher Educator of the Year Award from NAECTE/Allyn & Bacon. She is an advocate of high-quality early childhood teacher and administrator education. Among her publications are *Play and Meaning in Early Childhood Education*, *The Full-Day Kindergarten*, *Play from Birth to Twelve and Beyond* (co-edited with Doris Bergen), *The Encyclopedia of Early Childhood Education* (co-edited with L. R. Williams), and *The Successful Classroom* (with M. Driscoll).

Fergus Hughes, who earned his Ph.D. in psychology from Syracuse University, is a professor of human development and psychology at the University of Wisconsin–Green Bay. He teaches courses on life-span human development, adolescent development, and child development, and has taught a course on children's play for the past 27 years. His books include *Human Development: Across the Life Span*, *Child Development*, and *Children, Play and Development*. His articles have been published in such journals as *Developmental Psychology*, the *Journal of Genetic Psychology*, and *Young Children*. He is currently working on a research project dealing with college students' perceptions of their own learning experiences and on a book chapter on the role of play in the early childhood education curriculum.

John M. Johnston is professor of instruction and curriculum leadership at the University of Memphis, where he teaches courses in early childhood education, action research, and curriculum. Since completing his Ph.D. in teacher education at The Ohio State University, his research has focused on beginning teachers, early childhood teacher problems, and the effects of reduced class size in the primary grades. He helped develop the Early Childhood/Generalist standards for the National Board for Professional Teaching Standards and the initial and advanced teacher education standards for the National Association for the Education of Young Children; he also serves as a member of the National Council for the Accreditation of Teacher Education Board of Examiners.

Lea M. McGee is co-director of the High/Scope Early Childhood Reading Institute and a professor of literacy education at the University of Alabama. She teaches graduate and undergraduate courses in children's literature, beginning reading and language arts, and foundations of language and literacy development. She received her Ed.D. from Virginia Tech and has previously taught at Boston College and Louisiana State University. She is the co-author of three books: *Literacy's Beginnings: Supporting Young Readers and Writers* and *Designing Early Literacy Programs for At-Risk Preschool and Kindergarten Children* (both with Donald J. Richgels) and *Teaching Reading with Literature* (with Gail Tompkins). She has published numerous articles in a variety of journals, including *The Reading Teacher*, *Language Arts*, and *Reading Research Quarterly*. Her research interests include the role of fingerpoint reading in making the transition from emergent to conventional reading and young children's responses to literature. She frequently works with teachers in their classrooms and is currently vice president of the National Reading Conference.

Shirley C. Raines, the 11th president of the University of Memphis, is the first woman to hold that office. She is widely regarded as an expert in early childhood and teacher education, including the Distinguished Faculty Award at George Mason University and two distinguished research awards from the Eastern Education Research Association. Major themes of her higher education leadership have been interdisciplinary research; improving teaching, retention, and graduation rates; and building partnerships on and off the campus. Dr. Raines earned her doctorate in education from the University of Tennessee, Knoxville. She has served on the faculty or administration of universities in Florida, Virginia, Oklahoma, North Carolina, and Alabama. She has also been involved with early childhood education in Tennessee, Kentucky, and Indiana. Immediately before coming to Memphis, she was vice chancellor of academic services and dean of the college of education at the University of Kentucky.

Frances O'Connell Rust is professor and coordinator of early childhood and elementary education curricula in the Department of Teaching and Learning at New York University. She is the winner of the 1985 AERA Outstanding Dissertation Award, the recipient of the Teachers College Outstanding Alumni Award (1998), and the recipient of the Association of Teacher Educators 2001 Award for Distinguished Research in Teacher Education. Her research and teaching focus on teacher education and teachers' research. Her most recent books are *Taking Action Through Teacher Research* (co-edited with Ellen Meyers), *Guiding School Change: New Understandings of the Role and Work of Change Agents* (co-edited with Helen Friedus), *Changing Teaching, Changing Schools: Bringing Early Childhood Practice into Public Education,* and *Ensuring Teaching Quality* and *What Matters Most: Improving Student Achievement,* both of which are syntheses of teacher research co-edited with Ellen Meyers as part of her work as adviser to the Teachers Network Policy Institute. Rust completed her doctoral work at Teachers College, Columbia University.

Sudha Swaminathan is currently an associate professor of early childhood education at Eastern Connecticut State University in Willimantic. She received her doctorate degree in early childhood education from the State University of New York at Buffalo in 1995. Her specialization within the field includes the use of educational technology as a learning tool in the teaching and understanding of mathematics, particularly geometry. Her current focus includes teacher education, particularly the use of educational technology in the classroom. She has made over 30 national presentations, and her papers on young children and technology have been published in journals such as *Young Children, Childhood Education,* and the *Journal for Research in Mathematics Education.*

Kevin J. Swick is a professor of early childhood education at the University of South Carolina, Columbia. He received his Ph.D. in education in 1970 from the University of Connecticut. Professor Swick is very involved in working with family involvement programs in early childhood and has published more than 50 articles and 6 books on the topic. He is currently working with several Even Start programs on developing stronger family literacy programs. He is also involved with several school districts on developing programs for homeless families and students.

Louise Boyle Swiniarski is a professor of education, director of the Northeast Global Education Center, and coordinator of student teaching in England at Salem State College in Salem, Massachusetts. She teaches early childhood education, global education, and foundations of education in

Salem State College's graduate school, where she coordinated the Early Childhood Program for many years. She earned her Ph. D. at Boston College and has had appointments as a visiting practitioner at Harvard University's Graduate School of Education for its Principals' Center. The Salem State College Graduate School Award for Excellence and a Distinguished Service Award for Massachusetts State College Faculty recognized her for her commitment and achievements in education. Her interest in international education has taken her around the world to research, lecture, and write about global educational practices and policies. Support for her work has come from numerous private funding and governmental sources, including the Ministry of Education in Finland. She authors books and articles and has produced videos and photo exhibitions on early childhood education, global issues, international systems, and celebrations.

Edwina Battle Vold is professor emerita, Indiana University of Pennsylvania (IUP). She served as chairperson of the Department of Professional Studies in Education and professor of early childhood education at IUP. Dr. Vold has published extensively in the area of multicultural education and early childhood education. She co-authored (with Patricia G. Ramsay and Leslie R. Williams) the book *Multicultural Education: A Source Book* and is the editor of the books *Preparing Teachers for Diverse Student Populations* and *Multicultural Education in Early Childhood Classrooms*. She has authored and co-authored numerous chapters and articles in professional books and journals. She has received numerous research grants, including a $600,000 grant from the Dewitt Wallace–Reader's Digest fund to prepare paraprofessionals in the Pittsburgh public schools to become elementary teachers. Dr. Vold received her Ph.D. from the University of Wisconsin–Madison.

C. Stephen White is an associate professor of education and co-coordinator of literacy programs in the Graduate School of Education at George Mason University in Fairfax, Virginia. Dr. White received a Ph.D. in curriculum and instruction from Texas A&M University. Prior to teaching at George Mason University, Dr. White was a faculty member in the Department of Elementary Education at the University of Georgia for 10 years, where he served as director of the UGA Follow Through Project. Dr. White also has experience teaching preschool, kindergarten, and second-grade children. His research interests include young children's problem solving and analogical reasoning; teachers' knowledge, beliefs, and practices; and curriculum integration in kindergarten and the primary grades. Dr. White has co-authored an early childhood foundations textbook and a number of publications on analogical reasoning in young children. He currently serves as associate features editor for the American Educational Research Association publication *Educational Researcher*.

Sue C. Wortham is professor emerita of early childhood and elementary education at the University of Texas at San Antonio. She has published three textbooks and numerous articles on the topic of assessment of young children. She served as a Fulbright Scholar to Chile in 1992 and president of the Association for Childhood Education International from 1995 to 1997. Since retirement, she has continued working on textbooks and assisting in the development of a global self-assessment tool for early childhood education and care settings.

June L. Wright is professor emerita of early childhood education at Eastern Connecticut State University. She founded and directs the Computer Discovery Project, which researches young children's learning styles, parent–child relationships, and the role of technology in the classroom and the home. Dr. Wright represents the United States on the Early Childhood/Elementary Education Working Group of the International Federation of Information Processing (IFIP). Her publications include *Young Children and Technology: A World of Discovery* and *Young Children: Active Learners in a Technological Age*.

Index

Abuse, 14, 19, 24, 71, 72
Accountability, 90, 92, 93, 109, 186
Accreditation, 1, 86, 92
Achievement, 51–52, 54, 56–57, 64, 88, 97–98, 158
Adair, V. C., 189
Adcock, S. G., 24
Administrators, 24–25, 184, 186
Affective development, 17, 165
African Americans, 18, 37, 193. *See also* Multicultural education
Aid for Families with Dependent Children, 155
Ainsworth, M., 17
Alliance for Childhood, 139
Allington, R. L., 101
American Association of University Professors, 183
American Educational Research Association, 178
Anastasiow, N. J., 35
Anderson, R. C., 117
"Ani's Rocket Ride" (software), 144
Anti-bias concepts, 31, 32, 35, 36, 38, 39–40, 168
The Anti-Bias Curriculum (Derman-Sparks and A.B.C. Task Force), 31, 32, 39–40, 168
Arbaugh, F., 141
Armstrong, A., 137
Ashiabi, G., 23
Assessment: and achievement, 97–98; authentic and performance, 93, 105–7, 108, 109–10; benefits for children of, 103–4; categories of, 99; and cognition, 100, 102; and culture, 82, 99, 102; and DAP, 85, 91, 92, 93, 99; definition of, 98, 99; developmental, 97–98; and diversity, 99; evaluation of, 107–8; and how children's progress should be assessed, 103–7; and inclusion, 62; and language, 82, 99, 100, 102, 104; and learning, 97–98; and measurement, 98–99; overview of, 82, 97–98; and parents, 104, 107–8; persistent issues concerning, 108–10; and play, 103, 105; and portfolios, 108, 109; principles for, 104; and

profile of child, 108; purposes of, 98, 99–100, 101; questions about, 98, 109; reports about, 82, 107–10; and socioemotional development, 100; of special needs children, 82, 100, 101, 102–3; and standards, 108; and status of early childhood educators, 186, 188; and teacher assessment strategies, 105; types of, 99; and who are being assessed, 99; and why assessment is issue, 101–3. *See also* Standardized testing
Assimilation, 32, 37, 43
Association for Childhood Education International (ACEI), 174
Association for Persons with Severe Handicaps (TASH), 55
Association of Teacher Educators, 87
At-risk children/families, 71–72, 77, 100, 139, 155
Autonomy, 179, 182, 189

Bailey, D. B., 50, 52, 64
Baker, J. M., 53
Ballenger, C., 117
Banks, C.A.M., 37
Banks, J. A., 31, 32–33, 37, 41
Barbour, A., 106, 107
Barnette, M., 138
Barrera, I., 102
Barrera, M. T., 141
Beasley, W., 142
Beck, S. S., 105
Becker, H. J., 144
Belenky, Mary, 1
Bennett, S., 143
Bennett, William, 41
Bergen, Doris: chapter by, 12, 47–68; references to works by, 50, 52, 53, 57, 103, 105, 109
Bergin, D. A., 140
Berk, L. E., 15, 16, 21, 22, 23
Berliner, D. C., 185
Best practices, 90, 120, 165, 173
Bielefeldt, T., 142
Black Americans. *See* African Americans; Race

Bomholt, S. K., 141
Bowen, M., 71
Bowlby, J., 17
Bowman, B., 89, 143, 144, 177
Boyer, E. L., 21
Boyer, J., 37
Bracey, G. W., 188
Bradley, R. H., 15, 21, 22
Bransford, J., 89, 179
Bredekamp, S., 85, 86, 87, 88, 92, 127, 177
Breitborde, M., 165, 171, 174
Brennan, R. T., 178
Bricker, D. C., 57
Bridges, Ruby, 193
Bronfenbrenner, U., 15, 17, 73, 75, 76
Brooks-Gunn, J., 15, 18, 23
Browning, L., 23
Building Bridges for Excellence in the Early Grades (TV series), 171
Bureau of Labor Statistics, U.S., 156
Bureau of the Census, U.S., 159, 160
Buysse, V., 50, 52, 64

Caldera, Y. M., 130
Campbell, D. E., 41
Campbell, F. A., 88
Cannella, G., 91, 92
Caring, 12, 21, 22, 70, 73, 76, 77, 153–63, 167, 170, 188
Carnegie Corporation, 17, 18, 19, 20, 23
Case, R., 15
Casement, C., 137
Castle, C., 170, 172
Cauthen, N. K., 22
Certification, 177–78, 181, 184, 188, 189
Challenges, 4, 5–6, 22–25. *See also specific topic*
Charlesworth, R., 88, 91
Cheney, Lynne, 41
Child care: availability of, 156–57; and consequences of policies, 153–54, 156–59, 161, 162; and DAP, 87, 93; and development issues, 17, 18, 21; and inclusion, 63; quality in field of, 158–59; and status of early childhood educators, 183, 185, 189. *See also* Child-care workers; Early childhood educators
Child Care, Inc., 157
Child-care workers, 127–28, 158. *See also* Early childhood educators
Child Development Associate (CDA), 180
Child Observation Record, 108
Children: profiles of, 108; statistics on, 13–14; views of, 155. *See also specific topic*
Children's Defense Fund, 2, 13, 14, 15, 19, 20, 22, 23, 155, 157, 158, 159, 160
Chrisman, K., 74, 75
Clements, D. H., 138, 141, 144

Climate, classroom/school, 88, 132–33, 167, 170
Coalition of Essential Schools, 22
Cochran-Smith, M., 117, 178
Cognition, 14–15, 17, 33–34, 35–36, 41–42, 72, 88, 100, 102, 120, 137, 139–40
Cohen, N. E., 157, 158
Coles, Robert, 34, 193
Comer, J., 73, 75
Comer Schools, 22
Committee on the Prevention of Reading Difficulties, 120–21
Communication, 12, 74–75, 144, 145
Communities, 7, 12, 16, 20, 23, 76–77, 168, 171, 172, 188
Compensation, 158–59, 179, 183, 188, 189
Competition, fair, 56, 57
Conformity, 37, 38, 43
Connell, J. P., 101
Connolly, J., 130
Connor, J. A., 131
Controversy, 4, 5–6. *See also specific topic*
Copely, J., 90
Coping, 15, 20, 22–23
Copple, C., 87, 88, 92, 127
Cordes, C., 137, 139
Cornelius, M. D., 20
Couchenour, D., 74, 75
Council for Early Childhood, 182
Council for Exceptional Children, 86–87, 90
Covell, K., 173
Covert, S., 50
Critical thinking/pedagogy, 40, 43, 91–92, 165, 167
Cuban, L., 142
Cultural pluralism, 36, 37, 38, 39, 40, 42
Culture: and assessment, 82, 99, 102; and DAP, 91; and play, 82, 126–35; and status of early childhood educators, 188–89; variations across, 128; variations within, 129. *See also* Global education; Multicultural education; Sociocultural forces
Curriculum: appropriateness for young children of, 33–36; for caring, 73; and child development, 81; on diversity, 31–33; four F's, 37; "hidden," 82; and inclusion, 52; and multicultural education, 31, 32–33, 35, 36, 38, 39–40; origin of term, 81; questions about, 81; and standards, 82; ways of conceptualizing, 81–82. *See also* Anti-bias concepts; Assessment; Developmentally appropriate practices; Mandates; Play; Technology
Curriculum Standards for the Social Studies (NCSS), 170

Darling-Hammond, L., 183, 185
Davidman, L., 43

Davidman, P. T., 43
DeGarmo, D. S., 16
Delpit, L., 187
Denham, S. A., 15, 22, 23
Deno, S., 50
Derman-Sparks, Louise, 31, 32, 39–40, 168
Desjean-Perrotta, B., 106, 107
Development, child: adverse influences on, 17–21; and curriculum, 81; definition of, 15–16; and developmental needs of children, 2, 13, 14–15, 24–25; and diversity, 30–46; and family issues, 11–12; historical views of, 16–17; implications and recomendations for, 22–25; and multicultural education, 30–46; positive influences on, 21–22; questions about, 8, 12. *See also* Developmentally appropriate practices
Developmentally appropriate practices (DAP), 31, 48, 53, 64, 82, 85–93, 99, 173
Dewey, John, 16, 65, 88, 170, 187
Dickinson, D. K., 117, 120
Dickman, G. E., 52
Dimidjian, V., 71
Disabilities. *See* Special needs
Diversity, 8, 12, 30–46, 50, 56, 64, 65, 88, 89, 91, 99, 102, 165, 170, 173, 187
Dobrich, W., 117, 121
Doherty, K. M., 157, 158
Duke, N. K., 117
Dunn, L., 88, 92
Dunst, C., 72
Dwyer, D. C., 142

Early childhood education: historical and philosophical traditions of, 11–12, 16–17, 184–85
Early childhood educators: autonomy to practice of, 179, 182, 189; certification of, 177–78, 181, 184, 188, 189; compensation of, 158–59, 179, 183, 188, 189; competency of, 180; and consequences of policies, 158–59; ethics of, 179–80; expertise and skills of, 179, 180–82; goals of, 2; implications of multicultural education for, 42–43; status of, 152, 158–59, 177–92; traits of, 1–2. *See also* Professional development; Teacher preparation; Teachers
Early, D. M., 14
Education of All Handicapped Act (1975, 1986), 55
Educators for Social Responsibility, 170
Edwards, C. P., 128, 130
Ehri, L. C., 117
Eisner, Elliot, 194
Elementary and Secondary Education Act, 93
Elkind, D., 71
Emergent literacy, 82, 90, 114–25

Emotional development, 14, 21, 88, 100, 140
Empowerment, 12, 72–74, 75–77
Engel, B., 106
Environment, 73, 167, 171. *See also* Climate, classroom/school; Least restrictive environment
Epstein, J., 70
Equity, 7, 57, 64, 88
Erikson, E. H., 15, 17, 73, 88
Erikson Institute, 144
Ethics, 179–80, 186, 188
Ethnic revitalization, 28, 37
Expectations, 17, 21, 24

Fairness, 56, 57, 63–64, 102
Families: at-risk, 71–72, 77; communication with, 74–75; and communities, 76–77; and consequences of policies, 155–56, 159, 160–61; and development issues, 11–12; empowerment of, 12, 72–74, 75–77; and global education, 165, 168, 171, 172; historical context for working with, 71–72; and history of early childhood education, 11–12; importance of strong, 70, 76–77; as models, 76; partnerships with, 24, 73, 74–77, 92, 93; and political issues, 11–12; poor working, 160–61; questions about, 8, 11–12; and status of early childhood educators, 188; and technology, 145; working with, 69–80. *See also* Parents
Family and Medical Leave Act (1993), 157
Farr, R. C., 108
Farver, J. A., 128, 129, 132
Farver, J. M., 132
Federal Interagency Forum on Child and Family Statistics, 13, 14
Feeney, S., 180
Feinman, S., 56
Fereshter, M. H., 32
Ferguson, D., 144
Fewell, R. R., 103
Fields, J., 156
File, N., 75
Fincham, F. D., 18
Fisher, B., 89
Fleer, M., 87
Forgatch, M. S., 16
Forman, George, 145
Foster, J. E., 101
Fraiberg, S., 70
Freeman, N. K., 140
Friendships: development of, 50, 52, 64
Fromberg, Doris Pronin: chapter by, 152, 177–92; references to works by, 187
Fuch, L. S., 56
Fuch, S., 56
Fullan, M., 186

Galda, L., 120
Galinsky, E., 21
Garbarino, J., 13, 14, 19–20
Gardner, H., 88
Gartner, A., 50, 55
Gee, K., 64
Gender issues, 82, 129–31, 132–33
Generativity, 70, 73
Getty Center for Education in the Arts, 90
Giangreco, M. F., 60
Gibboney, R. A., 179
Giroux, H. A., 40
Giuliano, T. A., 131
Givens, K., 109
Glazer, S. M., 107
Glick, M., 103, 127
Global Connections, 170
Global education, 151–52, 164–76
Goffin, S., 88, 155
Golbeck, S. L., 23
Gonzalez-Mena, J., 75
Goodman, J. F., 131–32
Goodwin, L. D., 98, 101, 102, 109
Goodwin, W. L., 98, 101, 102, 109
Gordon, L., 155
Grace, C., 106
Grafwallner, R., 75
Grant, Carl, 31, 32, 33, 37, 39
Graue, M. E., 101
Graves, S., 71, 72, 73–74
Greendorfer, S. L., 131
Greenspan, S. I., 102
Greer, J., 20
Grieshaber, S., 91, 92
Grych, J. H., 18
Gullo, D. F., 141
Guralnick, M. J., 49, 50, 52, 56, 64
Guskey, T. R., 109

Haberman, M., 23, 189
Halverson, C. L., 130
Hanson, M., 75
Hamre-Nietupski, S., 50
Haugland, S. W., 139, 143
Haynes, M., 73, 75
Head Start, 11–12, 24, 32, 38, 54, 65, 154–55, 180
Health and safety: and consequences of policies, 157, 159–60, 161, 162; and development issues, 13, 14, 18, 19, 23–24; and working with families, 72
Healy, J. F., 137, 138
Helburn, S., 21
Hennessy, E., 24
Herman, J. L., 105, 109, 110
Heymann, J., 71

Hilliard, A. G., 178
Hirsch, E. D., 41
Hitchcock, C. H., 140
Hoffman, M., 70, 132
Horm-Wingerd, D. M., 108
HOST (Helping One Student at a Time), 76
Howe, E., 178, 185
Howe, R., 173
Hughes, Fergus, 82, 126–35
Humphreys, A. P., 130
Hupp, C., 72
Hutinger, P. L., 141
Hyson, M. C., 15, 21, 22, 24, 186

Identity, 32, 70, 133, 166
Ideology, 161
Inclusion, 12, 47–68
Individuals with Disabilities Education Act (IDEA) (1990, 1991), 56
Inhelder, B., 35, 42
Insight, 4–6
Instruction, 33, 40, 52, 110, 140. See also specific topic
International Kindergarten Union, 174
International Reading Association (IRA), 86, 90
International Society for Technology in Education (ISTE), 141
Isenberg, Joan Packer: chapter by, 12, 13–19; references to work of, 24
Issues, 3–4, 5–6. See also specific issue

Jenkins, J. R., 51
Johanson, J., 141
Johnson, I. D., 141
Johnston, John M., 82, 85–96

Kagan, S. L., 157, 158
Kahn, A. J., 157
Kaiser Commission on Medicaid and the Uninsured, 159
Kaiser Family Foundation, 159
Kamii, C., 106
Kammerman, S. B., 156, 157, 162
Katz, L. G., 15, 102, 179
Kays, J., 117
Kerr, M., 71
King, S. H., 189
Kipnis, K., 180
Kitzrow, M., 70
Klein, E. L., 14
Knitzer, J., 22
Knotos, S., 88, 92
Knowledge bases, 180, 185–87
Kohlberg, Lawrence, 34–35
Kohn, A., 101, 102, 178, 183
Kontos, J., 21

Kotre, J., 70
Kozol, J., 18
Krechevsky, M., 108

Labeling, 23, 52, 55
Language: and assessment, 82, 99, 100, 102,
   104; and DAP, 91; and literacy, 115, 117, 122,
   123; and technology, 140
Le Blanc, L., 172
Learning disabilities, 14. *See also* Special needs
Least restrictive environment, 56, 62, 63
Leave No Child Behind Act (2001/2002), 82, 93,
   161
Leavitt, R., 70
Lehrer, R., 89
Lens metaphor, 2–4, 5, 8, 194
Lever, J., 130
Lewit, E. M., 19, 20
Liebbrand, J., 179
Lindsey, G., 17
Lindstrand, P., 145
Lipsky, D. K., 50, 55
Listening to Children (film), 193
Literacy: domains of, 123; and domains of
   knowledge, 122; making decisions about
   programs of early, 121–22; and modeling, 115;
   and working with families, 72. *See also*
   Emergent literacy
Lonigan, C. J., 118, 119, 122
Lubeck, S., 91, 92, 174
Luckin, R., 144
Lundell, M., 193
Lynch, E., 75

Magid, K., 71
Mallory, B., 87, 92
Mandates, 24, 54, 55, 62, 63–64, 91, 93, 121,
   155
Marlowe, B., 60, 61
Marshall, K., 173
Martin, Jane Roland, 170
Maslow, A., 72
Mather, N., 51, 52
McCarthy, J., 184
McDonnell, A. P., 54, 59
McGee, Lea M.: chapter by, 82, 114–25;
   references to works by, 118
McGill-Franzen, A., 101
McKelvey, C., 71
McLoyd, V. C., 18, 19, 22
McMahon, R., 116
McMillan, J. H., 18
McNabb, M. L., 141
McWilliam, R. A., 58
Measurement: definition of, 98–99
Meisels, S. J., 101, 102, 106, 108

Melting-pot theory, 36–37, 38
Meyer, L. A., 117, 118
Miller, E., 137, 139
Minorities, 188–89
Minuchin, S., 73
Mitchell, Lucy Sprague, 172
Mobius Corporation, 144
Modeling, 76, 115, 189
Molinaro, J., 15, 21, 22, 24
Monson, D. L., 116
Montessori, Maria, 11–12, 170
Morals, 33–35, 36, 167
Morgenthaler, Shirley, 184–85
Morphett, M. V., 115
Morrow, L. M., 117, 120
Moskey-Howard, S., 57
Moss, Peter, 174
Multicultural education, 12, 30–46, 75, 167, 168
Muzi, M. J., 34
Myers, B., 169
Myers, M., 169

Nancy, J., 137, 140
National Academy of Early Childhood Programs,
   86, 92
National Association for the Education of Young
   Children (NAEYC), 1, 20, 21, 24, 54, 85, 86,
   87, 89, 90, 91, 92, 98, 127, 138, 145, 180, 182,
   183, 184
National Association of Early Childhood
   Specialists in State Departments of Education,
   98, 101, 177, 184
National Association of Early Childhood Teacher
   Educators (NAECTE), 177, 183–84
National Association of Elementary School
   Principals, 180
National Board for Professional Teaching
   Standards (NBPTS), 87, 90, 91, 184, 188
National Center for Health Statistics, 159
National Center for Youth Law, 21
National Council for the Accreditation of
   Teacher Education (NCATE), 180, 184, 189
National Council for the Social Studies (NCS),
   90, 169–70
National Council of Teachers of English, 86
National Council of Teachers of Mathematics,
   86–87, 90
National Early Childhood Assessments Resource
   Group, 104
National Education Goals Panel, 104
National Head Start Association, 144
National Institute of Child Health and Human
   Development Early Child Care Research
   Network, 158
National Institute on Early Childhood
   Development and Education, 187

National Institutes of Health, 158
National Research Council, 89, 90, 115, 121
National Science Foundation, 144
Neill, M., 106
New, R., 87, 92
Newacheck, P. W., 160
Newberger, J. J., 17
Nielsen, D. C., 116
Nieto, S., 31, 37, 40, 43
Nilsen, B., 183
Noddings, Nel, 170
Noonan, M. J., 140

O'Brien, M., 63
Odom, S. L., 50, 52, 64
Office of Special Education and Rehabilitative
  Services, 55
Olson, L., 156, 157, 158
Oravec, J. A., 138
Organization for Economic Co-operation and
  Development (OECD), 174, 180
Organizational systems and structures, 62–64
Otto, C., 193

Palmer, D. S., 51
Papert, S., 141
Parents, 12, 24, 51, 72–77, 92, 93, 104, 107–8,
  128, 132, 145, 157, 159. See also Child care;
  Families
Parker, S. T., 130
Parrette, P., 145
Partnership for the Educational Village, 171
Partnerships, 24, 73, 74–77, 92, 93
Patton, M. M., 24
Paul, R., 40
Peabody, Elizabeth, 174
Peck, C. A., 52
Peers, 52, 130, 132, 140. See also Inclusion
Peisner-Feinberg, E. S., 15, 88, 158
Pellegrini, A. D., 120, 130
Percell-Gates, V., 117
Perrone, V., 101
Personnel resources: implications of inclusion
  for, 59–62
Phillips, D., 21, 89
Phonemic awareness, 114–25
Physical development, 14, 15, 20–21, 33–34,
  100, 139
Piaget, Jean, 7, 17, 34, 35, 42, 88, 91
Pierson, C. A., 101, 105
Pipher, M., 70, 76
Play, 82, 103, 105, 106, 115, 126–35, 138, 172,
  187
Pogrow, S., 180
Policies. See Public policies

Poor working families, 160–61. See also Poverty
Portfolios, 107, 108, 109
Poverty: and consequences of policies, 155, 159,
  160–61; and development issues, 13, 14, 18–
  19, 20, 23, 24; and working with families, 72
Powell, D., 73, 74, 75
Powlishta, K. K., 132
Practices: autonomy in, 179, 182, 189; implications
  of inclusion for, 57–64; and status of early
  childhood educators, 179, 182, 189; and
  working with families, 77. See also Best
  practices; Developmentally appropriate
  practices (DAP)
Prenatal care, 17, 18, 19, 20–21
Primavera, J., 140
Professional development, 24–25, 58–59, 60, 61,
  86, 89, 92, 93, 142–43, 151–52, 180, 181, 186.
  See also Teacher preparation
Professional organizations, 24–25, 89, 90, 179,
  183–84, 188. See also specific organization
Professionalism: and defining knowledge bases,
  180, 185–87; paradox of, 178–79; and status of
  early childhood educators, 152, 177–92;
  working definition of, 179–84
Progress. See Assessment
Project Spectrum, 108
Psychology/psychological issues, 17, 22
Psychosocial development, 17, 73
Public policies: consequences of, 153–63; and
  defining the issues, 156–61; and ideology, 161;
  overview of, 151–52; questions about, 8; and
  status of early childhood educator, 178
"Pull-out" programs, 50
Purcell-Gates, V., 118

Quality Counts, 87
Quyen, G. T., 16, 22

Raag, T., 130
Race, 18. See also Multicultural education
Rackliff, C. L., 130
Rafferty, Y., 50
Raines, Shirley C., 82, 85–96
Ramsey, P. G., 37, 42
Rapport, M.J.K., 56, 62
Ratcliff, N., 86, 105
Raver, C. C., 56
Ravitch, Diane, 41
Readiness, 41–42, 53, 101, 115, 116
Reading: aloud, 114, 115, 116–18, 121–22, 123;
  and DAP, 89, 91; and literacy, 114–25;
  prevention of difficulties in, 120–21; shared,
  115, 121–22
Reading Recovery, 22
Reed, D. R., 18

Reflection, 40, 167, 188
Reform: and DAP, 90, 91, 92–93; and
    development issues, 16, 18, 23, 24; and global
    education, 169–70; importance of, 7; and
    inclusion, 65; and multicultural education, 32–
    33, 40
Regular Education Initiative, 55
Relationships: and development issues, 21, 22,
    23
Reports: assessment, 82, 107–10
Resources: and development issues, 23–24;
    implications of inclusion for personnel, 59–62
Retention, 101
Reynolds, M. C., 55
Reys, B. J., 141
Rhodes, S., 24
Rich, J., 103
Risk factors, 17–21. See also specific factor
Rivers, J. C., 158
Robbins, C., 117
Roberts, C., 52
Roberts, R., 51, 52
Robison, J. F., 31
Rogoff, B., 88
Roopnarine, J. L., 128, 129
Rosenblum, V., 106
Rousseau, J.-J., 16
Rubrics, 109–10
Rust, Frances O'Connell, 151, 153–63
Ryan, B., 70, 71

Sailor, W., 50
Sanders, W. L., 158
Saracho, O. N., 31
Sarama, J., 141, 144
Scarborough, H. S., 117, 121
Schlesinger, Arthur, Jr., 41
Schoenborn, C. A., 14
School reform. See Reform
Schorr, L., 18, 19, 22, 23, 71
Schweinhart, L. J., 108
Scriven, M., 40
Seefeldt, Carol, 106, 168–69, 170
Segal, M., 103, 105
Seifert, Kelvin, 36
Self-concept, 50, 51, 52
Self-confidence, 15, 23, 74, 76
Self-esteem, 21, 22–23, 32, 70, 72, 140, 144, 180
Semmel, M. I., 52
Senechal, M., 117
Serbin, L. A., 130, 131
Shannon, P., 161
Shapiro, J. P., 50
Shauble, L., 89
Shepard, L. A., 99, 101, 109, 178, 186

Shin, Y. L., 128
Shonkoff, J., 89
Shores, E. F., 106
Sleeter, Christine, 31, 32, 37, 39
Smart toys, 138–39
Smith, Anne, 173
Smith, B. J., 56, 62
Smith, J. K., 117, 120
Smith, M. W., 117, 120
Smith, P. K., 130
Snow, C. E., 89, 115, 118, 121, 122
Social action, 32, 33, 166
Social context: and play, 126–35; questions
    about, 8
Social development: and assessment, 102; and
    DAP, 88; and development issues, 14, 20–21;
    and global education, 165; and inclusion, 51,
    52, 53, 64; and multicultural education, 33–
    34; and technology, 137, 140
Social justice, 40, 41
Social reconstructionism, 32, 36, 39
Sociocultural forces, 17, 35–41, 91, 130, 186,
    188
Socioemotional development, 88, 100
Software, 137, 138, 140, 143–44
Somerindyke, J., 140
Sowell, Thomas, 41
Special needs: and assessment, 82, 100, 101,
    102–3; and DAP, 87, 91, 93; and development
    issues, 12, 15, 21, 23; and global education,
    166; and technology, 138, 140, 145; testing
    children with, 102–3. See also Inclusion
Spitz, R., 17
Spodek, B., 31
Spring, Joel, 42
Squires, B., 193
Stainback, S., 50, 55–56
Stainback, W., 50, 55–56
Standardized testing, 53, 54, 82, 86, 91, 92, 93,
    99, 101–4, 182, 184. See also Assessment
Standards, 24–25, 57, 85, 88, 89–90, 91, 92, 93,
    108, 141–42, 144, 169–170, 180, 182, 184,
    185, 189
Starnes, B. A., 180
State Children's Health Insurance Program
    (CHIP), 159–60
Stent, M. D., 37
Stereotypes, 32, 33, 39, 41, 43, 50, 57, 164, 168
Structure, organizational, 51, 62–64
Su, Z., 188
Success for All, 22
Sulzby, E., 115
Swadener, B. B., 32, 41
Swaminathan, Sudha, 83, 136–49
Swartz, S., 31

Swick, Kevin J.: chapter by, 12, 69–80; references to work by, 70, 71, 72, 73–74, 75, 76
Swiniarski, Louise Boyle: chapter by, 151–52, 164–76; references to works by, 165, 166, 171, 172, 173, 174
Swint, S., 139

Taking the First Steps: Parents as Educators (TV series), 171
Tamis-LeMonda, C. S., 128
Teacher preparation: and consequences of policies, 158–59; and development issues, 24, 25; implications of inclusion for, 58–59; and status of early childhood educators, 177, 178, 180, 184, 186, 187–88, 189; and technology, 142–43. *See also* Professional development
Teachers, 87, 93, 105, 115, 136–37, 140, 141–43, 145, 146, 151, 173–74, 187. *See also* Early childhood educators; Professional development; Teacher preparation
Teaching Tolerance Project, 170, 172
Teale, W. H., 115
Team approach, 23–24, 51, 53, 59, 60–61, 62, 65
Technology, 82–83, 136–46, 167, 169
Testing: as category of assessment, 99. *See also* Assessment; Standardized testing
Theokas, C., 132–33
Thomas, J. Y., 20
Thompson, A., 142
Thompson, T., 72
Thornton, A., 72
Tinker, R., 141
Torgeson, J. K., 119–20, 121
Toys: smart, 138–39
Tracy, D. M., 131
Trends, 3, 5–6
Tye, Kenneth, 165

Ukrainetz, T. A., 122
United Federation of Teachers, 183
United Nations Bureau of the Preparatory Committee for the Special Session of the General Assembly on Children, 174
United Nations Children's Fund (UNICEF), 170, 174
United Nations Convention on the Rights of the Child, 166, 170, 172–73
U.S. Department of Education, 144, 171

Values, 55, 56–57, 168. *See also* Morals
Van Dyck, R., 50
Violence, 18, 19–20, 24
Vold, Edwina Battle: chapter by, 12, 30–46; references to works by, 31, 32

Voyer, D., 131
Vygotsky, Lev, 7, 15, 17, 34, 35–36, 43, 88, 144

Waldrop, M. L., 130
Walker, A., 20
Walsh, K., 185
Wang, L.-C., 142
Wartella, E. A., 137, 140
Washburne, C., 115
Wasserman, S., 178
Waxler, T., 180
Webber, N. T., 103, 105
Weikart, D. P., 15
Wein, C. A., 7
Weissbourd, B., 14, 15, 16, 18, 22, 23
Wesson, K. A., 101
Wetzel, D. R., 142
Wheeler, E. J., 23
White, C. Stephen, 12, 13–19
Whitebook, M., 183
Whitehead, A. N., 181
Whitehurst, G., 117, 118, 120, 122
Whiting, B. B., 128, 130
Whole child concept, 2, 24, 88
Wiggins, G. P., 103, 105, 109–10
Wilds, M., 138
Will, J. A., 130
Will, Madeleine, 55, 62
Wilson, C., 88
Wimbarti, S., 128, 132
Winton, P. J., 24
Wise, A., 179, 180, 185
Wolery, M., 54
Wolpert, E., 42, 43
Wood, E., 142
Woodcock, R. W., 119
Work Sampling System, 108
World Organization for Early Childhood Education (OMEP), 174
Wortham, Sue C.: chapter by, 82, 97–113; references to works by, 100, 105, 107, 108
Wright, June L.: chapter by, 83, 136–49; references to works by, 143
Wrigley, J., 155
Writing, 115, 116, 121–22
Wuthnow, R., 76

Young Children Interest Forum Listserv, 145

ZERO TO THREE Work Group, 102
Zigler, E. F., 56
Zigmond, N., 52, 53
Zill, N., 14